Margaret Moran
W. Frances Holder

AP* SUCCESS
World History

2nd EDITION

THOMSON
★
PETERSON'S

Ariel Prybylo

Australia • Canada • Mexico • Singapore • Spain • United Kingdom • United States

THOMSON

PETERSON'S

About The Thomson Corporation and Peterson's

With revenues of US$7.2 billion, The Thomson Corporation (www.thomson.com) is a leading global provider of integrated information solutions for business, education, and professional customers. Its Learning businesses and brands (www.thomsonlearning.com) serve the needs of individuals, learning institutions, and corporations with products and services for both traditional and distributed learning.

Peterson's, part of The Thomson Corporation, is one of the nation's most respected providers of lifelong learning online resources, software, reference guides, and books. The Education Supersite℠ at www.petersons.com—the Internet's most heavily traveled education resource—has searchable databases and interactive tools for contacting U.S.-accredited institutions and programs. In addition, Peterson's serves more than 105 million education consumers annually.

Consultant: Margaret Martin, Arlington High School, Arlington, TX.
Graphics: Siren Design, Inc.

For more information, contact Peterson's, 2000 Lenox Drive, Lawrenceville, NJ 08648; 800-338-3282; or find us on the World Wide Web at www.petersons.com/about

ISBN 0-7689-0985-6

Printed in the United States of America

10 9 8 7 6 5 4 3 2 1   04 03 02

CONTENTS

CONTENTS

QUICK REFERENCE GUIDE

THREE IMPORTANT STRATEGIES

1. Highlight the key words in the question so you will know what you are looking for in the answer choices.
2. With a *not/except* question, ask yourself if an answer choice is true about the subject of the question. If it is true, cross it off and keep checking answers.
3. If you aren't sure about an answer but know something about the question, eliminate what you know is wrong and make an educated guess.

10 STRATEGIES FOR ACING THE TEST

PREPARING FOR THE TEST

1. Read the *Advanced Placement Program Course Description for World History* available from the College Board and the "10 Facts About the AP World History Test" on pages 3–8 in this book.

2. Choose your Practice Plan from pages 12–16 in this book.

3. Choose a place and time to study every day. Stick to your routine and your plan.

4. Even though they are time-consuming, complete the Diagnostic and Practice Tests in this book. They will give you just what they promise: practice—practice in reading and following the directions, practice in pacing yourself, practice in understanding and answering multiple-choice questions, and practice in writing timed essays.

5. Complete all your assignments for your regular AP world history class. Ask questions in class, talk about what you read and write, and enjoy what you are doing. The test is supposed to measure your development as an educated and analytical reader and writer.

THE NIGHT BEFORE THE TEST

6. Assemble what you will need for the test: your admission materials, four number 2 pencils, two pens, a watch (without an alarm), and a healthy snack for the break. Put these items in a place where you will not forget them in the morning.

7. Don't cram. Relax. Go to a movie, visit a friend—but not one who is taking the test with you. Get a good night's sleep.

The Day of the Test

8. Wear comfortable clothes. If you have a lucky color or a lucky piece of clothing or jewelry, wear it—as long as you won't distract anyone else. Take along a lucky charm if you have one.

9. If you do not usually eat a big breakfast, this is not the morning to change your routine, but it is probably a good idea to eat something nutritious if you can.

10. If you feel yourself getting anxious, concentrate on taking a couple of deep breaths. Remember, you don't have to answer all the questions, you can use EDUCATED GUESSES, and you don't have to write three perfect essays.

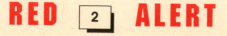

10 FACTS ABOUT THE AP WORLD HISTORY TEST

1. THE ADVANCED PLACEMENT PROGRAM OFFERS HIGH SCHOOL STUDENTS AN OPPORTUNITY TO RECEIVE COLLEGE CREDIT FOR COURSES THEY TAKE IN HIGH SCHOOL.

The AP program is a collaborative effort of secondary schools, colleges and universities, and the College Board through which students like you who are enrolled in AP or honors courses in any one or more of nineteen subject areas may receive credit or advanced placement for college-level work completed in high school. While the College Board makes recommendations about course content, it does not prescribe content. The annual testing program ensures a degree of comparability among high school courses in the same subject.

2. MORE THAN 2,900 COLLEGES AND UNIVERSITIES PARTICIPATE.

Neither the College Board nor your high school awards AP credit. You need to find out from the colleges to which you are planning to apply whether they grant credit and/or use AP scores for placement. It is IMPORTANT that you obtain each school's policy IN WRITING so that when you actually choose one college and register, you will have proof of what you were told.

3. THE AP WORLD HISTORY TEST MEASURES FACTUAL KNOWLEDGE, CONCEPTUAL KNOWLEDGE, AND A RANGE OF SKILLS, ESPECIALLY INTERPRETATIVE.

In the course description for AP World History, the College Board lists six themes specific to world history that the test covers:

- Themes
  - Impact of societal interactions
  - Change and continuity across world history periods
  - Impact of technology and demography
  - Social and gender structures
  - Cultural and intellectual developments
  - Functions and structures of states

 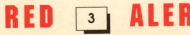

The College Board also lists seven habits of mind or skills that an AP world history course should foster and the test addresses. The first four are ways of thinking or skills relevant to any history course and the last three are specific to the study of world history.

- General historical habits of mind

  - Constructing and evaluating arguments

  - Using primary documents and data

  - Assessing change and continuity over time

  - Handling diversity of interpretations

- Specific to world history courses

  - Global patterns

  - Comparison within and among societies

  - Understanding of ideas and values

The focus of the test appears to be on conceptual knowledge rather than factual detail. The Acorn (The Advanced Placement Program Course Description) book notes the types of representative information that you will not be expected to know. If you analyze this listing for each chronological boundary, you will notice that the things you will be expected to know fall into the category of broad interpretative knowledge, the governing generalizations or concepts about a culture, civilization, or region rather than factual detail. As you read and study, ask yourself often what is the significance of this event, time period, person's actions, and so on.

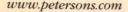

4. THE AP WORLD HISTORY TEST HAS TWO SECTIONS: MULTIPLE CHOICE AND A THREE-PART ESSAY SECTION.

Study Strategy

See Chapter 1 for multiple-choice strategies and Chapter 2 for strategies to use in writing your essays.

The total test is 3 hours and 5 minutes. "Section I: Multiple Choice" has 70 questions and counts for 50 percent of your total score. You will have 55 minutes to complete it.

In Section II, you are given three essay topics to write about. The first is a document-based question (DBQ) with from four to ten documents to analyze. The second essay question will ask you to trace change over time in relation to large global issues, and the third question is a comparative essay. You will need to compare developments in at least two societies.

You are allotted 50 minutes for the DBQ, of which the first 10 minutes are to be used for reading the documents. You will have 40 minutes apiece to answer the other two essays. You should use 5 minutes of each period to read and plan your essay.

All three essays are counted equally—33⅓ percent—in your score for Section II. This means that the DBQ is no more important in the final score than the other two essays.

5. THE AP WORLD HISTORY COURSE BREAKS WORLD HISTORY INTO FIVE CHRONOLOGICAL BOUNDARIES.

Study Strategy

See Chapters 6 through 10 for a brief review of world history.

In its course description for the AP World History Test, the College Board lists six broad areas of study through which the five themes listed above are interwoven. Each set of major developments includes work on diverse interpretations; that is, historians' divergent views about how to explain the causes of historical events and/or their significance. The basic course outline from the College Board is as follows:

- Foundations (to 1000 C.E.)*

  - Basic features of geography

  - Crises of late antiquity (third to eighth centuries C.E.)

  - Key cultural, social, and economic systems (prior to 1000 C.E.)

  - Principal international connections between 700 and 1000 C.E.

---

* The College Board uses B.C.E (Before Common Era) and C.E. (Common Era) rather than B.C. and A.D.

- 1000–1450

  - Questions of periodization

  - Interregional networks

  - Nature of philosophy and knowledge

  - China's internal and external expansion

  - The Islamic world

  - Changes in Christianity

  - Non-Islamic Africa

  - Demographic and environmental changes

  - Amerindian civilizations

- 1450–1750

  - Questions of periodization

  - Change in global interactions, trade, and technology

  - Knowledge of major empires and other political units and social systems

  - Demographic and environmental changes: Diseases, animals, new crops, and comparative population trends

  - Cultural and intellectual developments

- 1750–1914

  - Questions of periodization

  - Changes in global commerce, communications, and technology

  - Demographic and environmental changes

  - Changes in social and gender structure

  - Political revolutions and independence movements; new political ideas

  - Rise of Western dominance

- 1914–Present

  - Questions of periodization

  - The World Wars, the Cold War, nuclear weaponry, international organizations, and their impact on the global framework

  - New patterns of nationalism, especially outside the West

  - Impact of major global economic developments

- New forces of revolution and other sources of political innovations

- Social reform and social revolution

- Internationalization of culture and reactions

- Demographic and environmental changes

The College Board notes that the course in world history should not allot more than 30 percent of its coverage to European history. The course description also states that the United States should be included only in its relations with other nations, and lists, for example, colonization, the American Revolution, and expansion as well as the place of the United States in international politics, especially in the latter half of the twentieth century. As a result, you should not spend time reviewing U.S. domestic history or slight Asian, African, Eastern European, or Latin American history in favor of Western European history in your review.

In designing the test, the test writers allot a certain percentage of questions to each chronological boundary. Note, however, that one question may actually ask you about several time periods. The following list shows the range of questions that might appear on an AP World History Test:

- Foundations: 14 percent (approximately 9 questions)

- 1000–1450: 22 percent (approximately 15)

- 1450–1750: 22 percent (approximately 15)

- 1750–1914: 20 percent (approximately 14)

- 1914–Present: 22 percent (approximately 15)

6. THERE IS NO REQUIRED LENGTH FOR YOUR ESSAYS.

It is the quality, not the quantity, that counts. Realistically, a one-paragraph essay is not going to garner you a high score because you cannot develop a well-reasoned analysis and present it effectively in one paragraph. An essay of five paragraphs is a good goal. By following this model, you can set out your ideas with an interesting beginning, develop a reasoned middle, and provide a solid ending.

7. YOU WILL GET A COMPOSITE SCORE FOR YOUR TEST.

Test-Taking Strategy

See "Scoring High on the AP World History Test," pp. 9–11.

The College Board reports a single score from 1 to 5 for the two-part test, with 5 being the highest. By understanding that you can balance the number of questions you need to answer correctly against the essay score you need to receive in order to get at least a "3," you can relieve some of your anxiety about passing the test.

8. EDUCATED GUESSING CAN HELP.

Test-Taking Strategy

See "Scoring High on the AP World History Test," pp. 9–11.

No points are deducted for questions that go unanswered on the multiple-choice section, and don't expect to have time to answer them all. A quarter of a point is deducted for wrong answers. The College Board suggests guessing IF you know something about a question and can eliminate a couple of the answer choices. Call it "educated guessing." You'll read more about this in Chapter 1.

9. THE TEST IS GIVEN MID-MAY.

Most likely, the test will be given at your school, so you do not have to worry about finding a strange building in a strange city. You will be in familiar surroundings, which should reduce your anxiety a bit. If the test is given somewhere else, be sure to take identification with you.

10. STUDYING FOR THE TEST CAN MAKE A DIFFERENCE.

Study Strategy

Stop first at pp.12–16 and read "Practice Plan for Studying for the AP World History Test."

The first step is to familiarize yourself with the format and directions for each part of the test. Then you will not waste time on the day of the test trying to understand what you are supposed to do.

The second step is to put those analytical skills you have been learning to work, dissecting and understanding the kinds of questions you will be asked, and the third step is to practice "writing on demand" for the essays. So turn the page, and let's get started.

SCORING HIGH ON THE AP WORLD HISTORY TEST

Around early July, you and the colleges you designate will receive a single composite score from 1 to 5, with 5 being the highest, for your AP World History Test, and your high school will receive its report a little later. The multiple-choice section is graded by machine, and your essays are graded during a marathon reading session by high school and college teachers.

A different reader scores each of your essays. None of the readers knows who you are (that's why you fill in identification information on your Section II booklet and then seal it) or how the others scored your other essays. For each essay, the College Board works out grading criteria for the readers to use, much as English/language arts teacher uses a rubric to evaluate your writing.

WHAT THE COMPOSITE SCORE MEANS

The College Board refers to the composite score as weighted because a factor like 1.0000 for the multiple-choice section and another factor for the three free-response essays are used to determine a raw score for each section of the test. That is, the actual score you get on the multiple-choice questions—say 48—is multiplied by the factor for the multiple-choice section, and the actual scores you get for the three essays—say 20 out of a possible 27—is multiplied by the factor for the essays. These two weighted scores are added, and the resulting composite score—say somewhere between 0 and 150—is then equated to a number from 5 to 1.

WHAT DOES ALL THIS MEAN TO YOU?

Without going into a lot of math, it means that according to the College Board, you can leave blank or answer incorrectly some combination of multiple-choice questions that give you 35 correct answers (50 percent of the multiple-choice questions on this test), write three reasonably good essays, and get at least a 3. Remember that a majority of students fall into the 3 range, and a 3 is good enough at most colleges to get you college credit or advanced placement. A score of 4 certainly will. It takes work to raise your score a few points, but it is not impossible. Sometimes, the difference between a 3 and a 4 or a 4 and a 5 is only a couple of points.

The highest score you can receive on an essay is a 9, and all three essays are worth the same percentage (33.3 percent) of your total Section II score. It is possible to get a variety of scores on your essays—7, 5, and 6, for example. The chances are that you will not get a wide range of individual essay scores such as 6, 2, and 5. Even if you did, you could still get at least a 3 and possibly a 4, depending on how many correct answers you have in the multiple-choice section balanced against how many wrong answers you have.

AP Grade	AP Qualifier	Probability of Receiving AP Credit
5	Extremely Well Qualified	Yes
4	Well Qualified	Yes
3	Qualified	Probably
2	Possibly Qualified	Rarely
1	No Recommendation	No

EDUCATED GUESSING: A HELPFUL TECHNIQUE

You may be concerned about guessing when you are not sure of the answer or when time is running out. We have more to say about pacing in Chapter 1, but even the College Board recommends guessing IF you know something about the question and can eliminate one or more of the answer choices. But we call it "educated guessing." Here are some suggestions for making an educated guess:

Test-Taking Strategy

Remember that there is no penalty for unanswered questions, but an unanswered question won't get you a point either.

- Ignore answers that are obviously wrong.

- Discard choices in which part of the response is incorrect. Remember that a partially correct answer is a partially incorrect answer—and a quarter-point deduction.

- Reread the remaining answers to see which seems more correct.

- Choose the answer that you feel is right. Trust yourself. Your subconscious usually will guide you to the correct choice. Do not argue with yourself. This works, though, only IF you know something about the content of the question to begin with.

You may still be concerned about the quarter-point deduction, known as the "guessing penalty," for an incorrect answer and are wondering if taking a chance is worth the possible point loss. We are not advocating guessing, but we are advocating making an educated guess. Recognize that if you use this technique, your chances of increasing your score are very good. You will have to answer four questions incorrectly to loose a single point, yet one correct educated guess will increase your score by 1 point. IF you know something about the question and can eliminate one or more answer choices, why not act on your idea?

SOME REMINDERS ABOUT THE AP WORLD HISTORY TEST

Here are four important ideas to remember about taking the test:

1. The College Board states that for a student to receive a grade of 3 or higher on the typical AP test, the student has "to answer about 50 percent of the multiple-choice questions correctly and do acceptable work on the free-response section."

2. It is important to spend time practicing the kinds of questions that you will find in the multiple-choice section because 50 percent of your score comes from that section. You do not have to put all your emphasis on the essay questions.

3. You can leave some questions unanswered and still do well. Even though you will be practicing how to pace yourself as you use this book, you may not be able to complete all 70 questions on the day of the test. If you come across a really difficult question, you can skip it and still feel that you are not doomed to receive a low score.

4. There is a guessing penalty. If you do not know anything about a question or the answer choices, do not take a chance. However, if you know something about the question and can eliminate one or more of the answer choices, then it is probably worth your while to choose one of the other answers. Use EDUCATED GUESSING. Even the College Board advises this strategy.

Study Strategy

See Chapter 1 for strategies.

Study Strategy

See Chapter 1 for more on pacing.

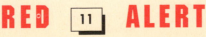

PRACTICE PLAN FOR STUDYING FOR THE AP WORLD HISTORY TEST

The following plan is worked out for nine weeks. The best study plan is one that continues through a full semester. Then you have time to think about ideas and to talk with your teacher and other students about what you are learning, and you will not feel rushed. Staying relaxed about the test is important. A full-semester study plan also means that you can apply what you are learning here to class work—your essay writing—and apply your class work—everything that you are reading—to test preparation. The plan is worked out so that you should spend about 3 hours on each lesson.

Week 1

First: Take the *Diagnostic Test,* pp. 21–44, and complete the self-scoring process. List the areas that you had difficulty with: timing, question types, writing on demand, etc.

Then: Reread pp. 3–11 about the basic facts of the test and its scoring.

Week 2

Lesson 1
- Read *Top 10 Strategies for Acing the Test,* pp. 1–2.

- Reread *Scoring High on the AP World History Test,* pp. 9–11.

- Review the list you made after the *Diagnostic Test* to see what you need to learn in order to do well on the multiple-choice section.

- Read Chapter 1, *Answering the Multiple-Choice Questions,* pp. 79–94.

- Do the set of practice questions at the end of the chapter, and review the explanations of the answers.

Lesson 2
- Review Chapter 1, *Answering the Multiple-Choice Questions,* pp. 79–94, including the practice questions and answers. Focus on the techniques explained in the answers.

- Read Chapter 6, *Foundations of World History,* and find out more about any of the peoples, places, terms, and concepts that are unfamiliar to you. Be sure to locate the places on maps.

Week 3

Lesson 1
- Read Chapter 2, *Writing an Effective Essay*, pp. 100–104.

- Read Chapter 3, *Writing the DBQ Essay*, pp. 105–142, and answer the practice DBQ at the end of the chapter.

- Complete the self-scoring process, and compare your score against your score on the *Diagnostic Test.*

- Ask a responsible friend, an AP classmate, or a teacher to evaluate your essay against the scoring guide. Where did you improve from the *Diagnostic Test*? What still needs improvement?

Lesson 2
- Read Chapter 7, *From 1000 to 1450*, pp. 203–227, and find out more about any of the people, places, terms, or concepts that are unfamiliar to you.

Week 4

Lesson 1
- Reread Chapter 2, *Writing an Effective Essay*, pp. 100–104.

- Read Chapter 4, *Writing the Change-Over-Time Essay*, pp. 143–160, and answer the Practice Change-Over-Time Essay 2 at the end of the chapter.

- Complete the self-scoring process, and compare your score against your score on the *Diagnostic Test.*

- Ask a responsible friend, an AP classmate, or a teacher to evaluate your essay against the scoring guide. Where did you improve from the *Diagnostic Test*? What still needs improvement?

- Rewrite the essay once, incorporating points for improvement, and rescore it. How did you do this time?

Lesson 2
- Read Chapter 8, *From 1450 to 1750*, pp. 229–256, and find out more about any of the people, places, terms, or concepts that are unfamiliar to you.

Week 5

Lesson 1
- Reread Chapter 2, *Writing an Effective Essay,* pp. 100–104.

- Read Chapter 5, *Writing the Comparative Essay,* pp. 161–175, and answer the Practice Comparative Essay 2 at the end of the chapter.

- Complete the self-scoring process, and compare the score with your score on the *Diagnostic Test* comparative essay.

- Ask a responsible friend, an AP classmate, or a teacher to evaluate your essay against the scoring guide.

- Rewrite the essay once, incorporating points for improvement, and rescore it. How did you do this time?

Lesson 2
- Read Chapter 9, *From 1750 to 1914,* pp. 257–276, and find out more about any people, places, terms, or concepts that are unfamiliar to you.

Week 6

Lesson 1
- Answer the multiple-choice section of the Practice Test, and complete the self-scoring process.

- Compare the score to your score on the *Diagnostic Test.* Which question types continue to be a concern?

- Reread Chapter 1, *About the Multiple-Choice Section,* pp. 79–94, as needed.

Lesson 2
- Read Chapter 10, *1914 to the Present,* pp. 277–291, and find out more about any people, places, terms, or concepts that are unfamiliar to you.

Week 7

Lesson 1
- Complete the DBQ on the Practice Test, and score your essay against the rubric.

- Again, ask a responsible friend, an AP classmate, or a teacher to evaluate your essay against the scoring guide.

- Compare your scores to the scores on the *Diagnostic Test*. Where did you improve? Where does your writing still need work?

- Reread Chapters 2 and 3 as needed.

- Answer the change-over-time and comparative essay questions on the Practice Test, and score your essays against the rubric.

- Ask a responsible friend, an AP classmate, or a teacher to evaluate your essays on the scoring guide as well. Compare these scores to your scores on the *Diagnostic Test*.

Lesson 2
- Review the lists and notes you made as you studied Chapters 6 through 10.

- Summarize the major trends in each period you have studied.

- List connections within periods and across time periods.

- Reread Chapters 2, 3, and 5 as needed.

Week 8

Lesson 1
- Reread Chapter 1, *Answering the Multiple-Choice Questions*, pp. 79–94, as needed.

- Complete the Practice DBQ Essay 2 in Chapter 3, and score your essay against the rubric.

- Again, ask a responsible friend, an AP classmate, or a teacher to evaluate your essay against the scoring guide.

- Compare your scores to the scores on the *Diagnostic Test*. Where did you improve? Where does your writing still need work?

- Reread Chapters 2 and 3 as needed.

Lesson 2
- Answer the Practice Change-Over-Time Essay 2 and the Practice Comparative Essay 2, and score your essays against the rubric.

- Ask a responsible friend, an AP classmate, or a teacher to evaluate your essays on the scoring guide as well. Compare these scores to your scores on the *Diagnostic Test*.

- Reread Chapters 2, 4, and 5 as needed.

Week 9

Lesson 1
- Answer the last set of practice essays in Chapters 3, 4, and 5, and complete the self-scoring process. Check your results against the other essays you have written. See how much you have improved.

Lesson 2
- If you are still unsure about some areas, review those chapters and the practice activities.

- Reread *Scoring High on the AP World History Test*, pp. 9–11, and *Top 10 Strategies for Acing the Test*, pp. 1–2.

THE PANIC PLAN

Eighteen weeks, nine weeks, how about two weeks? If you are the kind of person who puts everything off until the last possible minute, here is a two-week Panic Plan. Its objectives are as follows: to make you familiar with the test format and directions, to help you get as many correct answers as possible, and to write the best DBQ and change-over-time and comparative essays you can.

Week 1

- Read *Top 10 Strategies for Acing the Test*, pp. 1–2, and *Scoring High on the AP World History Test*, pp. 9–11.

- Take the *Diagnostic Test*. Read the directions carefully, and use a timer for each section.

- Complete the self-scoring process. You can learn a lot about the types of questions in the multiple-choice section by working through the answers.

- Read Chapter 6, *Foundations of World History*, pp. 177–201, Chapter 7, *From 1000 to 1450*, pp. 203–227; and Chapter 8, *From 1450 to 1750*, pp. 229–256.

Multiple Choice

- Read Chapter 1, *Answering the Multiple-Choice Questions*, pp. 79–94.

- Answer the multiple-choice section on the Practice Test.

- Complete the self-scoring process, and see where you may still have problems with question types.

- Read all the answer explanations, including those you identified correctly.

Essays

- Read Chapter 2, *Writing an Effective Essay*, pp. 100–104.

- Write one practice DBQ essay and two free-response essays using the practice questions in Chapters 3, 4, and 5, *Writing the DBQ Essay*, *Writing the Change-Over-Time Essay*, and *Writing the Comparative Essay*.

- Score each essay against the rubric, noting areas for improvement.

- Complete Section II on the Practice Test.

- Score each essay using the rubric. List your weaknesses.

- Ask a responsible friend, an AP classmate, or a teacher to evaluate your essays on the scoring guide as well. Compare them to your scores on the *Diagnostic Test*.

Week 2
- Reread *Top 10 Strategies for Acing the Test,* pp. 1–2, and *Scoring High on the AP World History Test,* pp. 9–11.

- Read Chapter 9 *From 1750 to 1914,* pp. 257–276, and Chapter 10, *From 1914 to the Present,* pp. 277–291.

Multiple Choice
- Reread Chapter 1, *Answering the Multiple-Choice Questions,* pp. 79–94.

Essays
- Complete Practice Essays 2 and 3 in Chapters 3, 4, and 5.

- Score each essay using the rubric. List your weaknesses.

- Ask a responsible friend, an AP classmate, or a teacher to evaluate your essays on the scoring guide as well. Compare them to your scores on the *Diagnostic Test*.

- List your weaknesses, and then list how you can overcome them in writing the real essays.

WHY TAKE THE *DIAGNOSTIC TEST?*

What do you know about the format and questions on the AP World History Test? If you knew all you needed to know, you probably would not be reading this book. Taking a practice test is one way to learn about the test and what it will be like taking it on the real test day. It is a long test, and you will need to pace yourself in answering the multiple-choice questions and in planning and writing your essays. Taking the *Diagnostic Test* will help you learn how much time you can spend on each item.

Practice may not make perfect, but you can improve your score with practice. The more you learn about your strengths and weaknesses in test-taking abilities and in analytical skills and the more you work on strengthening them, the better your score.

How should you take this test? Just as though it were the real test, so that means setting aside 3 hours and 5 minutes of uninterrupted, quiet time to take the test, plus the time to score your answers.

- Make a copy of an answer sheet and Self-Evaluation Rubric at the back of this book.

- Assemble four number 2 pencils and two pens along with the answer sheet and eight pieces of paper on which to make notes and write your essays.

- Use a timer or a stopwatch to time each section of the test.

- Follow the directions for both sections of the test—multiple choice and essay. Set your timer for the allotted time for each section.

- When you have completed the test, check how many questions you were able to answer on the multiple-choice section and how far you got in completing the essays. This information will help you in pacing yourself for the other practice tests and for the real test.

- Then check the multiple-choice questions against Quick-Score Answers, page 57.

- Read the explanation for each answer, even if your answer was correct. You might learn something you didn't know about the content of the question.

- Score each of your essays against the rubrics. Be honest in your evaluation. Knowing your weaknesses is the only way to turn them into strengths.

- Turn to the Practice Plan, and design your study plan from now until test day.

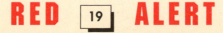

DIAGNOSTIC TEST

AP WORLD HISTORY

On the front page of your test booklet, you will find some information about the test. Because you have studied this book, none of it should be new to you, and much of it is similar to other standardized tests you have taken.

The front page will tell you that the following exam will take 3 hours and 5 minutes—55 minutes for the multiple-choice section and 2 hours and 10 minutes for the three essays. Ten minutes of the time for Section II is a mandatory reading period for the DBQ. There are two booklets for this exam, one for the multiple-choice section and one for the essays.

The page in your test booklet will also say that SECTION I:

- is 55 minutes.

- has 70 questions.

- counts for 50 percent of your total grade.

Then you will find a sentence in capital letters about not opening your exam booklet until the monitor tells you to open it.

Other instructions will tell you to be careful when you fill in the ovals on the answer sheet. Fill in each oval completely. If you erase an answer, erase it completely. If you skip a question, be sure to skip the answer oval for it. You will not receive any credit for work done in the test booklet, but you may use it for making notes.

You will also find a paragraph about the guessing penalty—a deduction of one-quarter point for every wrong answer—but also words of advice about guessing if you know something about the question and can eliminate several of the answers.

The final paragraph will remind you to work efficiently and to pace yourself. You are told that not everyone will be able to answer all the questions and it is preferable to skip questions that are difficult and come back to them if you have time.

SECTION I

> **Directions:** Each question or incomplete statement is followed by five suggested responses. Choose the best answer and fill in the correct oval on the answer sheet.

1. Which two of the following vied for influence in China during the Tang Dynasty?

   (A) Buddhism and Shintoism
   (B) Shintoism and Hinduism
   (C) Confucianism and Hinduism
   (D) Buddhism and Confucianism
   (E) Buddhism and Hinduism

2. Which of the following was not true of nomadic groups?

   (A) Nomadic societies were patriarchal.
   (B) They had some social hierarchy.
   (C) Most of the themes of nomadic art centered on their animals.
   (D) Nomadic societies had little positive influence on settled peoples.
   (E) Nomadic societies engaged in peaceful trade.

3. What happened in western Europe after the fall of the Roman Empire was similar to what occurred in

   (A) Byzantium after the end of the Eastern Empire.
   (B) China after the fall of the Han dynasty.
   (C) Japan after the end of the Tokugawa Shogunate.
   (D) the Holy Land after the unsuccessful Crusades ended.
   (E) the Andes when the Spanish ousted the Inca.

4. The most significant effect of Russia's conversion to Eastern Orthodox Christianity was

   (A) the trade network that Russia's acceptance of Christianity opened for it.
   (B) the way it slowed the development of a Russian national identity.
   (C) the way the Church's teaching that God vests power in the ruler strengthened the Russian tsars' control over the state.
   (D) the power it gave the Eastern Church in dealing with the Roman Catholic Church.
   (E) its influence on Russian architecture.

5. Which of the following developments most directly resulted from the Crusades?

   (A) Growth of Italian city-states
   (B) Spread of the Black Death
   (C) Vasco da Gama's voyage to India
   (D) Columbian Exchange
   (E) Restriction of European traders to treaty ports

6. All of the following are true of the major Amerindian civilizations in Central and South America prior to the arrival of Europeans EXCEPT

   (A) economies based on trade.
   (B) monumental building.
   (C) urban centers.
   (D) differentiation of labor.
   (E) social stratification.

7. All of the following are characteristics of western Europe in the 1400s and 1500s EXCEPT

    (A) the growth of capitalism.
    (B) the decline of the feudal system.
    (C) an increasingly urban population.
    (D) the development of improved weaponry.
    (E) the continued strength of the Roman Catholic Church.

8. Which of the following statements best describes the relationship between European and Asian commercial interests in the 1500s?

    (A) Europeans took over the Asian trading network by force.
    (B) The trading network in Asia was divided into three zones—Arab, Indian, and Chinese.
    (C) Europeans imposed a monopoly system on the spice trade.
    (D) Europeans abandoned any idea of colonizing or trading directly with Asians in favor of using Asian intermediaries.
    (E) Europeans found, after trial and error, that the only way to benefit from the Asian trading network was to join it as a peaceful partner.

9. Ghana in the 900s and France in the 1600s had which of the following characteristics in common?

    (A) Parliamentary government
    (B) Divine monarchy
    (C) Matrilineal descent
    (D) Islam
    (E) Trade based on gold and manufactured goods

10. "If man can, with almost complete assurance, predict phenomena when he knows their laws, and if, even when he does not, he can still, with great expectation of success, forecast the future on the basis of his experience of the past, why, then, should it be regarded as a fantastic undertaking to sketch, with some pretence to truth, the future destiny of man on the basis of his history?"

    The above statement most probably reflects the viewpoint of

    (A) scholar-gentry.
    (B) Machiavelli.
    (C) nationalists.
    (D) Enlightenment thinkers.
    (E) Social Darwinists.

11. Which of the following statements most accurately describes the short-term causes of the French Revolution?

    (A) The writings of the philosophes precipitated the French Revolution.
    (B) The bourgeoisie were willing to join with the aristocracy against the king until the aristocracy insisted that the three chambers of the Estates-General meet separately.
    (C) The support of the people of Paris created a general impression of discontent and upheaval but had little to do with the success of the French Revolution.
    (D) The French Revolution would not have occurred had the king not needed money.
    (E) The lack of interest among people in the countryside almost doomed the Revolution.

12. Which of the following countries practiced indirect rule in governing its colonies in Africa?

(A) Portugal
(B) France
(C) Germany
(D) Great Britain
(E) Belgium

13. Which of the following is not an accurate comparison of the Japanese and Russian reforms of the late nineteenth century?

(A) Both countries initiated reform of the military.
(B) Business leaders became an important part of the power structure of both countries.
(C) Both governments were reorganized to share power with lesser councils.
(D) The governments of both nations recognized the importance of fostering industrialization.
(E) Former serfs in Russia and displaced samurai in Japan in general suffered from the reforms.

Question 14 relates to the cartoon shown below.

"NEW CROWNS FOR OLD"

14. Which of the following is not an accurate interpretation of the cartoon?

(A) Disreali encouraged Queen Victoria to accept the title of Empress of India.
(B) The cartoon makes an allusion to the story *Aladdin and His Wonderful Lamp.*
(C) The cartoon implies that Queen Victoria is a weak monarch.
(D) The cartoonist portrays Disraeli as evil.
(E) The cartoonist questions the wisdom of accepting the crown of India.

15. Which of the following agreements renounced war as a vehicle of national policy?

(A) Five-Power Treaty
(B) Treaty of Versailles
(C) United Nations Charter
(D) Kellogg-Briand Pact
(E) Atlantic Charter

16. A major problem for developing countries in general is

    (A) stagnant population growth.
    (B) weak industrial base.
    (C) static rural/urban population distribution.
    (D) lack of natural resources.
    (E) lack of foreign economic aid.

17. Which of the following is a fundamental teaching of Islam?

    (A) The Shari'a is a compilation of the Sunna, the teachings of Muhammad, and the Quran.
    (B) Muslim converts may continue to worship their former deities.
    (C) The five-times-a-day prayer services that Muslims must observe are led by a priest called an imam.
    (D) Everyone is equal under Islam.
    (E) Social responsibility is less important than adherence to ritual.

18. A major influence on the development of western Europe was

    (A) the movements of the Mongols.
    (B) Attila's advance against Rome.
    (C) the spread of Islam into Spain by the Moors.
    (D) the pressure put on Germanic peoples by the movement of the Huns.
    (E) the emergence of a unified Frankish kingdom.

19. The introduction of papermaking into Europe is an example of cultural diffusion

    (A) from China by way of the Eurasian trade route.
    (B) from Japan by way of the Arab-Indian trade route.
    (C) through the Columbian Exchange.
    (D) through the Triangular Trade route.
    (E) from the Middle East as part of the Eurasian trade route.

20. A common stage in the early development of political units as diverse as England, France, China, Russia, and Japan was

    (A) manorialism.
    (B) divine right monarchy.
    (C) constitutional monarchy.
    (C) feudalism.
    (E) anarchy.

21. A major area of contention between the papacy and secular rulers was

    (A) the establishment of the Church of England by Henry VIII.
    (B) the rulers' determination to appoint Church officials in their nations.
    (C) the heavy tithes the rulers placed on churches within their borders.
    (D) the practice of trying clerics in secular rather than Church courts.
    (E) the rulers' disinterest in supporting the Crusades.

22. Which of the following statements most accurately describes the long-term significance of Europe's economic activity during the High Middle Ages?

    (A) Economic activity in medieval Europe was stagnant.
    (B) The roots of European capitalism and entrepreneurial activity were laid during the Middle Ages.
    (C) Most Europeans were farmers during the Middle Ages.
    (D) European economic activity was fueled by the Eurasian trading network during the Middle Ages.
    (E) Manorialism was in decline by the end of the Middle Ages.

23. All of the following statements are accurate about both the Mayan and Aztec civilizations EXCEPT

 (A) most of the ordinary people in both civilizations were farmers.
 (B) the priest class in both empires were powerful.
 (C) neither civilization had very advanced technologies or scientific understanding.
 (D) the Mayans lived in independent city-states, whereas the Aztecs had one ruler over the entire empire.
 (E) the exact nature of the decline of the Mayan civilization is unknown, whereas the Aztec empire fell to the Spanish.

24. Which statement most accurately describes Peter the Great's approach to reforming Russia?

 (A) He reorganized the bureaucracy but did not touch the military.
 (B) He chose to adopt technological modernizations but did not reform the governmental structure.
 (C) He adopted some aspects of western European political organization, such as political parties.
 (D) His many reforms improved the life of serfs, although he did not end the practice.
 (E) He used his modernization efforts to tighten his control over the country.

25. Which of the following statements most accurately describes the differences between the Spanish and Portuguese empires in the Americas?

 (A) Portuguese Brazil was more dependent on agriculture for its economic base than was Spanish America.
 (B) The Catholic Church had more influence over developments in Spanish America than in Brazil.
 (C) Portugal exercised direct governmental control over Brazil, whereas Spain put little structure in place to govern its colonies.
 (D) Spanish America, unlike Brazil, developed a multiracial society.
 (E) Spanish America had little in the way of local manufacturing, whereas Brazil became for the most part self-sufficient.

26. Which of the following was a problem common to the Abbasids, Ottomans, and Mughals?

 (A) European seizure of the African and Southeast Asian trading networks
 (B) Western technology
 (C) Lack of a shared land border with Europe
 (D) A rigid succession policy that invited conflict
 (E) The competing power structure of regional warrior aristocrats

27. Which of the following had a direct impact on the abolition of slavery?

 (A) Teachings of the Roman Catholic Church
 (B) Enlightenment thinking
 (C) Islamic teachings
 (D) Social Darwinism
 (E) Humanism

28. Which of the following statements describes the major difference between the way Brazil achieved independence and the way other states of Latin America became independent?

(A) Brazil did not end its colonial status until late in the nineteenth century, whereas the Spanish states had all achieved independence by mid-century.

(B) Creoles incited and led slave rebellions in Mexico and Brazil, but mestizos led them in the other Spanish colonies in Latin America.

(C) Brazil became a monarchy, whereas the Spanish states became republics.

(D) Slaves led uprisings in Brazil and in Haiti but not in the Spanish empire's holdings.

(E) The other nations had to fight for their independence, but Brazil under the prince regent simply declared its independence.

29. All of the following were effects of the Industrial Revolution EXCEPT

(A) the migration of large numbers of people from rural areas to cities.

(B) the redefinition of the role of middle- and upper-class women in western society.

(C) the drive for new sources of raw materials.

(D) the development of suburbs.

(E) the development of interchangeable parts.

30. Which of the following groups of nations competed for colonial empires in Africa in the last half of the nineteenth century?

(A) Germany, Belgium, and the United States

(B) France, Italy, and the Netherlands

(C) Germany, Belgium, and Great Britain

(D) Spain, Great Britain, and Japan

(E) Japan, Portugal, and Germany

31. How did the West influence the overthrow of both the Ottoman Empire and the Qing dynasty?

(A) Direct military intervention by the West resulted in the collapse of the governments.

(B) Western political ideas motivated younger men intent on reform to seize the governments.

(C) Western support of the opium trade had severe negative consequences on the local economies, thus weakening the structure that supported the empires.

(D) Neither empire had a strong cultural or religious center and thus was easily attracted to western ideas.

(E) Both empires had a strong tradition of the people overthrowing rulers whom they no longer considered governing in their best interests.

32. All of the following were results of World War II EXCEPT

(A) the loss of colonial empires by European nations.

(B) the creation of new states in Europe.

(C) Japan's adoption of a democratic constitution.

(D) the positioning of the United States as a world power.

(E) the adoption of the United Nations charter.

Question 33 relates to the graph shown below.

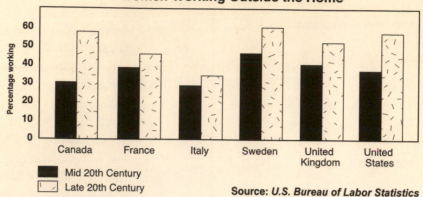

Women Working Outside the Home

Source: *U.S. Bureau of Labor Statistics*

33. Which of the following may explain the trend represented by the data in the graph above?

(A) Women's income helped improve their family's standard of living.

(B) Family stability declined and the divorce rate rose as a result of women working outside the home.

(C) Women who served as heads of households often lived in poverty.

(D) Women made progress toward legal and economic equality as a result of their economic activity.

(E) Women's pay lagged behind men's.

34. "Perestroika is an urgent necessity arising from the profound processes of development in our socialist society. This society is ripe for change."

Which of following spoke the words above?

(A) Adoph Hitler
(B) Lenin
(C) Karl Marx
(D) Boris Yeltsin
(E) Mikhail Gorbachev

35. Which of the following statements is an accurate description of both Buddhism and Hinduism?

(A) The caste system was an outgrowth of Hinduism but became identified also with Buddhism.
(B) Neither religion placed importance on the individual's efforts to seek release from rebirth.
(C) Nirvana was a major aspect of the belief system of both Buddhism and Hinduism.
(D) Both religions taught the importance of karma in affecting a person's fate.
(E) Buddhism made use of formal rituals, but Hinduism did not.

36. The Mandate of Heaven governed the relationship between the ruler and the ruled in

(A) China.
(B) Japan.
(C) France.
(D) Ghana.
(E) Russia.

37. Which of the following reasons motivated both the Abbasids and the Mongols to expand their empires?

(A) The conversion of nonbelievers to their faith
(B) The desire to attack first to keep invaders from their own territories
(C) The need to gain a port on the Baltic Sea
(D) The desire for wealth and plunder
(E) Population pressures within their own empires

38. All of the following characteristics are true of the Tang and Song dynasties EXCEPT

(A) Buddhism appeared in China for the first time.
(B) the Confucian-educated scholar-gentry increased its power in government and society.
(C) artistic and scientific innovations flourished.
(D) the subordinate role of women was symbolized by the practice of footbinding.
(E) the urban population continued to grow.

39. Which of the following best describes the spread of Islam in East Africa and Christianity in China?

    (A) Neither religion made inroads in the cities or the interior of either area.

    (B) Christianity was confined to the cities in China, while Islam made converts in the interior through the Swahili trading network.

    (C) Islam had a decided impact on the trading centers of East Africa but little impact on the interior, whereas Christianity had little impact on either urban or rural areas in China.

    (D) Through the trans-Saharan trading network, Islam reached West Africa, but Christianity, with its reliance on priests, did not travel as easily along the Chinese inland trade routes.

    (E) The East African trading centers became a blend of African and Islamic society and culture.

40. All of the following were characteristics borrowed by Kievan Russia from the Byzantine Empire EXCEPT

    (A) the Orthodox Church version of Christianity.

    (B) art and architectural styles.

    (C) having the church dependent on the state.

    (D) a large and highly trained bureaucracy.

    (E) the concept of divine monarchy.

41. Comparing Aztec and Inca political organization would identify differences in

    (A) the way they were structured.
    (B) the presence of a tribute system.
    (C) the power of the ruler.
    (D) the presence of a class of nobles.
    (E) the emphasis on military power.

42. Triangular trade referred to the network connecting

    (A) East Africa, the Arabian Peninsula, and India.

    (B) the west coast of Africa, North America, and western Europe.

    (C) the west and east coasts of Africa and India.

    (D) India, Southeast Asia, and China.

    (E) China, the Middle East, and the southern European coast of the Mediterranean.

43. Which of the following statements best describes the similarities between the economies of the African continent and Latin America in the latter part of the nineteenth century?

    (A) The economies of both the African colonies and Latin American nations depended on exports.

    (B) Both areas were distracted by internal conflicts.

    (C) Latin Americans and Africans resisted the intervention of foreign capitalists who wanted to invest in industrial development.

    (D) African colonies and Latin American nations both had middle classes that supported industrial development.

    (E) Neither area had developed an infrastructure to transport goods and raw materials quickly and over great differences.

44. The unification of which two nations in the nineteenth century ended the centralization of power begun in Europe in the Middle Ages?

    (A) Germany and Spain
    (B) Italy and Spain
    (C) Russia and Austria
    (D) Germany and Italy
    (E) Germany and Austria

45. Western European foreign policy in the late 1800s was characterized by

(A) Pan-Slavism, colonialism, and an arms race.
(B) détente, colonialism, and an arms race.
(C) imperialism, militarism, and deterrence.
(D) an arms race, imperialism, and a series of alliances.
(E) containment, détente, and the domino theory.

46. All of these factors contributed to the severity of the Great Depression EXCEPT

(A) the reparations demanded of Germany after World War I.
(B) the Stock Market Crash in the United States.
(C) agricultural underproduction.
(D) protective tariffs.
(E) unemployment.

47. All of the following are aspects of traditional Chinese culture and society that are present in modern China EXCEPT

(A) an attitude of cultural superiority.
(B) the Confucian belief that the government must govern for the good of the people.
(C) the reliance on a bureaucracy to run the government.
(D) a belief in the value of harmony.
(E) the Confucian system of civil service.

Question 48 relates to the table shown below.

Language Expansion in Eurasia and Africa

Estimated Date	Language Family or Language	Expansion	Ultimate Driving Force
6000 to 4000 BCE	Indo-European	Ukraine or Anatolia > Europe, Central Asia, India	Food production or horse-based pastoralism
6000 to 2000 BCE	Elamo-Dravidian	Iran > India	Food production
4000 BCE to present	Sino-Tibetan	Tibetan Plateau, North China > S. China, tropical Souteast Asia	Food production
3000 BCE to 1000 BCE	Austronesian	S. China > Indonesia, Pacific Island	Food production
3000 BCE to 1000 CE	Bantu	Nigeria and Cameroon > South Africa	Food production
1000 BCE to 1 CE	Austronesiatic	South China > tropical Southeast Asia, India	Food production
1000 BCE to 1500 CE	Tai-kadai, Miao-Yao	South China > tropical Southeast Asia, India	Food production
800s CE	Hungarian	Ural Mountains > Hungary	Horse-based pastoralism
1000 CE to 1300 CE	Altaic (Mongol, Turkish)	Asian Steppes > Europe, Turkey, China, India	Horse-based pastoralism
1480 CE to 1638 CE	Russian	European Russia > Asiatic Siberia	Food production

48. Based on the table above and your knowledge of world history, which of the following is a reasonable interpretation of the data?

 (A) Language developed as the procurement of food became more organized and complex.

 (B) Language families developed independent of outside forces.

 (C) Older languages eventually disappear.

 (D) New languages are really combinations of old languages.

 (E) Languages from Asia did not spread farther than Asia.

49. Monasticism was an important aspect of which two of the following religions?

(A) Islam and Buddhism
(B) Buddhism and Christianity
(C) Daoism and Shintoism
(D) Hinduism and Buddhism
(E) Christianity and Hinduism

50. Which of the following statements is accurate regarding feudalism in both Europe and Japan?

(A) Feudalism was an economic as well as a political system.
(B) The nature of feudalism was such that it created a strong central government.
(C) Feudalism weakened as cities developed.
(D) Feudalism needed a large agricultural base to support the system.
(E) The basic feudal relationship was between lord and vassal.

51. The blending of Islamic culture traits with Indian practices resulted in

(A) the use of Indian art styles to render Islamic subjects.
(B) the end of the caste system in the Delhi sultanate.
(C) the loss of Urdu as a language of the Indian subcontinent.
(D) the development of a new religion, Sikhism.
(E) the end of Sufism.

52. The placing of upper-class Russian women into quarters separate from men was an outgrowth of Russia's contact with

(A) the Mongols.
(B) the Byzantine Empire.
(C) the Chinese.
(D) the Abbasids.
(E) Indian traders.

53. All of the following are differences between the Sudanic empires and the kingdoms and states of the interior EXCEPT

(A) the Sudanic empires were in a savannah region, and the interior states were in the rain forest.
(B) the Sudanic empires embraced Islam, whereas the interior kingdoms practiced animism.
(C) Bantu-speaking peoples founded the interior kingdoms, whereas the Sudanic kingdoms traced their founding to several different groups.
(D) the economy of the Sudanic empires was based on agriculture and herding, whereas the interior kingdoms reaped the wealth of the slave trade.
(E) the Sudanic empires developed centers of advanced learning, whereas the kingdoms of the interior did not.

54. All of the following were long-term causes of the Protestant Reformation EXCEPT

(A) religious wars in Europe.
(B) the emergence of European nation-states.
(C) the political power of the papacy.
(D) the lax morals of many clergy.
(E) the call by humanists to simplify Catholic practices.

55. "We have seen that kings take the place of God, who is the true father of the human species. We have also seen that the first idea of power which exists among men is that of the paternal power; and that kings are modeled on fathers."

The above definition of kingship could fit the monarchs of all the following states, kingdoms, and empires EXCEPT

(A) Great Britain.
(B) Union of Akan States.
(C) France.
(D) Spain.
(E) Japan.

56. The price revolution in Europe was the direct result of

(A) mercantilism.
(B) a combination of scarce goods and an increase in the gold and silver in circulation.
(C) the growth of global trade in the 1500s and 1600s.
(D) population growth.
(E) joint-stock companies.

57. All of the following were reforms passed by the French National Assembly in reaction to earlier abuses EXCEPT

(A) confiscation of Church property.
(B) limitations on the power of the monarchy.
(C) revocation of special privileges of the nobility.
(D) ended papal authority over French clergy.
(E) abolishment of the Legislative Assembly.

58. Which of the following statements best describes Latin American nations after independence in the 1800s?

(A) Although they had won their independence, Latin American nations remained plagued by their colonial pasts.
(B) Latin America's economic dependence shifted from Spain to the United States and Great Britain.
(C) The newly independent nations continued to be troubled by inequality, rule by a small elite, and limited land ownership.
(D) Although each nation had a constitution that granted the vote to certain males, typically the new nations simply exchanged rule by peninsulares for rule by creoles.
(E) In addition to their old problems of inequality and racism, local peasant revolts led by caudillos began to unsettle the political stability of nations.

59. After World War II, the influence and power of which world region declined?

(A) United States
(B) Soviet Union
(C) Asia
(D) Western Europe
(E) Africa

60. Which of the following problems did Russia and its former Eastern European satellite nations not have in common?

(A) High unemployment
(B) Ethnic tensions
(C) Lack of experience of a market economy
(D) High inflation
(E) Privatizing state-run industries

61. "And what, O priests, is the noble truth of the path leading to the cessation of misery?

    It is . . . right belief, right resolve, right speech, right behavior, right occupation, right effort, right contemplation, right concentration."

    These words describe a teaching of which religion?

    (A) Judaism
    (B) Hinduism
    (C) Christianity
    (D) Buddhism
    (E) Islam

62. Which of the following is an example of an event or situation around 1000 C.E. that helps to mark this as a new period in world history?

    (A) The invasions of the Huns expanded the boundaries and composition of the former Roman Empire.
    (B) The split between the Roman Catholic Church and the Byzantine Empire set the stage for the supporters of each to develop very different religions.
    (C) The breakdown of feudalism in Europe beginning in the 1100s occurred for a number of reasons, including the growth of towns and the efforts of some monarchs to centralize political power in their own hands.
    (D) The collapse of the Delhi sultanate left India in a state of constant upheaval as new waves of peoples moved into the area from Central Asia.
    (E) Buddhism entered China during the Sung Dynasty and for a time supplanted Confucianism.

63. The Aztec civilization's militaristic tone and use of human sacrifice was based on the earlier culture of the

    (A) Inca.
    (B) Maya.
    (C) Mound Builders.
    (D) Toltec.
    (E) Khazars.

Question 64 relates to the map shown below.

Europe in the Medieval Trading Network

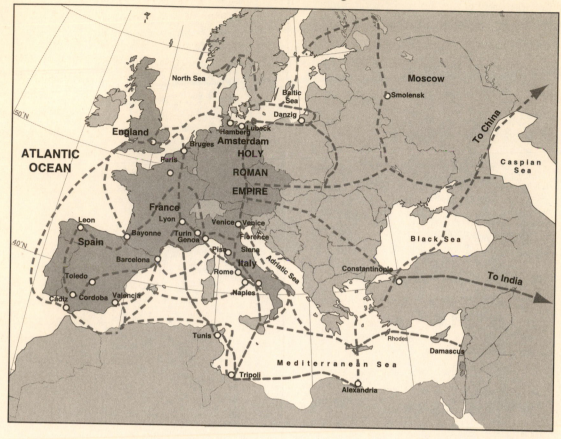

— O — Major trade routes

64. The map above demonstrates which of the following about the trade network that involved medieval Europe?

(A) European trade in this period was restricted to Eurasia.

(B) The pope had no influence on the trading network.

(C) Italian city-states were in an excellent position to capitalize on the trading network that developed in the late Middle Ages.

(D) The trading network facilitated cultural exchanges among Europe, Asia, and the Middle East.

(E) The influx of goods from the Americas would seriously disrupt this network by the 1600s.

65. Which of the following decisions by the Portuguese affected the Arab-African cities of the east coast of Africa?

(A) To trade only from coastal centers

(B) To monopolize trade with Asia

(C) To use force if necessary to ensure favorable trading conditions

(D) To set up an African trading network that included the interior trade routes as well as the coastal cities

(E) To allow Christian missionaries to evangelize in the cities of the east coast

66. All of the following are true about the Enlightenment EXCEPT

(A) the Enlightenment spawned the Scientific Revolution.

(B) according to the thinking of the Enlightenment, religion was based on superstition and should be discarded.

(C) Enlightenment thinkers believed in the power of reason to discover natural law.

(D) Enlightenment thinkers owed much to the earlier Scholasticism for their view of the value of education.

(E) the influence of the Enlightenment can be seen in the Latin American independence movements of the early 1800s.

67. The major significance of the Boxer Uprising was

(A) the halt it brought to Chinese reform efforts.

(B) the division of China by European powers into spheres of influence.

(C) the increased intervention of European powers in Chinese affairs.

(D) the campaign against Christians that occurred in the aftermath of the uprising.

(E) the United States' drafting of the Open Door Policy.

68. Which of the following statements most accurately describes why the United States and other European nations did not stop Hitler before a war could begin?

(A) None of the countries had the money or resources after the Great Depression to arm themselves should Hitler fight back.

(B) These nations were still trying to revive from the Great Depression and paid little attention to Hitler.

(C) These nations were reluctant to make munitions makers any wealthier by rearming.

(D) The United States adopted a policy of isolation after World War I and determined to let Europe deal with its own problems.

(E) Appalled by the destructiveness of modern war, these nations were reluctant to engage in actions that might bring about another war.

69. Which statement most accurately describes the economies of Japan and the city-states of the Pacific Rim compared with the economy of the United States?

(A) The Asian governments of Pacific Rim countries provide economic planning, whereas the United States relies on the market and private business to make economic decisions.

(B) The Asian Pacific Rim nations typically have a low rate of economic growth, whereas the United States has a high GDP.

(C) The Asian Pacific Rim nations have a chronic unemployment problem, whereas the United States does not.

(D) The Asian Pacific Rim nations have an unfavorable balance of trade with the United States.

(E) Industrial pollution is not a problem for Asian Pacific Rim countries, whereas pollution control is an economic drain on U.S. companies.

70. The primary problem facing developing nations in Africa is

(A) lack of a skilled workforce.

(B) their status as dependent economies.

(C) their mounting debt.

(D) the AIDS epidemic.

(E) drought and famine.

SECTION II
PART A

(Suggested planning and writing time—50 minutes)

> **Directions:** The following question asks you to write a coherent essay that incorporates your interpretation of documents 1–4. (Some editing of the documents have been done for this test.)
>
> This question will assess your skill in working with and understanding historical documents. Consider both the sources of the documents and the authors' points of view. Do not summarize the documents individually, but integrate your analysis. Cite relevant evidence from your outside knowledge of world history.

1. The period from 1000 C.E. to 1450 C.E. experienced a number of cultural and social changes. Explain how the following passages reflect the events and ideas that caused change during this period.

   What other documents would you include to discuss change and why?

DOCUMENT 1

SOURCE: The following are selected provisions of the Magna Charta, which English barons forced King John to sign in 1215.

John, by the grace of God, king of England, lord of Ireland, duke of Normandy and Aquitaine, count of Anjou; to the archbishops, bishops, abbots, earls, barons, justiciars, foresters, sheriffs, reeves, servants, and all bailiffs and his faithful people greetings. . . .

12. No scutage [money paid by a vassal to his lord in lieu of military service] or aid shall be imposed in our kingdom except by the common council of our kingdom, except for the ransoming of our body, for the making of our oldest son a knight, and for once marrying our oldest daughter, and for these purposes it shall be only a reasonable aid. . . .

20. A freeman shall be amerced [fined] for a small offence only according to the degree of the offence; and for a grave offence he shall be amerced according to the gravity of the offence, saving his contenement [property necessary for support his family] And a merchant shall be amerced in the same way, saving his merchandise; and a villein in the same way, saving his wainage [seed crops]—should they fall into our mercy. And none of the aforesaid amercements shall be imposed except by the oaths of good men from the neighborhood.

28. No constable or other bailiff of ours shall take grain or other chattels of any one without immediate payment therefor in money, unless by the will of the seller he may secure postponement of that payment.

29. No constable or other bailiff shall distrain [require] any knight to pay money for castle-guard when he is willing to perform that service himself, or through another good man if for reasonable cause he is unable to perform it himself. And if we lead or send him on a military expedition, he shall be quit of castle-guard for so long a time as he shall be with the army at our command.

30. No sheriff or bailiff of ours, nor any other person, shall take the horses or carts of any freeman for carrying service, except by the will of that freeman.

31. Neither we nor our bailiffs will take some one else's wood for repairing castles or for doing any other work of ours, except by the will of him to whom the wood belongs.

39. No freeman shall be captured or imprisoned or disseised [deprived] or outlawed or exiled or in any way destroyed, nor will we go against him or send against him, except by the lawful judgment of his peers or by the law of the land.

41. All merchants may safely and securely go away from England, come to England, stay in and go through England, by land or by water, for buying and selling under right and ancient customs and without any evil exactions. Except in time of war if they are from the land at war with us. And if such persons are found in our and at the beginning of a war, they shall be arrested without injury to their bodies or goods until we or our chief justice can ascertain how the merchants of our land who may then be fount in the land at war with us are to be treated. And if our men are to be safe, the others shall be safe in our land.

DOCUMENT 2

SOURCE: Buddhist missionaries were sent from India to what is now Sri Lanka, Burma [Myanmar], Thailand, Laos, and Cambodia. The excerpt below tells the story of one mission.

The wise Majjhima preached in the Himalaya region whither he had gone with four theras [religious teachers]. . . . The five theras separately converted five kingdoms; from each of them a hundred thousand persons received . . . doctrine. . .

Together with the thera Uttara, the thera Sona of wondrous might went to Suvannabhumi [lower Burma or Bengal]. Now at this time, whenever a boy was born in the king's palace, a fearsome female demon who came forth out of the sea was wont to devour [the child] and vanish again. And at that very moment a prince was born in the king's palace. When the people saw the theras they thought: "These are companions of the demons," and they came armed to kill them. And the theras asked: "What does this mean?" . . . Then the demon came forth from the ocean with her following, and when the people saw them they raised a great outcry. But the thera created twice as many terrifying demons and therewith surrounded the demon and her following on every side. She thought: "This [country] is come into possession of these [people]"and, panic-stricken, she took flight.

When the thera had made a bulwark round the country he pronounced in the assembly the [Buddhist doctrine.]

. . . [S]ixty thousand were converted to the true faith.

DOCUMENT 3

SOURCE: The selection, written by Francis Bacon in 1620, discusses the discoveries and inventions of previous centuries.

It is well to observe the force and virtue and consequences of discoveries. These are to be seen nowhere more conspicuously than in those three which were unknown to the ancients [Greeks], and of which the origin, though, recent, is obscure and inglorious; namely, printing, gunpowder, and the magnet. For these three have changed the whole face and state of things throughout the world, the first in literature, the second in warfare, the third in navigation; whence have followed innumerable changes; insomuch that no empire, no sect, no star, seems to have exerted greater power and influence in human affairs than these mechanical discoveries.

DOCUMENT 4

SOURCE: Ibn Battuta, an Islamic jurist and historian in the 1300s, describes the devastation caused by the bubonic plague in Southwest Asia and North Africa.

Early in June we heard at Aleppo that the plague had broken out at Gaza, and the number of deaths there reached over a thousand a day. On travelling to Hims I found that the plague had broken out there: about three hundred persons died of it the day I arrived. So I went on to Damascus, and arrived there on a Thursday. . . . The number of deaths among them reached a maximum of 2,400 a day. . . . We revisited Hebron, and then went to Gaza, the greater part of which we found deserted because of the number of those who died there of the plague. I was told by the qadí that the number of deaths there reached 1,100 a day. We continued our journey overland to Damietta, and on to Alexandria. Here we found that the plague was diminishing in intensity, though the number of deaths had previously reached a thousand and eighty a day. I then traveled to Cairo, where I was told that the number of deaths during the epidemic rose to twenty-one thousand a day.

SECTION II

PART B AND PART C

(Suggested planning and writing time for each part—40 minutes)

Directions: You are to answer the following question. In writing your essay, use specific examples to support your answer.

2. Explain how the globalization of commerce brought about major changes over time among the peoples of two of the regions listed below between 1450 and 1750. Note major developments, exchanges, shifts of power, and demographic changes.

   - Eurasia
   - Africa
   - The Americas

Directions: You are to answer the following question. In writing your essay, use specific examples to support your answer.

3. Compare and contrast the impact of the Mongol invasions on each of the three regions listed below. In writing your essay, explain each region's response to the invasion and discuss whether the original society was strengthened or weakened by the invasion.

   - China
   - India
   - Russia

SUGGESTIONS FOR THE DOCUMENT-BASED QUESTION

PART A

Study Strategy

Revise your essay using points from this list that will strengthen it.

Be sure that you analyzed each document. Notice that you are asked to identify first the events, then the changes caused by the events described in each document, and third, any significance to the contemporary world. You might have noticed that the documents were not in chronological order. However, you might have chosen to order them chronologically and write about them in that order. Did you also notice that the Bacon excerpt was written at a later time but about earlier events? Or you may have preferred to classify the documents by their importance and discuss them beginning with the least important and ending with the most important for a powerful ending. The rubric for the DBQ states that documents should be grouped in one, two, or three different ways for a basic score and in additional ways for expanded points.

Regardless of the form of organization you chose, you should have incorporated references to all the documents in your essay. You should also have noted any documents that you think would present other events or other points of view that you may consider more important or that present a more balanced view than those included in the question. Be sure to mention such documentation in your essay. As you analyze your essay, consider the following points about Documents 1 through 4.

Document 1

Magna Charta

- Signed by King John I, who was forced by his barons to agree

- Though bearing his signature, not his point of view

- The point of view of his subject vassals

- Example of pressure that organized opponents could apply even to a liege lord

- Guaranteed rights of barons; no attention to serfs

- Implicit in the document, justice depended on the observance of law by all, including monarchs

- Opened way for later extensions of freedom

Article 12

- No money levied in lieu of military service except by general consent

- No taxes without consent of barons

Through time:

- All taxation must be by consent

- Taxation without representation, tyranny

Article 20

- Fined according to severity of offense

Through time:

- Punishment to fit the crime

Article 28

- Seizing of property illegal without prompt payment

Through time:

- No governmental right to take property without legal process

Article 39

- Trial by peers, other barons

Through time:

- Doctrine of due process before the law

- Everyone entitled to trial by peers

Article 41

- Safe passage for foreign merchants

- Reasonable treatment in time of war

Through time:

- Trade protected

- Foreign nationals protected from unreasonable treatment

- Merchants and trade valued

Effects Today

- Principles found in U.S. Constitution and other nations' constitutions

- Considered foundation of present liberties in Great Britain and North America

- Constitutional principles extended throughout the world

- Some of the principles source of conflict regarding human rights

Document 2

Test-Taking Strategy

Don't forget to discuss the authors and their points of view.

- Author unknown, time period unknown

- Whether eyewitness or second-hand account unknown

- Could be much a later recounting of a myth

- Whether writer believed unknown and unknowable from source

- Credibility and validity unknown and unknowable from source

- Spread of religions throughout the world; in this case, Buddhism

- Conversions because test shows religion's power

- Proven ability to overcome evil

- Benefits followers

- Religions transmitted through

  - Commerce

  - Missionaries

  - War

  - Adoption by elites

- Religion governed

  - Daily life

  - Morals

  - Values

- Buddhism to China, Japan

Larger Context of Spread of Religions

- Islam into Africa, India, Southwest Asia, Pacific islands

- Christianity to western hemisphere

- Cause of misunderstanding and conflict among peoples and nations

Effects Today

- Unites and divides nations and groups of nations

- Old conflicts affect current political situation

- Jews and Muslims in the eastern Mediterranean

- Islamic fundamentalism in North Africa, Southwest Asia, South Asia

- Hindu, Sikh, and Muslim conflicts in Indian subcontinent

- Protestant and Catholic conflict in Ireland

- Muslims and Catholics in Philippines

Document 3

- Essay by seventeenth-century philosopher and statesman
- Influential in the Scientific Revolution, important in conceptualizing scientific research through observation
- Question if biased because of use of terms *obscure* and *inglorious,* meaning of unknown origin, in referring to inventions noted
- Gunpowder, printing (block type), and compass—all originally Chinese innovations
- Perhaps not personally biased, but why weren't origins of inventions known in seventeenth-century Europe?
- Eurocentric view possibly expressed by use of ancient Greeks as standard for knowledge

- Transmission of technology and ideas
- Contact with Eurasia and Africa
- Techniques and inventions from the East to the West and the West to the East
- Chinese trading links throughout Asia, Africa, and Europe
- Preservation of classical literature and philosophy

Effects Today
- Many technologies used today based on earlier inventions
- Greater possibility of exchanges of ideas and technologies

Document 4

- Historian as chronicler of events
- Unknown whether idea of objectivity on the part of a historian true in 1300s as is today
- Consider not just historian but also eyewitness
- Note other sources such as statistics from outbreak of plague in Europe

- Outbreak of the Black Death in Southwest Asia
- Possibly spread by Mongols invading from Central Asia
- Outbreaks in Europe and China also
- One third or more of the population in plague areas died

- Little known about effects of plague outside Europe
- Altered the socioeconomic pyramid
- Severe labor shortage in some areas
- Depressed economy
- Hastened end of serfdom
- Psychological effects
  - Fascination with death and dying
  - Death as centerpiece of dance, decoration, art, and public ceremony
  - Accepted causes: demons, wrath of God
- Along with famine, war, schisms, and Turkic invasions, added to sense of waning Middle Ages as a time of calamity and fatalism

Effects Today
- Weakened feudal system in western Europe
- Resulted in stronger monarchies
- Indirectly affected development of European political system

You might have asked for documents suggesting other important aspects of the time period:

- Roman Catholic Church
- Eastern Orthodox Church
- Missionaries
- Famine
- The feudal system in Europe
- China's voyages of exploration and their end
- Turkic invasions

SUGGESTIONS FOR THE CHANGE-OVER-TIME ESSAY

Review Strategy

Skim Chapter 8 for additional information.

You might have chosen the following points to include in your essay on changes over time during the period from 1450–1750 brought about by the globalization of commerce.

Major Developments

- Scientific Revolution

- Acceleration of change, cultural diffusion

- Columbian Exchange

- Transoceanic linking of major regions

- Shift in trade routes from Mediterranean to Atlantic

- Globalization of trade

- Spanish conquer/colonize Central and South Americas

- British in North America

- Dutch and Portuguese in Africa and Asia, island nations

- Global demand for Asian goods

- Global demand for African slaves

- Capitalism emerges as dominant system for

  - Organizing labor

  - Production

  - Trade

- Urbanization

Exchanges

Europe to Americas
- Slavery, plantation system

- Disease

- Genocide

- Plants: wheat, melons, grapes

- Animals: cattle, pigs, goats, chickens, donkeys, horses

- Western clothing

- Carpentry, locksmithing

- Wheeled vehicles

- Organized education

- Christianity, especially Roman Catholicism

- Spanish, Portuguese, and English language and culture as predominant

Africa to Americas
- Plants: bananas, coconut palms, coffee, sugar cane, okra

- Farming methods

- Cooking styles

- Ironworking

- African languages and culture

Americas to Europe
- Gold

- Silver

- Other jewels

- Plants: corn, beans, squash, tomato, chocolate

Europe to Asia
- Cartography

- Astronomy

- Mathematics

- Plants: corn, potatoes from Andes Mountains

- Christianity, especially Roman Catholicism

Asia to Europe
- Guns

- Gunpowder

- Silk

- Porcelain

- Metalwork

- Block printing

- Paper

Shifts of Power

- Spain most powerful country in Europe

  - Spain conquers/colonizes Americas

  - Spain seizes Philippines (link to Asia)

  - Gold and silver from Americas disrupt economy, price revolution

- Portuguese power declines globally

- Chinese

  - Decline of Ming power

  - Rise of Qing power

- French power declines in

  - India

  - Africa

  - North America

- African power declines

  - Negative effects of slave trade

- British power rises in

  - India

  - Africa

- European competition in Caribbean, North America, Africa

  - Dutch

  - French

  - Spanish

  - English

Demographics

- Slave trade ravages African populations

- Enslaved Africans transported to Americas

- Catastrophic decline of Native Americans

  - Genocide

  - Enslaved

  - Disease

- Migration of Europeans to Americas
- Global population rises
  - Agricultural Revolution, higher food production
  - Better crops
  - More known about disease

Other Points to Consider

Mercantilism

- Dominant country must export more than it imports
- Colonies provide
  - Resources
  - Raw materials
  - Markets for goods exported from dominant country
- European effort to control and manage
  - Regulation of trade
  - Selling of trade monopolies
  - Establishment of protective tariffs

Economic Changes in Europe
- Upsurge in prices (price revolution)
- Population increase
  - Greater demand for goods
  - More need for services
  - Urbanization
- Rise of modern capitalism

SUGGESTIONS FOR THE COMPARATIVE ESSAY

You might have chosen the following points to include in your essay on the impact of Mongol invasions on China, India, and Russia. Consider these points as you complete your self-evaluation.

China

- Yuan dynasty

- Few foreigners, caste society, Chinese considered beneath Mongols

- Tolerated other religions, respected scholars and artisans

- Mongol improvements

  - Renovated grand canals

  - Water projects

  - Everyday life for Chinese

- Trade revived between Middle East and Central Asia, then to Europe

- Renewed interest in China and Chinese goods

- Imports

  - Foods

  - Tools

  - Ideas

  - Inventions

- Exports

  - Porcelain

  - Tea

  - Medicines

  - Silks and other textiles

- Mongols despised by native Chinese

  - Bore rule

  - Driven out late 1300s

  - Then Ming Dynasty

India

- Mughals, mixed Mongol and Turkic people

- 1526 to early 1700s, rulers of all India but very southern portion

Test-Taking Strategy

Remember that planning your essay is the most important part. You won't be able to write a logical, well-reasoned essay with pertinent examples if you don't plan first.

- Hindus
- Buddhists
- Led to collapse of Buddhism in India
- Many Hindus converted to Islam
  - Avoidance of taxes
  - Desire for political positions
- Mongols encouraged
  - Education
  - Architecture
  - Arts
  - Culture flourished
- Trade between India, Muslim world increased
- Foreign interest in India
- Exports
  - Indian spices
  - Textiles
- Imports
  - Muslim culture
  - Foods
  - Tools
  - Inventions
- Tolerance of Hindus increased
  - Cultural blending
  - Language, Urdu
  - Arts, miniature paintings
  - Literature
- Interchange and absorption of and by Hinduism and Islam
  - Muslims take on marriage rules
  - Caste ideas

Russia

- Mongols tolerated Russian Orthodox Church
- Levied taxes, tribute system
- Importance of Moscow as tax collector
- Russian princes continued to rule locally
- New trade routes
    - China
    - Central Europe
    - Little or no trade with western Europe
- Decreased interchanges with Europe
- No access to advances in science and arts from western Europe
- Model for later Russian rulers
    - Absolute power
    - Harsh laws
    - Severe penalties
- Absorption by Russians
    - Some Mongol foods
    - Clothing
    - Customs
- Mongol decline in power
- Moscow rise in power, mid-1400s

Other Points to Consider

- Mongol conquest brought devastation and horrible suffering to conquered people
- Mongols fierce conquerors but not oppressive rulers
- After Mongol conquest, political stability, peace, economic growth, cultural growth
- Welcomed by Mongols
    - Foreigners
    - Cultural diffusion
    - Increased foreign interest
- All conquered lands considered source of tribute

ANSWERS AND EXPLANATIONS

QUICK-SCORE ANSWERS

1. D	11. B	21. B	31. B	41. A	51. A	61. D
2. D	12. D	22. B	32. B	42. B	52. A	62. C
3. B	13. B	23. C	33. A	43. A	53. D	63. D
4. C	14. C	24. E	34. E	44. D	54. A	64. C
5. A	15. D	25. B	35. D	45. D	55. A	65. B
6. A	16. B	26. E	36. A	46. C	56. B	66. D
7. E	17. D	27. B	37. D	47. E	57. E	67. C
8. E	18. D	28. E	38. A	48. A	58. E	68. E
9. B	19. A	29. E	39. C	49. B	59. D	69. A
10. D	20. D	30. C	40. D	50. E	60. C	70. B

DIAGNOSTIC TEST

Test-Taking Strategy

Remember that all parts of an answer must be correct in order for the choice to be correct. Half a right answer is still a quarter-point deduction.

1. **The correct answer is (D).** Confucianism is indigenous to China, having originated in the 500s B.C.E., whereas Buddhism arrived in China around the 600s C.E., coming over the trading network from India by way of Central Asia. Even before the Tang Dynasty (618–907), Confucianism had become the predominant ethical system of the Chinese. Many Chinese, however, were attracted to the aspect of salvation in Buddhism and were converted. Because Buddhism was a monastic religion, many monasteries were built in China, thus depriving the government of tax revenue on the land. In time, the government, concerned by the loss of government revenue, the potential lack of population growth because of monks' and nuns' vows of celibacy, the loss of able-bodied men to lives as monks, and the growing influence of Buddhist scholars, fought back. At the instigation of the scholar-gentry, who had lost power and influence, the government set about destroying Buddhist monasteries and temples, confiscating their lands, and forcing monks and nuns to return to secular life. The scholar-gentry solidified their hold on the government and Confucianism on Chinese life. Choices (A) and (B) are incorrect because Shintoism is a Japanese religion. Choices (B), (C), and (E) are incorrect because Hinduism is a religion indigenous to India that did not influence Chinese developments.

2. **The correct answer is (D).** Choices (A), (B), (C), and (E) are true. Choice (D), that nomadic peoples had little positive influence on settled cultures, may seem like a good choice if you think only about Huns and Mongols waving swords and demanding tribute. In reality nomadic peoples were also the ones who protected the trade networks across Central Asia, even if it was for a price. Nomads were also the transmitters of ideas and technologies, both scientific (Muslims) and military (Toltec) in nature. If you did not know the wrong answer immediately (remember this is *not/except* question), you could eliminate choices (A) and (C) fairly quickly as being correct answers. It stands to reason that a culture that relied so heavily on animals would use them as subjects in their art. It also stands to reason that a culture that required physical prowess, especially warrior cultures, would define their society in terms of its male members.

3. **The correct answer is (B).** After the collapse of the Roman Empire in the West in 473 C.E., local leaders became the focus of power. Ordinary people began to turn to them for protection from criminals and from invaders. In this way, the feudal system became established. The invasions of nomadic peoples that had begun in the 200s continued for another 400 or so years. Some invaders like the Franks stayed, and others like the Vandals were driven off. China in the period after the fall of the Han in 220 C.E. suffered a similar experience. The empire was split into rival warring territories and invaders, including the Huns, moved into China. Choice (A) is incorrect because Byzantium fell to the Ottomans who established their rule. Choice (C) is incorrect because after the fall of the Tokugawa Shogunate in 1867, the emperor retained his position, but new bureaucrats, businessmen, and military leaders wielded power and set the country on a path of modernization. Choice (D) is incorrect because the Arabs retained control. Choice (E) is incorrect because the Spanish forced their rule on the Inca.

Idea Bank

Be sure to add Russia to your list of monarchies ruled by what is referred to as divine right in Europe.

4. **The correct answer is (C).** The tsars were eager to adopt the concept that they ruled because of power vested in them by God's authority. The Orthodox Church, choice (E), did influence Russian architecture, but that is not more important to the development of Russian history than the way the tsars used the idea of divine kingship to wield autocratic power. Choice (A) is incorrect because Russia was already involved in long-range trade, so its acceptance of Eastern Orthodoxy did not open any new trade opportunities. In fact, Russia's trade with the Byzantine Empire is how the Eastern Orthodox religion came to

Russia. Choice (B) is also false; the adoption of a single religion helped speed the development of common culture traits. Choice (D) is also false because by 988, when Russia made the Eastern Orthodox Church its official state religion, the Eastern Orthodox and Roman Catholic churches had been growing apart since the Roman Empire was divided in the 400s.

5. **The correct answer is (A).** The question asks you to choose the most direct result. Choice (C), da Gama's voyage around Africa to India; choice (D), the exchange of people, animals, plants, technology, and disease that is characterized as the Columbian Exchange; and choice (E), China's restriction of European traders to treaty ports are indirect results of the Crusades. Choice (B) is simply incorrect. The Black Death was a fourteenth-century occurrence. Only choice (A), the growth of Italian city-states, directly resulted from the Crusades. City such as Genoa and Venice shipped Crusaders and supplies to the Holy Land and on the return voyage brought back spices, silks, and other goods to Europe for sale. After the Crusades, these cities kept up this trade and enlarged it. The Crusades fueled an interest in the other events or situation, but were not the direct cause. A desire for the goods that Asia offered, which the Crusades brought to the attention of Europeans, without the need for intermediaries—Italian or Arab—was the direct cause of da Gama's voyage. The Columbian Exchange resulted from Columbus's voyage west that discovered the Americas in the path to Asia. While European trade with China is an outgrowth of this same interest in the goods that Asia had to offer, segregating Europeans did not occur until the 1500s.

Test-Taking Strategy

For not/except questions, ask yourself if the answer choice is correct in the context of the question. If it is, check it off, and go to the next answer. In these questions, you are looking for the wrong answer.

6. **The correct answer is (A).** Although various cultures had extensive trade networks, like the Mayans, the economies of the Amerindian civilizations in Central and South America prior to 1492 were based on agriculture. Choices (B), (C), (D), and (E) are all true. Remember that differentiation of labor and social stratification are often complementary. Hierarchical political (ruler, councilors) and social structures (nobility, priests) provide markets for foodstuffs (farmers) and manufactured goods (craftworkers)—whether made by hand or by machine—and often require some show of force (soldiers) to ensure governmental continuance or expansion (enemies as slaves).

Test-Taking Strategy

The key words are 1400s and 1500s.

7. **The correct answer is (E).** The Roman Catholic Church's practices were coming under growing criticism as the 1400s wore on, and in 1517 Martin Luther published his Ninety-Five Theses, thus beginning the Protestant Reformation. Choice (A), growing capitalism; choice (B) declining feudalism with the concomitant growth of centralized government; choice (C), an increasingly urban population as commerce took hold; and choice (D), improvements in weaponry are all true about the 1400s and 1500s.

Test-Taking Strategy

The key words are best describes, European and Asian *and* 1500s.

8. **The correct answer is (E).** Choice (B) is a correct statement about trade in Asia, but it does not tell you about how Europeans related to this trade, so eliminate it immediately. Choice (A), the use of force, and choice (C) are incorrect. Europeans determined that they could not enforce a monopoly on the spice trade because they were too few in number to counteract Asian resistance. Choice (D) is also incorrect because Europeans did set up trading centers in various parts of Asia, including the Philippines and India. Choice (E), joining the existing trade network, was the eventual outcome of Europeans' early attempts at controlling the spice trade.

9. **The correct answer is (B).** Both the French monarch and the ruler of Ghana held their throne based on the concept of divine monarchy, that is, the ruler's power came directly from God, choice (B). Choice (C) is incorrect; neither throne was based on matrilineal descent. Islam was the chief religion of Ghana, but France was considered a Roman Catholic country, making choice (D) incorrect. Choice (E), the trade base, describes Ghana, but not France. Remember that although France had a parliament, choice (A), the monarch and the royal advisers made all government decisions.

10. **The correct answer is (D).** If you had circled the key words in this quotation, you would have seen that they relate to the Enlightenment—*phenomena, laws, truth, destiny of man, history.* Choice (A), the scholar-gentry, is not a reasonable assumption because Confucianism bases its principles on such things as right behavior, right thinking, and relationships between people. There is no mention of any of these ideas, making choice (A) incorrect. Machiavelli, choice (B), also deals with behavior and how men should use their power to rule; neither of these is the subject of this quotation. A quotation by a nationalist, choice (C), would probably discuss independence, patriotism, a sense of a nation's destiny rather than that of *man.* You might have considered choice (E), Social Darwinists, for a minute, but if you had highlighted the key words, you would see that they relate better to the Enlightenment than to the theory of natural selection.

11. **The correct answer is (B).** You can immediately eliminate choices (C) and (E) as incorrect statements. Think of the French Revolution as four revolutions in one. The third stage was the uprising of the *sans culottes* or people of Paris; their participation was central to the success of the Revolution. The fourth and simultaneous stage was the revolution of the peasants in the countryside. Choice (D), Louis XVI's need for money, was the direct cause of the convocation of the Estates-General, but the discontent of the French would have erupted into conflict at some point, so eliminate choice (D). Choice (A), the influence of the philosophes, was a long-term cause. The king's insistence reinforced by the nobility themselves that the three estates meet and vote separately was the event that caused the bourgeoisie to break with the aristocracy in the latter's fight against the king. The bourgeoisie, in turn, were joined by the people of Paris, and the French Revolution became a popular revolt and turned violent.

12. **The correct answer is (D).** Great Britain, choice (D), used a system of indirect rule in its African colonies. A British governor and a council of British advisers were at the top of the colonial hierarchy. Government positions below them were held by local rulers, some of whom over time were educated in England. Portugal, choice (A); France, choice (B); Germany, choice (C); and Belgium, choice (E) used an indirect system of colonial governance in which official positions were held by men sent out from the European homelands and local laws were replaced by the European codes of law. Within this system, there were variations. France, for example, believed in the policy of assimilation, whereby its colonial populations would abandon their native language and culture for French and French culture. Belgian rule on the other hand was far more authoritarian and violent, caring little for making the people it ruled Belgian.

13. **The correct answer is (B).** Both Japan and Russia initiated military reforms, so choice (A) is incorrect because this is a *not/except* question. You are looking for the wrong answer choice. Russia introduced *zemstvoes,* or local councils, to provide advice on local matters, whereas Japan established a House of Peers for the nobility and a lower house of elected representatives with limited powers. Choice (C) then is a wrong answer. Choice (D) is also correct but the wrong answer. Both nations promoted industrialization. Choice (E) is incorrect as well because the serfs in Russia and the displaced samurai in Japan suffered as a result of the reforms. That leaves choice (B) as the fact that does not reflect the reforms in Russia and Japan.

Japan's new leaders welcomed wealthy industrialists into positions of power and influence. When it began its reforms, Russia had little in the way of industry or a middle class, and while its reforms fostered industrialization, much of it came through foreign investment, not through the development of the middle class or a class of wealthy businessmen.

14. **The correct answer is (C).** This question asks you to find the choice that represents an inaccurate interpretation of the cartoon. Choices (A), (B), (D), and (E) reflect the attitude of the cartoonist. There is no indication that the artist feels that Queen Victoria is a weak monarch, so choice (C) is correct.

15. **The correct answer is (D).** Ultimately sixty-two nations signed the Pact. It had little practical effect since there were no provisions for enforcing it other than popular opinion. Choice (A), Five-Power Treaty, was signed as part of the Washington Conference; the signatories agreed to limit production of large warships. Choice (B), Treaty of Versailles, included the provisions for the League of Nations, which would settle international disputes peacefully and punish errant nations. Choice (C), United Nations Charter, established a world organization to promote peace and cooperation and to work to improve the welfare of poor countries. Choice (E), Atlantic Charter, was a World War II document signed by Winston Churchill and Franklin Roosevelt declaring the nations' cooperation.

16. **The correct answer is (B).** In general, developing countries suffer from lack of industrial development and the capital to establish their own industries and infrastructure, choice (B), which in turn leads to large debt loads or foreign domination of segments of the economy. A major problem for developing nations is rapid population growth, so choice (A) is incorrect. Another common characteristic of developing nations is the shift of population from rural areas to urban areas, so choice (C) is incorrect. Although there are exceptions, such as Chad, most developing nations have some natural resources—whether good soil for agricultural use, mineral resources, or energy sources—making choice (D) incorrect. Foreign economic aid from nations and from the World Bank and International Monetary Fund is available, choice (E), although not necessarily enough or without strings attached.

17. **The correct answer is (D).** Choice (A) is incorrect because although it is a true fact about Islam, it is not a teaching or principle. Choice (B) is incorrect. Muslims did not force anyone to convert to Islam, but once a person converted, he or she was to abide by the principal teaching of Islam, "There is no God but Allah." Choice (C) is incorrect because Islam does not have priests. Imam may be translated as leader. Any man may lead the prayers and function as the imam, or leader, of those prayers. A mullah is a teacher or interpreter of the law. Choice (E) discusses a principle of Islam, social responsibility, but incorrectly, so it is wrong.

18. **The correct answer is (D).** It was the Huns' pressure on Germanic groups that pushed them into the Roman Empire, where they contributed to its collapse and set up their own kingdoms. The Frankish kingdom, choice (E), that Charlemagne unified rested on these earlier attempts at unification so that it was a result, not a cause, of the development of western Europe. Choice (A), the Mongols, is incorrect because they did not begin their invasions until the 1200s and drove into Russia and eastern Europe—Poland and Hungary—not western Europe. Choice (B), Attila's advance on Rome, was short-lived, so it could not have been a major influence. Choice (C), the spread of Islam into Spain, had an impact on a part of western Europe, but not the entire area, so eliminate it.

19. **The correct answer is (A).** Papermaking originated in China during the Han Dynasty and made its way west along the Eurasian trade route. Choice (B), from Japan, and choice (C), by way of the Columbian Exchange, should be easily eliminated. Japan had limited trading interests early in its history, and those were with China. The Americas were not "discovered" by Europeans until the end of the 1400s, and paper was already in use in Europe. Choice (D), the Triangular Trade route, is incorrect for the same reason. It was established in the late 1600s. Choice (E), from the Middle East, is incorrect but is there as a distracter because it was Muslims who introduced papermaking into Europe from China as a result of their position on the Eurasian trade route.

20. **The correct answer is (D).** All five countries experienced feudalism, although it varied in time from the 700s to 1300s in Europe, from the 800s to the 1800s in Japan, and from the 1600s to the 1800s in Russia. Manorialism, choice (A), was a European characteristic, so eliminate this answer. Divine right monarchy, choice (B), was practiced in some form in all the nations but England, so it is incorrect. England, on the other hand, developed a constitutional monarchy, choice (C), making it incorrect. Anarchy, choice (E), is the lack of an organized government.

21. **The correct answer is (B).** The Roman Catholic Church appointed bishops and other important Church officials such as the abbots of monasteries. Monarchs wanted this power for themselves because the Church through these posts controlled vast amounts of tax-exempt lands and wielded great influence in European nations. Choice (A), Henry's establishment of the Church of England, was a result of a controversy between Henry and the pope, not a cause of conflict, and it did not involve other monarchs. Choice (C) is the reverse of what was true; secular rulers could not tax Church property, which was another source of conflict between the monarchs and the Church. Choice (D), in whose courts clerics could be tried, was a third source of conflict, but of less importance than choice (B). Choice (E) is incorrect; European rulers supported the Crusades, even participating in some.

22. **The correct answer is (B).** As the Middle Ages progressed, Europe became less subject to invasions, the population increased, urban areas grew, and Europe was able to tap into the Asian trade network. With the latter came the evolution of banking and credit and a slowly developing middle class. Choice (C), that Europe had an agricultural economy, is true, but its significance—short-term or long-term impact—is not evident. Choice (E), the decline of manorialism, is true also, but it is a result of and a contributing factor to choice (B), the changing nature of European economic activity, so choice (B) is a better, broader answer. Choice (D), the influence of the Eurasian trading network, is true, but its significance is limited compared to choice (B). The qualifier for choice (D) also is that it is true for the latter part of the Middle Ages, not the entire period. Choice (A), a stagnant European economy, is incorrect and the opposite of what was happening.

23. **The correct answer is (C).** Both the Mayans and the Aztecs had high levels of technology and science. They both built monumental buildings such as pyramids. The Mayans had a complex calendar and could predict eclipses. Both knew techniques for metalworking and weaving and had writing systems. Choice (A), an agricultural economy, was common to both; don't be confused because Mayans also had a trading network that may have stretched north to what is today the southeastern United States. In both civilizations, the priests, choice (B), had great influence with the rulers. The contrast in types of political units, choice (D), is true. The Aztecs lived in a single empire, whereas the Mayans lived in independent city-states. Choice (E) is also true. The fall of the Aztec Empire to the Spanish is well recorded by the Spanish, whereas exactly how and why the Mayan ceremonial centers declined is unknown, although historians speculate about disease, soil exhaustion, and conquering neighbors.

24. **The correct answer is (E).** Peter the Great was interested in those westernization efforts that would modernize his nation, not loosen his grip on power. In fact, he used the changes to exert even greater control, so choice (E) is the most accurate description of his use of reforms. Choice (A) is incorrect because Peter reorganized both the bureaucracy and the military. Choice (B) is incorrect because Peter adopted technological changes and also reorganized the government by replacing the council of nobles with advisers of his choosing and by appointing provincial governors. Choice (C) is incorrect because Peter adopted nothing from western political tradition, such as political parties, that would weaken his power. The lives of serfs did not improve under Peter, so choice (D) is incorrect.

25. **The correct answer is (B).** The Catholic Church had less direct influence on the running of Brazil than it had in the Spanish colonies, making choice (B) correct. Choice (B) is incorrect because both Portuguese Brazil and Spanish America were agricultural economies. Don't be confused by the silver and gold that were extracted from Mexico and the Andes or the gold from Brazil. The majority of colonists made their livings by agriculture. Both Portugal and Spain exercised control over their colonies, so choice (C) is incorrect. Both Brazil and Spanish America developed multiracial societies, so eliminate choice (D). Choice (E) can also be eliminated because Spanish America developed self-sufficiency except for luxury goods.

Test-Taking Strategy

One way to approach a question in which you need to determine whether each answer choice is correct for each item to be compared is to ask yourself if the question is true for the first item. If it is, go to the second answer choice and check it against the first item. If it isn't, cross off the answer choice and go to the next answer. An answer has to be incorrect for just one item in your comparison list to be incorrect.

26. **The correct answer is (E).** All three empires suffered from regional warrior aristocrats who sought to usurp the power of the caliphs and then the sultans. But before you decide this, you need to go through the answer choices in relation to each item to be compared in the question stem. Choice (A) is incorrect because the Europeans were not able to seize control of the trading networks during the Abbasid dynasty, so cross off choice (A) regardless of whether it may be true for the Ottoman Empire or Mughal Empire (it isn't). Western technology was not superior during the Abbasid Dynasty, so eliminate choice (B). (European weaponry and then industrial developments outpaced technological developments of the Ottoman and Mughal Empires.) Choice (C) is correct for the Abbasid Empire, because it spread over Iraq and Syria, but the Ottoman Empire did abut Europe, so rule out choice (C). (The Mughal Empire was on the subcontinent of India.) Choice (D) is incorrect for the Abbasid Empire (and the other two). The problem was that none of the three empires had a succession policy, which led to internal rivalries and intrigues over succession.

27. **The correct answer is (B).** The Enlightenment had a direct influence on the abolition of slavery by focusing people on the ideas that society could be perfected and that injustices, such as slavery, could and should be ended. Choice (A), the teachings of the Catholic Church, and choice (C), Islamic teachings, are incorrect. While both religions taught equality, slavery flourished in countries that considered themselves Catholic or Islamic. Social Darwinism, choice (D), dealt with applying the theory of natural selection in the plant and animal kingdoms to humans. Don't confuse humanism, choice (E), the Renaissance interest in classical literature that developed into a philosophy focused on the study of humans and human values, with humanitarianism, an interest in improving the welfare of people, which was an outgrowth of Enlightenment.

Test-Taking Strategy

Be sure you know what the question is asking. Highlight the important parts of the question.

28. **The correct answer is (E).** In 1822, Dom Pedro declared Brazil independent of Portugal and ruled as Emperor Pedro I. In 1889, the reigning emperor abdicated under pressure and Brazil became a republic. Choice (A) is incorrect. Although Brazil was termed an empire, it was no longer a Portuguese colony after 1822. Choice (B) is incorrect, but it may confuse you because it has a glimmer of truth, which all good distracters have. Creoles led the uprisings—not slave rebellions—in the Spanish colonies, whereas mestizos led the uprising in Mexico. Choice (C) is a partially true statement in that the Spanish colonies became republics, but while you may wonder if monarchy and empire are the same or different, you can eliminate this answer because the statement does not answer the question. The question asks how the colonies achieved their independence, not what kind of nation-state each became. Choice (D) again has some truth. Slaves led an uprising in Haiti that won the colony's independence, but no slave uprising was successful in Brazil or Spanish America.

Test-Taking Strategy

For not/except questions, ask yourself if the answer is correct in the context of the question. If it is, cross it off and go on to the next answer choice.

29. **The correct answer is (E).** The development of interchangeable parts was one of the factors that brought about the Industrial Revolution, not a cause, so in this reverse answer question, choice (E) is the correct answer. Choice (A), the shift of large numbers of people from rural areas to cities, is true of the Industrial Revolution. In places this shift was also encouraged by the enclosure movement. Middle- and upper-class women found their public roles narrowed as work and domestic life separated, so choice (B) is true, but it is the wrong answer. The need for both raw materials, choice (C), and new markets in which to sell manufactured goods encouraged European countries and the United States to seek colonies, so cross off choice (C). As cities grew and transportation systems developed, the middle class moved out of the cities into suburbs, making choice (D) also true but incorrect.

Test-Taking Strategy

All parts of an answer must be correct in order for an answer to be correct.

30. **The correct answer is (C).** Germany, Belgium, and Great Britain all added to their colonial holdings in Africa in the last half of the nineteenth century, making choice (C) correct. Choice (A) is incorrect because while Germany and Belgium took parts of Africa, the United States focused its imperialist interests elsewhere. Both Italy and France helped carve up Africa, but the Netherlands did not, making choice (B) incorrect. Eliminating choices (D) and (E) should have been easy if you remembered that Japan had been isolated from the rest of the world and had not begun its modernization efforts until 1868. Spain, choice (D), and Portugal, choice (E), had been involved in dividing up Africa in the late 1800s.

Test-Taking Strategy

Be careful of distracters. They can confuse you because they are half-truths or true but not in context.

31. **The correct answer is (B).** The Young Turks were motivated by a sense of nationalism and western liberal ideas and the Chinese revolution was led by U.S.-educated Sun Yat-sen and his followers. Choice (A) is incorrect because western forces did not invade China. World War I had an indirect influence on the Ottoman Empire, which fought on the side of Germany against the Allies. At the end of the war, as a result of the Treaty of Sèvres, the Empire was divided up among Great Britain, France, Italy, and Greece, and a Kurdish state and Armenia were created. The Allies controlled the Turkish government, thus setting the stage for rebellion. Choice (C), the opium trade and its consequences, is true about China, but not the Ottomans. Choice (D) is incorrect because both China with its Confucian system of behavior and the Ottoman Empire with its basis in Islam had strong cultural and religious centers. Choice (E) is true about the Chinese but not the Ottoman Empire. The Chinese believed in and had practiced the concept of the "mandate of heaven" to overthrow rulers.

32. **The correct answer is (B).** The states of Eastern Europe were created after World War I, not World War II. While the movements for independence within colonial empires began after World War I, they gained momentum after World War II, choice (A). Choice (C) is correct; the United States forced Japan to accept the abdication of the emperor and the adoption of a democratic constitution. After World War II, the United States did not retreat from international alliances, choice (D), as it had after World War I. The establishment of the United Nations, choice (E), was an indirect result; unlike the League of Nations, which was a part of the Treaty of Versailles, the United Nations had a separate charter. Discussion of the need for such an organization began during the war, however; it was the subject of the Dumbarton Oaks Conference in October 1944.

33. **The correct answer is (A).** All of the responses are true of the late twentieth century. However, only one answer, choice (A), answers the question of why women increasingly worked outside the home.

34. **The correct answer is (E).** These words were spoken by Mikhail Gorbachev, the last president of the USSR, who initiated the policy of perestroika in an attempt to reform the Soviet government and economy. He wanted to reduce government bureaucracy and introduce some elements of the free-market economy into the Soviet Union. He was not, however, ready to disavow communism, which led to his downfall and the establishment of the Russian republic in 1991. The word *socialist* might make you think of Hitler, choice (A), and the National Socialist German Workers' Party, the Nazi party; Lenin, choice (B); or Marx, choice (C), but they are all incorrect. Choice (D), Yeltsin, was the first president of the Russian Republic and might seem like a reasonable choice, but he was not the originator of perestroika.

Test-Taking Strategy

Remember that all parts of an answer must be correct in order for the answer to be correct. A partially correct answer is a partially incorrect answer.

35. **The correct answer is (D).** Both Buddhism and Hinduism teach that how a person acts in this life affects his or her fate in the next life. Choice (A) is correct in that the caste system was an outgrowth of Hinduism, but it is incorrect because it did not become identified with Buddhism. Buddhism embraces all people and their work toward nirvana, or release from rebirth, so choice (A) is incorrect. Choice (B) is incorrect. Buddhism does stress release from rebirth through achieving nirvana. Hinduism stresses release from rebirth through union with brahman, known as mosksha. Choice (C) is incorrect because nirvana is an aspect of Buddhism but not Hinduism. Choice (E) is the opposite of what is correct. Hinduism uses formal rituals but Buddhism does not.

36. **The correct answer is (A).** The Mandate of Heaven refers to the Chinese concept that the ruler had to govern for the benefit of the people or they could overthrow the ruler. Choice (B) is incorrect because the Japanese believed that the emperor was descended from the Sun goddess and, therefore, divine and could not be overthrown. Choice (C), France; choice (D), Ghana; and choice (E), Russia, also had rulers who, while not considered divine, were believed to rule through the intervention of God. In Europe this is known as the concept of the divine right of kings. It resulted in absolute rule, or absolutism.

37. **The correct answer is (D).** Both empires were motivated by the desire for wealth and plunder. Choice (A) is incorrect because conversion was not the focus of the expansion efforts of either group. Choice (B), strike first, was not a motivating force for either the Abbasids or the Mongols. While choice (C), a port on the Baltic Sea, might have been attractive to the Mongols because of their location, it was not a motive for the Abbasids. Choice (D), population pressure, is also incorrect.

Test-Taking Strategy

For not/except *questions, ask yourself if the answer is correct in the context of the question. If it is, cross it off and go to the next answer choice.*

38. **The correct answer is (A).** The Tang ruled from 618 to 906 C.E. and the Song from 960 to 1279, but Buddhism appeared in China around the first century C.E., so choice (A) is incorrect. During both dynasties the scholar-gentry increased their power and influence, choice (B), and both dynasties experienced sophisticated artistic and scientific advances, choice (C). Choice (B), the rising influence of scholar-gentry, is both a cause and a result of the dominance of neo-Confucianism in Chinese life. The female role became subordinate to males in Chinese society; footbinding, choice (D), was an outward manifestation of this subordination and reliance on men. Choice (E), the continued growth in urban population, is also true.

39. **The correct answer is (C).** Islam did not impact the interior of East Africa, but the trading ports of the coast became African-Islamic cities. Christianity, on the other hand, won few converts in either the cities or rural areas of China, although where there were converts it was in cities. Choice (A) is incorrect because Islam did have an impact on the cities of East Africa. While it is true that Christianity where it existed in China was largely an urban phenomenon, choice (B) is incorrect because Islam made few converts in the interior. It is true that Islam reached West Africa along the trans-Saharan trading network, but that network did not connect West Africa and East Africa, so choice (D) is incorrect. Choice (E) is a true statement but does not relate to the question of how Islam spread in East Africa and does not address Christianity and China at all.

40. **The correct answer is (D).** The Byzantine Empire had a large and well-trained bureaucracy that Kievan Russia lacked when it tried to adopt various aspects of Byzantine society and culture. Choice (A), the Orthodox Church, had a great influence on Russia's development, including the state's political evolution—choice (E), the concept of divine monarchy—even though the church was dependent on the state, choice (C). Other influences included art (icons) and architecture (onion dome churches).

41. **The correct answer is (A).** The Aztec empire was a confederation of city-states with the emperor demanding tribute from surrounding states, whereas the Inca empire was more unified with a central ruler, the Inca, who appointed regional governors who, in turn, appointed local governors. Each empire had a tribute system, choice (B), and a single, supreme ruler, choice (C), although nobles had influential roles in the government, choice (D). Both empires emphasized force in acquiring and maintaining conquered peoples and territories, choice (E).

42. **The correct answer is (B).** Choice (C) does not describe a three-legged trade network, so that answer can be eliminated immediately. Don't be fooled by distracters. Trade was conducted along routes that stretched from India to East Africa to the Arabian Peninsula, choice (A), but that was not the Triangular Trade. Neither was the trade carried on among India, Southeast Asia, and China, choice (D), nor trade among China, the Middle East, and southern Europe, choice (E), the Silk Road.

43. **The correct answer is (A).** African colonies and Latin American nations had dependent economies. Their reliance on world markets for such export commodities as foodstuffs and minerals put them at the mercy of changes in these markets. Choice (B) is correct in that both areas experienced conflict—Mexican revolutions and the Zulu War, for example—but the question asks about economic activity, not warfare, so this answer choice is incorrect in context. Choice (C) is incorrect because Latin Americans welcomed foreign investment in the second part of the century; Africans did not have a choice as colonial subjects. Latin American nations did have an urban middle class that supported industrial development, but African colonies did not have such a middle class, making choice (D) incorrect. Choice (E) is also incorrect because each area had some infrastructure in place to transport goods and raw materials to internal and external markets. They may not have been very large and in both cases were backed by foreign investment.

44. **The correct answer is (D).** The Risorgimento, the nationalist movement in Italy, succeeded in uniting all of Italy except Venetia and Rome under Victor Emmanuel II in 1861. By siding with Prussia, Italy received Venetia at the end of the Austro-Prussian War in 1866. In 1870 France lost the Franco-Prussian War and withdrew from Rome. Italy was once again unified—for the first time since 473. Prussia under Bismarck increased its influence and power through a series of wars that resulted in German princes requesting that William I of Prussia become kaiser of a united Germany in 1871. Germany is correct, but choice (A) is incorrect because Spain had become a unified nation by 1504 when it had ousted the last of the Moors. Choice (B) is incorrect because while Italy was unified in the late 1800s, Spain was already a single nation. Choice (C) is incorrect because Russia was a single nation by the nineteenth century, whereas Austria was not created until the Treaty of Versailles. Beginning in 1866 it had been part of the Austro-Hungarian Empire. Choice (E) is incorrect for the reasons stated above.

45. **The correct answer is (D).** You might have been confused by choices (A) and (D), but if you read the question carefully, you have seen the phrase *western European.* Pan-Slavism was a nationalist movement supported by Russia in eastern, not western, Europe, thus eliminating choice (A) because the question asks about *western* Europe. Choice (B) is incorrect because détente is a mid-twentieth-century element of U.S. foreign policy. Choice (C) is incorrect for a similar reason; deterrence is part of U.S. policy regarding nuclear weapons. Choice (E) is incorrect because all three factors are twentieth-century foreign policies. Containment refers to Harry Truman's view of how to deal with communism, and the domino theory refers to a principle articulated during the Eisenhower administration that if one country in Southeast Asia fell to communism, all would—like dominoes.

Test-Taking Strategy

For not/except *questions, ask yourself if the answer is true in the context of the question. If it is, cross it off and go on to the next question.*

46. **The correct answer is (C).** The problem was not agricultural underproduction but overproduction, which drove prices down, making it difficult for farmers to repay their creditors. Choice (A), German reparations, created inflation, so it is true but the wrong answer to this *except* question. Choice (B), the Stock Market Crash, weakened world markets because the United States had become Europe's major creditor, so eliminate this answer as being incorrect. Protective tariffs, choice (D), were a two-edged sword. They kept foreign goods from home markets, thus cutting the flow of local currency out of the country but also making it more difficult to find foreign markets for locally produced goods—and cash flowing into the economy. Eliminate it as the right answer to the question. Choice (E) is true, so rule it as out as the right answer. As more people became unemployed, there was less money to spend

47. **The correct answer is (E).** While there is a reliance on the bureaucracy to run the government, choice (C), that bureaucracy is no longer based on the Confucian examination system, choice (E), so that is the correct answer to this *except* question. Modern China still exhibits a certain degree of cultural superiority in dealing with foreigners, choice (A), so it is the wrong

answer. There is an element of the Confucian belief that the government must govern for the good of the people found in Chinese communism, choice (B), and a belief in the value of harmony, choice (D), so these too are incorrect answers.

Test-Taking Strategy

Be sure you read the title and all the data on a table or graph before reading the question and answer choices. See if you can answer the question before you read the answer choices.

48. **The correct answer is (A).** That a steady food supply and language development were simultaneous is a logical conclusion that can be reached based on the data on the table. There is no evidence on the table to support choice (B), outside forces. Nor is there any evidence to support choice (C), the disappearance of older languages. Choice (D), that new languages are a combination of old languages, may seem logical, but the table does not have any data to support that conclusion. The table contradicts choice (E) because it shows the spread of Asian languages into Europe. The title of the table even uses the term *Eurasia.*

49. **The correct answer is (B).** Monasticism was an important aspect of Buddhism and Christianity, both of which are religions. You could eliminate choice (C) immediately because Daoism is a philosophy, not a religion. Islam, choice (A), does not have monks. Hinduism, choices (D) and (E), has priests but not monks.

Test-Taking Strategy

This question asks you to compare feudalism in Europe and Japan. The correct answer must be true not in general terms but in terms specific to practices in Europe and Japan.

50. **The correct answer is (E).** Only choice (E) is true for both areas; the basic feudal relationship was between lord and vassal. Choice (B) is incorrect because feudalism in Europe may have spread out power among many lords, but in Japan the shoguns used the feudal system to create a strong central government. A lord in Europe such as Louis IX who wished to create a strong central government had to reign in the other French lords. Choice (C) is correct only for Europe where the growth of cities weakened feudalism, whereas in Japan urbanization did not affect the viability of feudalism. Choice (D) is correct for Europe but not for Japan, where a very small agricultural base in comparison fed a growing population. Choice (A) is simply incorrect. Feudalism was a political and administrative system, not an economic one. That was manorialism.

51. **The correct answer is (A).** The blending of Islamic culture traits and Indian practices resulted in the use of Indian art styles to render Islamic subjects. Choice (B) is incorrect, although it might give you pause since Islam teaches the equality of all people. Choice (C) is incorrect because Urdu continued to be an important language of the subcontinent and is one of the official languages of modern Pakistan and India. Sikhism did develop in the 1500s but independently of Islam, so choice (D) is incorrect. Choice (E), the end of Sufism, is also incorrect because Sufis continue to practice their mystical form of Islam.

52. **The correct answer is (A).** The Mongols were a male-domi-
nated society, so it is logical that the Russians would have
modeled on their society a practice such as isolating upper-class
women. Choice (D), the Abbasid Empire, might have given you
pause because of the practice of the harem, but Russians did not
have contact with the Abbasids. The same is true of choice (C),
the Chinese. Even if you did not know that Chinese women
were not formally isolated, you could rule out choice (C)
because of the lack of contact between the two cultures. Choice
(E), Indian traders, is also incorrect and illogical for the same
reason.

53. **The correct answer is (D).** Remember that for a *not/except*
question, you are looking for the answer that is *not* true in
relation to the context. The Sudanic empires' wealth was based
on the salt and gold trade, whereas kingdoms of the interior in
general had economies based on agriculture and herding. Later
the slave trade played an important part in the economies of the
interior states. Choice (A) is true about the geographic location
of each region and, therefore, incorrect. Choice (B) is also a true
statement about the predominant religion of each area and,
therefore, incorrect. Choice (C) is also a true statement about
the origins of each set of states and an incorrect answer. Choice
(E) is also correct about the intellectual attainments of the areas
and an incorrect answer choice. Knowing the correct answer to
choice (B) would have helped you to answer choice (E) correctly since Islamic scholars established these centers of learning.

54. **The correct answer is (A).** This is another *not/except* question, so you are looking for the answer that is not true. Religious
wars in Europe were a result of the division between Catholics
and Protestants, not a cause, so that makes choice (A) an
incorrect statement and the correct answer. Secular heads of
state wanted to dilute the political power of the papacy by
appointing men to such important positions within the Church
in their nations as bishops and abbots rather than having the
pope make these choices. These heads of state also wanted to
be able to tax the vast holdings of the Church within their
nations. As a result, both choices (B) and (C) are causes of the
Protestant Reformation and, therefore, neither is the correct
answer choice to the question. Choice (D), the lax morals of
some of the clergy, and choice (E), the call by humanists to
simplify Catholic practices, are also both true and, therefore,
wrong answers to the question.

55. **The correct answer is (A).** Great Britain alone among the nations listed had a constitutional monarchy and did not adhere to a policy of divine right monarchy. All the other states listed—the African Union of Akan States, choice (B); France, choice (C); Spain, choice (D); and Japan, choice (E)—viewed the monarchy as somehow invested with a divine right to rule. The Japanese believed that the emperor was descended from the Sun goddess and was actually divine.

56. **The correct answer is (B).** Most historians believe that the price revolution occurred because of the vast amounts of gold and silver put into circulation as a result of the importation of these precious metals from the Americas combined with an increasing scarcity of goods to be bought with the additional money. (Some later historians think that the price revolution was the result of the increase in population in Europe in the period between the 1600s and 1700s. This in turn would have led to a scarcity of goods to satisfy the larger population.) Choice (A) is incorrect because mercantilism was the practice of using high protective tariffs to maintain a favorable balance of trade for one's own country as well as a large reserve of gold and silver. Choice (C) is incorrect. While the growth of trade in the 1500s and 1600s had important consequences, the price revolution was not a direct result. Although capitalism, choice (D), was becoming increasingly important, it was not the cause of the price revolution. Joint-stock companies, choice (E), were a vehicle of capitalism.

57. **The correct answer is (E).** The Legislative Assembly was established in 1791 by the National Assembly as the new law-making body of France, so choice (E) is incorrect and, therefore, the correct answer. The other answer choices are all correct in the context of the French Revolution and, therefore, none are the correct answer to this *not/except* question. The National Assembly confiscated Church property, choice (A), in order to divide it up and sell it, thereby gaining tax revenue and breaking the power of the clergy. The National Assembly set severe limits on the powers of the monarchy, choice (B), in order to end royal absolutism and increase the influence of the bourgeoisie in government. The latter was also the purpose in the Assembly's revocation of the aristocracy's special privileges, choice (C). The Assembly also ended papal authority over the clergy, choice (D), and made them dependent on the French government for their salary in an effort to end the lax ways and political abuses of the clergy.

Test-Taking Strategy

In answering a question that asks for the best *description, look for the most inclusive statement, which may mean choosing a generalization.*

58. **The correct answer is (E).** Choice (E) is the best general statement about the problems that Latin American nations faced after independence. None of the other statements is complete in its listing of problems, so although choice (E) is general, it is broadly enough stated to include many ideas. If you were writing an essay on this topic, it would be a good topic sentence, or thesis statement. Choices (B) through (D) could be your supporting details. Choice (B) is a true statement of how the economic dependence of these nations changed, but it is only one aspect of their problems. Choice (D), rule by creoles, is only one aspect of the political problems faced by these nations. Choice (C) includes the idea in choice (D) in its phrase "rule by a small elite," but the statement is still not all-inclusive of the problems. Choice (E) lists two old problems and an additional problem, but it is still not complete.

59. **The correct answer is (D).** The United States and Soviet Union emerged from World War II as the two world superpowers. With physical destruction everywhere, Western Europe was exhausted by war and preoccupied with rebuilding after the war. The United States, removed from Europe and the Soviet Union by the Atlantic and Pacific Oceans, had escaped the war with far less suffering than had either Europe or the Soviet Union. It also had developed and used the first atomic weapons. Shortly after the war, the Soviet Union too had the technology needed for making atomic bombs. It had also surrounded itself with a ring of satellites and appropriated equipment from the West to rebuild its own industries. Western Europe, especially Great Britain and France, was never able to regain the position of power and influence it held before World War II. Choice (A), the United States, and choice (B), the Soviet Union, are incorrect for the reasons stated above. Choice (C) is also incorrect. For example, while Japan lost its position as a military power, its importance in the global economy far eclipsed its former position. The Asian "tigers" of the Pacific Rim likewise have risen in importance since the end of World War II. China, too, has a worldwide importance—both politically and as a market for foreign investment—that it lacked before World War II. Choice (E), Africa, is incorrect, because with independence these new nations have come to play a role in world affairs that they did not have before World War II.

60. The correct answer is (C). Unlike Russia that had been living with state-run businesses and central planning since the Russian Revolution, the nations of Eastern Europe had experience with free-market economies. They had not become Communist states until after World War II. This made the transition to privately run companies and a market economy easier for them. To some degree, Russia and the nations of Eastern Europe in general experienced unemployment, choice (A); ethnic tensions, choice (B); high inflation, choice (D); and the problems associated with turning state-run industries into privately managed businesses, choice (E).

61. The correct answer is (D). The other clue is the word *path* in the first sentence. You could also count the number of right actions listed. The number eight might remind you of the Noble Eightfold Path, a principle set of teachings of Buddhism. The teachings as stated do not match the other religions listed: Judaism, choice (A); Hinduism, choice (B); Christianity, choice (C); or Islam, choice (E).

62. The correct answer is (C). Feudalism probably developed among the Franks in the 700s and began to decline in the 1100s and 1200s. The end of feudalism is one benchmark on the path from the European Middle Ages to the development of a global age in the period from 1450 to 1750. Choice (A) is incorrect because the Huns had invaded the former Roman Empire some 400 to 500 years before 1000 C.E. Choice (B) is incorrect because the Christian Churches in the West and in the East had begun developing separately long before their official split in 1054. The Delhi sultanate did not come to power until 1206 and ended in 1526, so choice (D) is incorrect. Buddhism entered China in the first century C.E., so choice (E) is also incorrect.

63. The correct answer is (D). The Aztecs considered the Toltecs to be their mother culture. The Toltecs were highly militaristic and practiced human sacrifice, two traits that also characterized the Aztecs. Choice (A) is incorrect because the Inca were contemporary with the Aztec. Choice (B), the Maya, were at their cultural peak several centuries before the Aztec moved into the Valley of Mexico. It is possible, however, that the later Mayan centers also were influenced by the Toltecs, which would explain the use of human sacrifice and certain themes like skulls in the artwork of their late city-states. Choice (C), the Mound Builders, is also incorrect; their contact seems to have been with the Maya rather than the Aztec. Khazars, choice (E), may seem like a possibility because of the sound of their name, but Khazars were nomads who invaded Kievan Russia.

Test-Taking Strategy

Be sure to read the title, the map key, and the content of the map before you read the question and the answer choices. See if you can answer the question before you read the answer choices.

64. **The correct answer is (C).** Their position in the Mediterranean enabled a number of Italian city-states to prosper from trade with North Africa and the Middle East. The map contradicts choice (A) because it shows trade routes between European cities and the Middle East. The map does not have enough information for you to know whether the pope exercised any influence on trade or not, so do not select choice (B). The same is true for choice (D). While it is undoubtedly true, the map does not contain any information about cultural exchanges. Again, there is no information on the map to confirm or refute choice (E), so eliminate it. (The statement in choice (E) is not true—the discovery of a sea route to Asia would disrupt the old medieval trade routes more than the influx of goods from the Americas.)

65. **The correct answer is (B).** When the Portuguese determined to control trade with Asia, they spelled the end of the importance of the Arab-African cities of the east coast of Africa, which had traded for several centuries with the Indian subcontinent. Some of them, however, stepped up their trade in slaves from the African interior. Choice (A), to trade only from coastal centers, and choice (C), to use force, were both decisions by the Portuguese, but in relation to the slave trade on the west coast of Africa. Choice (D), to set up a series of interior trade routes, is incorrect—on either coast. Choice (E), the work of Christian missionaries, is incorrect in relation to the work of African-Arab traders.

66. **The correct answer is (D).** Choice (D) is a good distracter but incorrect and, therefore, the right answer choice for this *not/except* question. Scholastics like the Roman Catholic scholar and philosopher Thomas Aquinas sought to use reason to prove the existence of God. Many Enlightenment thinkers were Deists who believed in a supreme being, God as the source of natural law. It is the duty of humans to live virtuously according to these laws of nature. The Scientific Revolution, choice (A), was an outgrowth of the Enlightenment with its emphasis on reason and inquiry, so it is the wrong answer to this *not/except* question. Choice (B), institutional religion as superstition, is correct and, therefore, also the wrong answer. That humans can discover natural law through reason, choice (C), is a principle tenet of the Enlightenment, so eliminate it. The Enlightenment was known by and influenced some of the leaders of the Latin American independence movements of the early 1800s, so rule out choice (E) as incorrect.

Test-Taking Strategy

The key word is major.

67. **The correct answer is (C).** The European powers did divide China into spheres of influence, so choice (B) is correct. However, choice (C)—that the European powers intervened more in Chinese affairs after the Boxer Uprising—is a better choice. It is more inclusive. Choice (A) is incorrect; the Uprising spurred a series of reforms. Choice (D) is incorrect because Chinese Christians were killed along with missionaries and Chinese who worked for foreign import companies as part of the Uprising. The United States began its campaign to force European countries to accept the Open Door Policy in 1899 before the Boxer Uprising.

Test-Taking Strategy

In answering questions that ask you for the best *or* most accurate *description, check for accuracy among the answers but check also to see if any are broad statements or generalizations. Other choices may be details that support the broader, more inclusive statement.*

68. **The correct answer is (E).** While several of the answer choices have truth to them, choice (E)—the appalling destructiveness of World War I—seems to have been the major reason why the United States and European powers did not confront Hitler as he rebuilt the German war machine. Rebuilding and rearming had begun after World War I so that the Great Depression, choices (A) and (B), did not totally account for the reluctance of the former Allies to confront Hitler. Choice (C), the part munitions makers had in precipitating World War I, was an issue that isolationists in the United States used to refuse Europeans aid in resisting Hitler and was motivated by choice (E). Choice (D) is also true and motivated by choice (E). But be alert because choice (D) is incorrect in the context of this question because it deals only with U.S. actions; the question asks about both the United States and Europe.

69. **The correct answer is (A).** A basic difference between the economies of the United States and Pacific Rim nations in general is the presence of economic planning by the governments of Asian Pacific Rim nations. Choice (B) is incorrect because the Asian Pacific Rim nations in general have high GDP (gross domestic products). The nations of the Pacific Rim, including the United States, generally have a low unemployment rate, choice (C). Choice (D) is incorrect because it is the United States that has an unfavorable balance of trade with the Asian nations in general. Industrial pollution, choice (E), is a problem for both Asian Pacific Rim countries and the United States.

70. **The correct answer is (B).** Choice (A), lack of a skilled workforce, and choice (C), their debt load, arise from the status of African nations as dependent economies. Choice (D), the AIDS epidemic, does not face all African nations. In those nations where it is an issue, it contributes to problems related to the workforce and the need for economic aid to combat AIDS, but it is not the primary problem. Not all African nations are faced with drought and famine, choice (E).

Chapter 1

ANSWERING THE MULTIPLE-CHOICE QUESTIONS

Study Strategy

Check the Practice Plan for Studying for the AP World History Test, *pp. 12–16.*

This chapter provides some basic information about Section I of the AP World History Test as well as suggestions for developing a strategy for attacking the multiple-choice portion of the test. You have answered hundreds, probably thousands, of multiple-choice items during your time in school. The multiple-choice questions on the AP World History Test are not that different, and like other tests, if you have studied and know some test-taking techniques, you can do well.

PRACTICE PLAN

Use the *Diagnostic Test* as a tool to improve your objective test-taking skills. Check where you had difficulty on that test in figuring out what questions were asking or how to narrow answer choices, and then use the techniques explained in this chapter to practice answering the multiple-choice questions on the *Practice Tests.*

Always correct your responses with the *Quick-Score Answers* provided for each test. If you don't understand why an answer is correct, refer to the explanations given after the *Quick-Score Answers.* It is generally a good idea to read the answer explanations to all the questions because you may find ideas or tips that will help you better analyze the answers to questions in the next Practice Test you take. The answers often have additional information about the topic that could come in handy to answer a future question.

After you have finished reviewing all the answers for each *Practice Test,* ask yourself what are your weak areas and what can you do to improve—not just in test-taking techniques but in your knowledge of particular chronological boundaries. Are there some periods on which you need to spend time brushing up? Review the strategies in this chapter before you take each *Practice Test,* and also read Chapters 6 through 10, a brief review of world history.

BASIC INFORMATION ABOUT THE MULTIPLE-CHOICE SECTION

FAST FACTS

Test-Taking Strategy

Be sure to take a watch with you to the test, so you can pace yourself. Always take the Practice Test *with a timer, so you get used to the time limits for each section of the test.*

1. Section I consists of 70 multiple-choice questions. There are five possible answer choices for each question.

2. You will have 55 minutes to answer the questions in Section I.

3. You will receive one point for each correct answer that you give. Points are not deducted for questions that you leave blank. If you answer incorrectly, a quarter of a point is subtracted. This is the guessing penalty.

4. Section I counts for 50 percent of your final composite score.

5. The AP World History Test covers world history from the third century C.E.* to the present. The College Board includes "diverse interpretations" as a topic under each chronological boundary listed below, so it is important to review historiography, not just factual information.

   - Foundations (to 1000 C.E.)

     - Basic features of geography

     - Crises of late antiquity (third to eighth centuries C.E.)

     - Key cultural, social, and economic systems (prior to 1000 C.E.)

     - Principal international connections between 700 and 1000 C.E.

   - 1000–1450

     - Interregional networks

     - Nature of philosophy and knowledge

     - China's internal and external expansion

     - The Islamic world

     - Changes in Christianity

     - Non-Islamic Africa

     - Demographic and environmental changes

     - Amerindian civilizations

---

* The College Board uses the designations B.C.E and C.E, Before Common Era (pre-1 A.D.) and Common Era. (post–A.D.)

- 1450–1750

  - Change in global interactions, trade, and technology

  - Knowledge of major empires and other political units and social systems

  - Demographic and environmental changes: diseases, animals, new crops, and comparative population trends

  - Cultural and intellectual developments

- 1750–1914

  - Changes in global commerce, communications, and technology: the Industrial Revolution

  - Demographic and environmental changes

  - Changes in social and gender structure: end of the slave trade

  - Political revolutions and independence movements; new political ideas

  - Rise of Western dominance

- 1914–Present

  - The World Wars, the Cold War, nuclear weaponry, and international organizations and their impact on the global framework

  - New patterns of nationalism, especially outside the West

  - Impact of major global economic developments

  - New forces of revolution and other sources of political innovations

  - Social reform and social revolution

  - Internationalization of culture and reactions

  - Demographic and environmental changes

Diverse interpretations and the factors that define periodization for each chronological boundary are also to be part of any AP World History course.

6. The College Board further breaks down the categories to show approximate percentages of test items in each broad area of study. The following list shows the range of questions that might appear on an AP World History Test:

- Foundations: 14 percent (approximately 9 questions)

- 1000–1450: 22 percent (approximately 15)

- 1450–1750: 22 percent (approximately 15)

- 1750–1914: 20 percent (approximately 14)

- 1914–Present: 22 percent (approximately 15)

Because history in reality does not separate into neat categories, you will find that any given question may straddle several chronological boundaries.

7. According to the College Board course description, only about 30 percent of a world history course should be allotted to European history, and the United States should figure in the course only in its relations with the world. So, don't spend any time reviewing U.S. domestic history or a disproportionate amount of time on European history.

8. Expect to find questions that are based on the six themes that the College Board lists as the structure upon which AP World History courses should be built.

- Impact of societal interactions

- Change and continuity across world history periods

- Impact of technology and demography

- Social and gender structures

- Cultural and intellectual developments

- Functions and structures of states

9. In addition to factual knowledge, the AP World History Test will assess the seven habits of mind or skills that a world history course should foster.

General historical habits of mind include the following:

- Constructing and evaluating arguments

- Using primary documents and data

- Assessing change and continuity over time

- Handling diversity of interpretations

Specific world history skills include the following:

- Discerning global patterns over time and space

- Making comparisons within and among societies

- Developing understanding of ideas and values in cultural and historical context

10. There are four question types: graphics (maps, cartoons, tables, graphs, and pictures), short quotations, and either statements to complete or questions to answer. The majority of multiple-choice items will be of the basic statement or question type. The graphics questions are basically straightforward read-and-interpret questions. You may also find an additional question related to the graphic that asks for an answer that requires outside knowledge.

11. Generally, the questions at the beginning of the test tend to be easier, and the questions become more difficult as you progress through the test.

12. The questions are not randomly ordered. They are clustered in groups that go from the Foundation period to the present. That is, you will notice a progression forward in time to approximately the present, and then the questions will jump back to the earlier period.

13. If you answer approximately 50 percent of the multiple-choice questions correctly (35) and do reasonably well on the essays, you should get at least a 3.

It is important to remember these last three facts. They mean

(1) that you should try to answer as many of the questions at the beginning of the test as possible,

(2) that you can use this chronological order to help you answer questions, and

(3) that you do not have to answer all the questions.

PACING

Answering 70 questions in 55 minutes may seem like running a marathon. It is important to remember that you may not be able to answer all the questions, even with educated guessing. But you should pace yourself, so you can

(1) read all the questions,

(2) answer the easier ones,

(3) and leave the harder ones to return to later.

Because the questions at the beginning of the test tend to be easier, you might plan to spend more time on those questions and less time on the final questions. For example, rather than allotting yourself 47 seconds to read and answer each question, think about dividing your 55 minutes into 18-minute segments. Then divide up the questions so that you tackle more in the first 18 minutes when you are fresh than in the last 18 minutes when you are tired and the questions are more difficult. Or if you start slowly, surge in the middle, and lag at the end, you might try to pace yourself to answer more questions in the middle of the test. One of the benefits of taking the *Diagnostic Test* and *Practice Test* in this book is that you can devise a pacing schedule that fits how you work.

In developing your plan, however, understand that when we say you may be working on fifteen questions in the final 18 minutes, we do not necessarily mean that you are doing the last fifteen questions on the test in those final 18 minutes. We mean that you are working on the last questions that are the most difficult for you. You should skip truly difficult questions on your first pass through the test rather than spend time trying to figure them out. Even the College Board suggests this.

Test-Taking Strategy

Don't make marks on the answer sheet except to fill in answer ovals. Stray marks confuse the machine that scores the tests.

Here are some other suggestions to help you pace yourself:

- Don't spend too much time on a difficult question.

- If you read a question and the content and none of the answer choices seem familiar, skip the question. Put an "X" next to it in the test booklet and be sure you skip the answer oval.

- If you read a question, don't know the answer immediately, but at least one of the answer choices seems wrong, try the steps listed on page 10 for making an educated guess. If you can't immediately eliminate any other answer choices, don't spend any more time. Put a check (✓) next to the question and move on, skipping the answer oval for the question.

- When you have read through the entire test and answered what you can immediately or with a few seconds' thought, go back first to the questions marked with a check and try those again. If you still have time, try the questions you marked with an X.

One word of advice: don't worry if a question at the beginning of the test seems difficult to you. Although we say the earlier questions tend to be easier, all things are relative. What may be a snap question for some students because the subject was a favorite of their teacher may be a blank to other students because their teacher spent only one class period on it.

ANALYZING QUESTIONS

The following examples illustrate how the test writers mix and match question types and content to assess what you know and can do.

QUESTIONS AND SENTENCE COMPLETIONS

A test item may be in the form of a question:

- What European nation challenged Spain's power in the Americas?

Or the test item may require you to complete a sentence:

- Spain found that its chief rival in the Americas was

TEST ITEM QUALIFIERS

A test item may use a qualifier such as NOT or EXCEPT:

- Which of the following is NOT a consequence of the fall of the Ottoman Empire?

- All of the following are consequences of the fall of the Ottoman Empire EXCEPT

These test items want you to find the wrong answer; that is, they want you to select the answer choice that does not belong in each set of answers. To answer these reverse questions, read each answer and ask yourself if the answer choice is correct in relation to the content. If it is, cross it off and try the next response. Keep going until you find a response that is not true in relation to the content of the question.

KEY WORDS

Although most questions follow the questioning format or the sentence completion format, not all ask for straightforward recall. Some require analysis and interpretation.

- Look for words that signal cause-and-effect relationships such as *because of, direct result of, consequence of, primary reason, major reason, primary purpose.*

  - As a result of the slave trade, African nations

- Look for words that ask you to analyze or interpret, such as *most significant, significance of, most characteristic of, most accurately describes, best describes, most accurate description of, best known for, primarily, most influential.*

  - The most significant outcome of the slave trade for African nations was

A word like *significant* means you should be looking for why something is important in the larger context of world history, possibly an underlying concept or a generalization. Words like *best describes* or *least likely* are asking you to analyze the information and come up with an opinion based on facts. In both instances, one or more of the answer choices may be correct; you need to look for the one that is most inclusive, giving the broadest view of the subject.

- Look for words that ask you about comparisons such as *both, most accurate comparison of, shared which of the following.*

  - Which of the following characteristics were present in both English and Japanese feudalism?

First, take the first event, nation, person, or movement in the question stem and compare it to each answer choice. Mark "y" or "n" next to each answer as you go down the five choices. Then take the second item in the question stem and repeat the process. You should come up with just one answer choice that is true for both elements. (Or four if the question is *not/except.*)

- A comparison question might also ask you about the differences between or among events, movements, or cultures. Look for words such as *differentiate* and *distinguish.*

  - The most significant difference between Japanese and English feudalism was

Follow the same process as you do for test items that ask you to compare two or more things or people. Only this time, you are looking for an answer that is true for one element in the relationship but not for the other.

- Sometimes a test item may list several people or events and ask about some movement or event that relates to all of them. This is a disguised comparison question also. Before you can answer it, you must determine which of the answers is true in relation to all the items in the question stem.

  - The governments of France, Spain, and Russia in the seventeenth and eighteenth centuries were

Remember that the AP World History course is supposed to be dynamic in nature. Students are supposed to be learning about interactions and interconnections among societies and cultures. The summary course description even lists major comparisons for each chronological boundary that students should know, so expect to see various kinds of comparison questions on the test.

STIMULUS-RESPONSE QUESTIONS

Stimulus-response questions are based on visuals or on short quotations. Most often, the visuals are political cartoons, tables, and graphs. The quotations may be taken from documents or from the writings of famous people. To help you answer these kinds of questions,

- read the quotation and highlight the key words in it

- restate the quotation to be sure you understand it

- read the question and highlight the key words in it

- relate the question to the quotation

- keep this restatement in mind as you read the answer choices.

Questions based on visuals usually ask you to choose the answer that is best supported by the data. The test item may use words such as *proves* or *demonstrates*.

- According to the two pie charts, the fastest growing source of revenue for the British Empire between 1700 and 1750 was

The problem comes when you try to read too much into the data and choose an answer that may be true but that the given data does not support. When confronted with a question based on a table or graph, follow these helpful hints:

- read the question stem first and highlight key words

- read the title of the graphic

- read the categories on the *x* and *y* axis of line graphs or bar graphs

- read all the labels identifying the data

- look for trends in the data

- read the question again and then read the answer choices

In the end, knowing the type of question you are being asked is less important than paying attention to what the question is asking you. Circle, underline, or bracket the key words in the question. Use them to guide you to the correct answer.

EDUCATED GUESSING

Remember what we said about educated guessing in "Scoring High" on page 9. As you practice taking the tests in this book, use the strategies for making educated guesses when you know something about a question but are not sure of the answer. Once you see how educated guessing can help you raise your score, you will feel more confident using the strategies during the real test.

PRACTICING

Study Strategy

When you have finished the Practice Set, *read all the explanations. The reasoning involved and the additional information may help with questions on the real test.*

Read and answer the *Practice Set* on the next page. Jot down your answers to the questions in the margin or on a separate sheet of paper. If you do not understand a question, you may check the explanation immediately. You may refer to the answers question by question, or you may wish to score the entire set at one time. Either is acceptable, but be sure to read each answer explanation and see how following the strategies in this chapter can help you to answer questions successfully.

PRACTICE SET

> **Directions:** Each question or incomplete statement is followed by five suggested responses. Choose the best answer and fill in the correct oval on the answer sheet.

1. Which of the following civilizations is the exception to the generalization that cities began in river valleys?

   (A) Indus
   (B) Nile
   (C) Huang He
   (D) Inca
   (E) Tigris

2. All of the following are similarities between Buddhism and Christianity EXCEPT

   (A) belief in an afterlife.
   (B) the practice of monasticism.
   (C) the concept of holy people whose intercession can aid others.
   (D) the development of a hierarchical organization.
   (E) the concept of a savior.

3. The most significant change brought about by the rise to power of the Abbasids was

   (A) the decline of cities within the empire.
   (B) the development of an artistic tradition.
   (C) the acceptance of the mawali on an equal basis with the original converts to Islam.
   (D) the defeat of the Umayyad Empire.
   (E) the rise of absolutism in the government of the empire.

4. The empires of West Africa, Ghana, Mali, and Songhay rose to power between the 300s and 1500s

   (A) because they straddled the main trade route between north and south.
   (B) because of the dominance of Islamic power in the region.
   (C) as a result of the establishment of a series of forts by the Portuguese, which supported the West Africans against neighboring peoples.
   (D) because the slave trade had not yet become important.
   (E) because the kings centralized government practices so that their subjects had an advantage in the trans-Sahara trade.

5. Portugal's colonization of its South American colonies lagged behind that of Spain because

   (A) the climate of Brazil was less hospitable than that of Spain's territories.
   (B) the sugar cane that the Portuguese introduced did not grow well in the tropical climate.
   (C) the Native American population was better organized to resist the Portuguese than the Native Americans that the Spanish had faced.
   (D) Portugal's trade with Asia seemed more profitable than what Brazil offered.
   (E) English raiders made trans-Atlantic voyages for other nations' ships dangerous.

6. "I contend that we are the first race of the world and that the more of the world we inhabit the better it is for the human race. I contend that every acre added to our territory means the birth of more of [us] who otherwise would not be brought into existence."

The above was most likely written by

(A) a French revolutionary in 1792.
(B) a Russian Marxist in 1917.
(C) a British imperialist in the 1880s.
(D) a Chinese Communist in 1949.
(E) an American Patriot in 1776.

7. All of the following were causes of the Great Depression that can be traced back to World War I EXCEPT

(A) the U.S. stock market crash.
(B) the decline in the prices of agricultural goods.
(C) deficit financing of the war by European nations.
(D) uncontrolled inflation.
(E) the loss of market share by the United States to European nations.

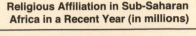

Religious Affiliation in Sub-Saharan Africa in a Recent Year (in millions)

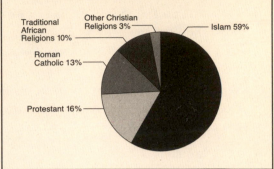

8. Which of the following is not supported by the data on the table?

(A) Traditional African religions have lost most of their believers.
(B) Almost one third of sub-Saharan Africans belong to some Christian denomination.
(C) Most sub-Saharan Africans who consider themselves part of a religion identify themselves as Muslims.
(D) Newer religions to the subcontinent have more believers than traditional African religions.
(E) Christianity, like Islam, spread throughout sub-Saharan African.

ANSWERS AND EXPLANATIONS

Quick-Score Answers							
1. D	2. D	3. C	4. A	5. D	6. C	7. E	8. E

Test-Taking Strategy

This is a factual information question. If you were not sure of the answer, you could probably have eliminated several choices immediately just because you know they are rivers. Choosing them would have been illogical.

1. **The correct answer is (D).** The general observation is that civilizations began in river valleys, and the proof can be found in choice (A), Indus River Valley in India; choice (B), Nile River Valley in Egypt; choice (C), Huang He, or Yellow River, in China; and choice (E), the Tigris and Euphrates Rivers in Mesopotamia in the Middle East. The civilizations of the Americas were the exception. The Inca in the highlands of the Andes, choice (D), developed a highly complex society, but they too needed water to irrigate their fields and built a large system of irrigation ditches to bring water to their land. The Aztec in Mexico and the other civilizations and cultures of North and South America typically did not develop in river valleys, but they all had abundant sources of food and some source of water.

Test-Taking Strategy

For not/except questions, ask yourself if the answer is true in the context of the subject. If it is, then it's the wrong answer to the question.

2, **The correct answer is (D).** Whereas Christianity developed a structured organizational pattern with first elected, and later appointed, officials (bishops), Buddhism remained a system of beliefs rather than adopting a structured governing body, choice (D). However, the two religions share similarities in their beliefs in the afterlife, choice (A), and the development of monastics within each group, choice (B). The bodhisattvas for Buddhists and the saints for Christians represent holy people whose intercession can help others gain holiness. In addition, both religions believe in the concept of a savior, Jesus to Christians and Buddha to Buddhists, choice (E).

Test-Taking Strategy

This question asks you for an opinion. Determine which answers are true about the subject and then decide which is the most important.

3. **The correct answer is (C).** The conquests of the Umayyads and then the Abbasids brought into the Islamic world many different peoples. The Abbasids encouraged the conversion of these peoples to Islam and gave them equal status with the first converts under Muhammad. This policy encouraged the spread of Islam among both Arabic and non-Arabic peoples. In time, Islam spread around the world, thus making choice (C) the most significant result of the Abbasid empire. Choice (A) is incorrect; the rise of the Abbasids fostered the revival and growth of the trading network between Africa and Europe, and with that came

increased wealth for merchants and craftworkers, both city-dwellers. While choice (B), the development of an artistic tradition, is true about the Abbasid empire, it is less significant—had less of an impact on the world—than the growth of Islam through the conversion and adoption of equal status for former nonbelievers. Like choice (B), choice (E), the development of absolutism, is correct about the Abbasids, but it does not have the importance in the course of world history that enlarging the pool of Muslims has had. Choice (D), the defeat of the Ummayyads, is tricky. This is the cause of the rise of the Abbasids, not a change that the Abbasids effected once in power.

Test-Taking Strategy

This is a disguised comparison question. It asks you to compare the three empires and decide what they had in common that enabled them to dominate trade.

4. **The correct answer is (A).** The location of the three empires—Ghana in the 300s to the 1076, Mali in the 1300s, and Songhay in the 1500s—enabled them to dominate the trade in salt from the north and in gold from the south, choice (A). In time, Mali and then Songhay controlled the salt fields and the gold mines. Through trade and invading armies, Islam became dominant in West Africa beginning around 1000, choice (B), but that was not the cause of the rise of the three empires; trade was. Whether or not you knew that the Portuguese established a presence in West Africa, choice (C), you could discard this answer because the Portuguese did not arrive in West Africa until the 1400s and the empires of Ghana and Mali both predate their arrival. Choice (D) makes no sense in the context of the question, nor does choice (E). Sunni Ali in Songhay centralized government organization, but it was the empire's location that made it dominant in the trans-Sahara trade of the time.

Test-Taking Strategy

This is a comparison question with a twist. Only two of the five answer choices relate to both Portugal and Spain. Before you can select an answer, you will need to decide if either of those are true as well as read and determine the accuracy of the other three statements about Portugal alone.

5. **The correct answer is (D).** The truthfulness of choice (A) is debatable. The territories that both Portugal and Spain claimed had rain forests, so that neutralizes that answer. In addition, Spain claimed large areas of Mexico that were arid. Choice (B) is incorrect. Brazil's prosperity was finally built on the introduction of sugar cane in the 1530s and the development of the plantation system. By the early 1600s, Brazil produced more sugar than any other area in the world. Choice (C) is also incorrect. Whereas the Spanish faced the highly organized societies of the Aztecs and Incas, the Portuguese met only scattered groups of Native Americans. Choice (E) is true but not the reason for Portugal's lack of interest in developing Brazil. If you think about it—would a European nation in the 1500s choose not to develop an area because it might lose some ships?—the answer makes no sense. Choice (D), the profitability of Portugal's trade with Asia, deflected attention from Brazil.

6. **The correct answer is (C).** The author of these words is Cecil Rhodes, the businessman for whom Rhodesia, now Zimbabwe, was named. He began the De Beers Mining Company in South Africa, founded a company to open area to British business, and was premier of the Cape Colony in the 1890s. While you probably will not know these facts, you should be able to recognize the words and the tone of superiority—even arrogance—as belonging to a British imperialist of the nineteenth century. They simply do not match the typical message of any of the other advocates, choice (A), the French revolutionary; choice (B), the Russian Marxist in 1917; choice (D), the Chinese Communist in 1949; or the American Patriot in 1776, choice (E).

7. **The correct answer is (E).** European nations had lost market share to the United States and Japan during World War I, thus making choice (E) incorrect and the right answer for this *not/except* question. You may have been tempted by choice (A), the U.S. stock market crash, but this was both a result of the worldwide economic problems of the 1920s and a cause of them. When banks could no longer support the wild speculation of investors and began calling in loans, investors could not make good and the market crashed. Banks began calling in debts that they had financed in Europe during and after the war, choice (C). Europeans could not pay; inflation soared, choice (D); and the worldwide depression worsened. One reason that Europeans could not pay was the drop in the prices of agricultural goods after the war, which also occurred in the United States, choice (B).

8. **The correct answer is (E).** This is a straightforward comprehension question. Read the title, the labels, and the pie graph. Then read the question. It's a *not/except* question, so you know that you are looking for what the pie graph does *not* show. Check the pie graph again to be sure you understand what it does show. Now read the answer choices. Choice (A), that traditional African religions have lost most of their believers, is true. Only about 10 percent of sub-Saharan Africans now practice traditional African religions. Choice (B), that one third of sub-Saharan Africans are Christians, is true. If you add up Protestants, Roman Catholics, and the category of "Other Christian Religions," it comes to 32 percent, almost one third. It is also true that most sub-Saharan Africans who identify themselves as affiliated with a religion identify themselves as Muslims, 59 percent, choice (C). Choice (D) is also correct. Only 10 percent of the people consider themselves as practicing traditional, that is, older, African religions as opposed to 90 percent

who consider themselves either Muslims or Christians. You have now worked your way through choices (A) through (D), and they can all be supported by the data on the pie graph. So in this *not/except* question, you should have crossed each one off as the wrong answer. Choice (E) cannot be supported by the data on the pie graph and, therefore, is the right answer to the question. There is no data on the pie graph that talks about how great the spread of either Christianity or Islam was through sub-Saharan Africa. The distracter here is that it makes sense that these two religions spread throughout the subcontinent, but the pie graph does not say that.

Chapter 2

WRITING AN EFFECTIVE ESSAY

Section II of the AP World History Test consists of three essay questions. You will have 2 hours and 10 minutes to answer all three questions. There are no optional questions in this test. Together, the essays make up 50 percent of your composite score. The document-based question (DBQ) counts for the same amount as the other two questions, so don't worry needlessly about it. Just keep in mind that you have to write three effective essays. An effective essay is one that answers the question clearly and coherently, sets out a reasonable thesis, and uses examples to prove your points. To perform well on the essay portion, you need to plan and to practice now so that on the day of the test, you will have the self-confidence to excel.

PRACTICE PLAN

Study Strategy

Check the Practice Plan for Studying for the AP World History Test, *pp. 12–16.*

In this chapter, you will have an opportunity to review the specifics of good essay writing and to learn some helpful techniques to use when you take the test. Use the *Diagnostic Test* and *Practice Test* as tools to improve your writing, too. Apply the techniques described in this chapter to plan and write each essay within the approximate time allowed per question on the actual Advanced Placement exam—50 minutes for the DBQ and 40 minutes for each of the other two essays.

When you have completed the essays, turn to the *Answers and Explanations* section following each test. First, score your essay with the *Self-Evaluation Rubric*, and use it to score your essay. Then compare your work against the list of suggested points that you might have discussed in your essay. Look for your weak points, and ask yourself how you can improve. Take several of the points from the list, and rework your essay using those points to strengthen ineffective areas.

Reevaluate your essay. Again, compare the points you made with the ones we suggest. Were you better able to dissect the question and discern what was required to answer it more effectively? By using our suggestions, did you improve your response by writing a more focused and more clearly developed answer? Ask yourself how much your work improved. Determine any remaining weak points, such as lack of supporting detail or weak close, and concentrate on improving them in subsequent essays.

Don't continue to revise your essay. You will not have the opportunity to polish your work to perfection on the test, and the evaluators know that you cannot write a perfect essay in 40 or 50 minutes. The purpose of reworking a practice essay is to help you pinpoint what the question is really asking and how you can best answer it with a clear, coherent, and unified essay.

Keep in mind what you learned on your first attempt at the essay. Then go to the next essay question and repeat the process, building confidence each time in your analytical skills and your ability to develop effective essays.

BASIC INFORMATION ABOUT THE ESSAY SECTION

Study Strategy

Use a watch to pace yourself as you write the practice essays. That way, you will become comfortable with the time limits of the test.

1. Section II contains three essay questions, all of which you must answer.

2. You may be given a choice of several cultures or regions within the change-over-time essay question and asked to choose one to write about.

3. You have 50 minutes to plan and write your response to the DBQ and 40 minutes each to plan and respond to the comparative essay and the change-over-time essay questions.

4. The 50-minute period for the DBQ includes 10 minutes for reading the documents and planning what you will write.

5. The College Board recommends that 5 of the 40 minutes that are allotted to answer each of the other two essays be used for reading and planning what you will write.

6. The essay directions remind you to "use specific examples to support your answer."

7. The questions may ask you to discuss and explain, analyze, assess, or evaluate. You will need to distinguish similarities and differences or identify causes and effects.

8. Each essay is scored from 1 to 9, with 9 being the highest.

9. The readers, using a scoring guide developed by the College Board, evaluate each of the essays holistically.

10. The essays together account for 50 percent of your final composite score.

11. The DBQ accounts for the same percentage of your essay score as the other two essays.

12. The essays will not have a single correct answer. Your answers will come from what you have learned in class. In addition, the essays often ask for your point of view, which you must support with evidence.

13. Your three essays will be read by three different people; you do not have to worry that one weak essay will pull down the scores for the other essays.

SOME PRACTICAL ADVICE

Red Alert

If you answer more than half the multiple-choice questions correctly and score in the middle or higher on the essays, you will receive at least a 3.

If you consider these facts, you will realize that you need to do some planning and practicing. You have 50 minutes to write the DBQ and 40 minutes apiece for the other two essays, so when you write the practice essays in this book, follow the actual time limits of the test. Take 10 minutes to read and plan the DBQ and 5 minutes each to read the other two questions carefully and then plan what you will say. Use the remaining time to write your essay, but save the final 1 to 2 minutes for a quick revision.

THE ESSAY: A QUICK REVIEW

You will recall that an essay is a group of paragraphs that work together to present a main point, or thesis. An essay contains an introductory paragraph, separate paragraphs that develop the thesis, and a concluding paragraph. You can see the parts of a five-paragraph essay—the beginning, called the introduction; the middle, called the body; and the ending, called the conclusion—on the next page. Your AP essays may require more than three body paragraphs to make and prove your points. However, keeping this structure in mind will give you direction and help you organize your essay.

WRITING AN OUTSTANDING ESSAY

Test-Taking Strategy

Spend a little more time on your opening paragraph and your conclusion. You want to make a good first and last impression on your scorer.

As obvious as it seems, you accomplish the results you want—a good score—not only by demonstrating your knowledge of world history but also by communicating your expertise in a well-constructed essay. You may have to plan and write your essays in a short period of time, but the characteristics of these essays are no different from those of any good writing: unity, coherence, and adequate development. First, you must determine your audience. Second, you need to establish your purpose. Third, you have to choose the appropriate tone. You can determine these three with a great deal of certainty even before you see the questions.

INTRODUCTION

Interesting Material and Background Information on Topic

Thesis Statement

*The introduction should catch the reader's attention,
establish the purpose and tone, and
present the thesis statement,
or the main idea.*

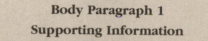

Body Paragraph 1

Supporting Information

*Each paragraph within the body of the essay should develop a subtopic
of the main point by providing strong supporting information.*

Body Paragraph 2

Supporting Information

*Each paragraph within the body of the essay should develop a subtopic
of the main point by providing strong supporting information.*

Body Paragraph 3

Supporting Information

*Each paragraph within the body of the essay should develop a subtopic
of the main point by providing strong supporting information.*

CONCLUSION

Reminder of Thesis Statement

Summary or Final Remarks

*The conclusion of an essay should bring the essay
to a satisfactory close and remind the reader of the main point.*

AUDIENCE

Study Strategy

We provide a Self-Evaluation Rubric and answer suggestions to help you prepare. Our rubric singles out the various descriptors, so you can pinpoint your weaknesses to work on and increase your overall score.

PURPOSE

TONE

STYLE

You have an audience of one—a College Board-trained reader who teaches high school or college world history and who will be reading hundreds of similar papers. She or he will have a scoring guide, or rubric, to aid in evaluating your paper. The reader will consider every aspect of your writing for its impact on the overall impression of your essay.

Your purpose is to get a score of 5 or better. To do that, you need to write a unified, coherent, and consistent essay that answers the question. A well-written essay that misses the point of the question will not get you a good score. That is why you need to read this chapter.

Your tone is the reflection of your attitude toward the subject of the essay. A writer's tone, for example, may be lighthearted, brusque, or serious. The safest tone to adopt is formal, and if you are asked to take a position and support it, persuasive. You do not want to be stuffy and pretentious by using phrases such as "one understands" or "we can surmise." On the other hand, do not be too casual either by writing things like "you know what I mean." Most students, however, err on the side of "faux" erudition, using big words and convoluted constructions. When in doubt, write what you mean simply and directly.

Remember we said that you could determine your tone even before you walk into the test site. Perhaps you wonder how to create that proper tone. You achieve the tone you want through style. Your style should be your own natural style that you use for school essays. That means

- using proper grammar and punctuation

- choosing words that convey your meaning in an interesting rather than a pedestrian or vague way: "The outcome hinged on the bureaucracy's ability to maintain a united front against the maneuverings of the reformists" versus "The bureaucracy had to unite against the reformists to survive."

- avoiding the use of several words when one will do: "There were a number of factors involved that added to the problem . . ." versus "The four factors most responsible for the problem were . . ."

Your style adds interest to the paper. Fresh words and phrasing as much as a unique point of view about a subject can make a paper interesting to read.

UNITY AND COHERENCE

Unity is extremely important to ensure that you communicate effectively. Unity is another word for clarity. A unified paper is one that is clearly developed. Each paragraph has a topic sentence, and every sentence in the paragraph relates to every other and adds to the development of the topic sentence.

In the same way, each paragraph relates to every other, and every paragraph supports the overall thesis. This means, of course, that you need a thesis to develop. This chapter and the next two will help you with developing thesis statements that answer the essay questions.

Remember that your thesis statement contains the central argument that you have developed from brainstorming ideas to answer the essay question. As the *Harbrace College Handbook,* that venerable college English manual, states: "[Your thesis statement] is basically a claim statement; that is, it indicates what you claim to be true, interesting, or valuable about your subject."

Although you can place your thesis statement anywhere in your essay, it is probably safest to put it in the first paragraph, so you can refer to it as you write to be sure that everything you are writing develops and supports it. Putting the thesis first also gets you started writing.

ADEQUATE DEVELOPMENT

Test-Taking Strategy

While neatness and legible handwriting don't count, they do matter. The scorer has to be able to read your essay in order to score it.

What is adequate development? You have a limited time to read and plan and then develop your ideas—neatly. The five-paragraph structure presented earlier will give you a format to work with: a one-paragraph introduction, a three-paragraph middle, and a one-paragraph ending. In the body of the essay, develop only one idea for each paragraph, and be sure to include information from your reading where relevant. You need examples to illustrate your points. You may need more than three paragraphs in the body of the essay to make your points, but this format provides a framework to begin.

You may be wondering why we include all this information about writing when the test is about world history. Remember that you must show the evaluators you can work at a college level. Knowledge about the facts and concepts is not enough. You must communicate to your readers what you know and understand. Graders are not mind readers. If you cannot write the information in a manner comprehensible to them, you cannot demonstrate your expertise. A well-written essay that clearly communicates your knowledge and your position will impress the evaluators and earn you a good score.

WHAT TO EXPECT IN THE AP ESSAYS

In order to answer the essay question that is asked and not what you think is asked, you have to understand what the question is asking. The following table lists some representative question types that you might encounter on the test and how to identify them. You will notice that certain words offer clues to the kinds of support you will need in order to develop an appropriate essay. The AP World History Test is demanding, and you will find that some questions combine two or more types of questions. However, by learning the clue words, you can apply the appropriate support and development strategies.

SOME KEY PHRASES FOR ESSAY QUESTIONS

QUESTION TYPE	WORDS THAT OFFER CLUES	REQUIRED SUPPORT
Evaluation	assess, evaluate, judge the validity	Use your knowledge of world history to substantiate your opinion. For the DBQ, look for evidence in the documents.
Compare	contrast, differ, differences	Look for and stress similarities with specific examples.
Contrast	contrast, differ, differences	Identify and stress differences with specific examples.
Definition	define, explain	Explain what something, such as a policy or a situation, is or does.
Description	describe	Provide the main features with specific details and examples.
Discussion	discuss, explain	Make a general statement that shows you understand the concept in the question. Then support your main idea with examples, facts, and details.
Explanation	explain, why, what, how	Offer examples, details, and facts that illustrate how something happened, what it is, or why it is so.
Illustration	illustrate, show	Provide concrete examples and explain each one to demonstrate the truth or significance of the main idea.
Interpretation	significance, meaning of quotations or events, influence, analyze	State a main idea about meaning. Give examples, facts, and reasons to explain and support your interpretation.
Opinion	what do you think, defend an idea or position, state your opinion	State your opinion clearly. Support and develop it with examples, facts, and reasons.
Prediction	If . . . , then; What . . . if	Predict and state a logical outcome based on your knowledge. Offer arguments to support your opinion.

In all instances, use your knowledge of world history to provide examples to support your thesis. When you are answering the DBQ, find evidence in the documents themselves to substantiate your interpretation. But also use outside examples from your general knowledge of the subject for support.

PLANNING AND WRITING YOUR ESSAYS

Here are specific techniques to help you master Section II. The following advice works both for the DBQ and the other two types of essays.

PLANNING YOUR ESSAY

- Read the question carefully. If it is a document-based question, read the documents carefully.

- Determine if you are required to give an opinion.

- Underline what the question is asking you to do (compare, contrast, analyze, assess, and so on). Circle any terms, events, and people that the question mentions.

- Restate to yourself what the question is asking. Look at your underlining to verify that you understand what you are to do.

Test-Taking Strategy

Use the test booklet to jot down your quick list.

- Do not take time to write a formal outline, but make a list by brainstorming all the ideas and supporting evidence as well as counterarguments that come to mind as you read.

- If you need to compare and contrast data or argue pros and cons, create a table to list the information.

- Be sure to include in your outline relevant outside information, especially for the DBQ if it asks you for additional sources that could be used.

Test-Taking Strategy

One way to write a thesis statement is to restate the question as a definitive statement.

- Create a thesis statement from the ideas you generated.

- Turn this brainstorm into an informal working plan by numbering the items that you want to include in your essay in the order in which you want to include them. Do not be afraid to cross out some that no longer apply now that you have a thesis.

WRITING YOUR ESSAY

- Begin writing your first paragraph by stating the thesis clearly. Take a minute or two to be sure that you are writing a clearly stated and interesting introduction.

- Once you have written the first paragraph, read it to be sure that your ideas follow one another logically and support the thesis.

- Write a transition into the second paragraph. Check your list of ideas.

- Use the vocabulary of world history, but do not overdo it or use words with definitions you are not sure of. Using the terminology of the subject lets your reader know that you are comfortable and familiar with the subject.

- Define your terms as you use them and any terms that have several denotations or connotations.

- Use transitions.

- Write one paragraph for each major idea or concept. Include examples to substantiate the points you make in the paragraph.

- Keep writing until you have used all the RELEVANT ideas on your list. Check how well you are doing at incorporating supporting evidence and refuting counterarguments.

- Allow time to write a solid concluding paragraph. There are several ways to approach the conclusion: rephrasing the thesis, summarizing the main points of your argument, referring in some way back to your opening paragraph, or using an appropriate quotation.

- Pace yourself so that you have at least 1 or 2 minutes to reread your essay for proofreading and revision. Cross out any irrelevant ideas or words and make any additions—neatly. If you have been following your plan to develop your thesis, this time should be spent making sure that your grammar and mechanics are correct and your handwriting is legible.

Your final product should include the following:

- A solid introductory statement: formal thesis, explanation of what is asked of you, and references to the data

- Adequate support

- Specific examples as support

- A response that answers the question completely and accurately

- Satisfactory concluding remarks

Review Strategy

Transitions are words or phrases that connect sentences and paragraphs; for example such words as second, in the third place, in addition, moreover, however, more importantly, next.

Test-Taking Strategy

If you think of additional ideas as you write, quickly jot them down in the margin or by your quick list. That way you will not lose your train of thought. Then, you can include the new ideas where appropriate.

Test-Taking Strategy

Take a watch on test day to ensure you keep within the time frame.

A WORD OF CAUTION

Test-Taking Strategy

If you draw a blank, take a deep breath, think about the topic, and jot down anything that comes to mind about the subject. That will help get you over your nervousness.

You have read extensively about what to do when writing the essays. The following are some suggestions about what NOT to do:

- Do not write an improbable, vague, or unrelated thesis.
- Do not be wordy in an effort to appear knowledgeable and impress the readers. They won't be.
- Do not make unsupported statements.
- Do not include irrelevant data, no matter how interesting.
- Do not use incorrect information. If you are not sure of your facts, leave them out.
- Do not use your opinions, thoughts, and feelings as fact. Express your opinion only when asked, and then support it with evidence.

A WORD OF ENCOURAGEMENT

Your readers know that the writing time is limited, so you cannot produce three perfect, insightful, ground-breaking, definitive essays. They are looking for responses that show that you have the ability and knowledge to produce college-level work. If you

- address the question,
- define your terms,
- thoroughly explain the issues,
- express yourself clearly and logically,
- support your position with evidence, and
- recognize other points of view,

you will do well on your essays. Be positive.

Test-Taking Strategy

Express your personal opinion where appropriate, but be sure to support it with evidence.

PRACTICE

Practice is important. The techniques described above for making sure you understand the question, brainstorming a quick list from which to write, and developing your essay will work for essays you write for your AP class as well as for the essays on AP test day. Practice these techniques when you take essay tests in class and when you write the practice essays in this book, and on test day you will find it much easier to write your essays. Using these techniques will have become second nature to you.

Chapter 3

WRITING THE DBQ ESSAY

After the 5- to 10-minute break following the multiple-choice section, you will begin the 50-minute DBQ—or document-based question—portion. The DBQ is the first part of the essay section. You will receive a booklet in which you will find the question and the documents. After you fill out your identification information, you will be told that for the first 10 minutes of the session you are to read the documents and take notes. You may not start to write your essay until the 40-minute writing session begins.

DEFINING THE DBQ

The DBQ has from four to ten primary-source documents. The documents and possibly the authors may be unfamiliar to you. The purpose of the DBQ is to see how well you can analyze and evaluate information found in primary sources and then synthesize this evidence to develop a well-reasoned essay. According to the College Board, the DBQ

- evaluates students' skills in analysis and synthesis by

  - requiring that students read and analyze each document in order to

    - plan and develop an essay that uses the documents to build a unified and coherent argument to answer the question.

You may be asked to identify additional documents that would help to round out the points of view represented and fill in evidentiary information. You may also be asked what points of view might be needed to give a more complete picture of the issue.

Either of these will provide you with an opportunity to include outside historical content. To get an 8 or 9, you will need to include some reference to relevant information in addition to what the documents provide. Note the word *relevant.* Don't just throw in an interesting fact or event; all additions must relate to the historical context of the period under discussion and the issue in the question.

The course description and the sample rubric for the DBQ state that not all documents need be used but "strong essays will use all of the documents." Since you want a "9," it would be best to plan to use all the documents if at all possible. You should certainly use at least half the documents plus one.

What does using all the documents mean? It does not mean summarizing the documents. The College Board states in boldface type that students are not to "summarize the documents individually." The emphasis in the DBQ is on synthesis and seeing the connections between and among documents. These can be negative connections as well—differences in point of view, for example.

The College Board goes on to state that a writer should "group the essays in as many appropriate ways as possible." This means that when you read each document, analyze it not only for what it says but also for how it relates to the other documents—for what light it may shed on the other documents. For example, a letter to the editor of a London newspaper in 1899 applauding the fight against the Boers could be used to illustrate a point made in a member's speech in Parliament championing the right of British sovereignty over its colonies. This is what "grouping" means.

When you are analyzing the documents, you should look for the following three things:

- context

- bias

- frame of reference

Paying attention to the content, tone, author, audience, and date of the piece will help you to identify all three elements. In planning your essay and then writing it, think about which essays have similar points of view or contrasting points of view or points of view that build from one document to another. As you have probably figured out by now, the DBQ assesses how critically you think about what you read.

THE GAME PLAN FOR THE DBQ

Study Strategy

You can find general strategies for writing effective essays in Chapter 2.

Study Strategy

See the table Some Key Phrases for Essay Questions, *p. 101, Chapter 2.*

Now that you understand what the DBQ consists of, you need a game plan, or essay-preparation strategy, to help specifically with writing a DBQ essay response.

1. Analyze the Question

   As you read the question, analyze what it is asking you to do. Circle, underline, and use brackets to highlight key words, such as the action(s) you are to do—explain, discuss, analyze, compare— the event, situation, issue, or condition that is the subject of the question; and any qualifying or identifying information, such as culture region or actors in the issue. If the time period, culture region, and theme are not stated directly, write them down.

2. Take Notes.

   This step probably seems out of place to you, but it isn't. Most students want to read the documents immediately after reading the question. However, many students experience difficulty generating their own ideas because they focus exclusively on the documents. All they can think about is what they have read.

   We suggest that before you begin to read the documents, you brainstorm the background and outside information you already know about the subject. Take a minute or 2 and jot down everything you can recall about the subject. Don't worry if it's relevant or not. Some of the information from your brainstorming may be included in the documents. Actually, that is a good thing because it shows your thinking is pertinent.

Test-Taking Strategy

You may find contradictions even within a document.

3. Read the Documents.

   Now you are ready to read the documents. As you read, look for inconsistencies among the documents. Since the purpose of the DBQ is to assess your ability to combine historical research and analytical skill, documents will undoubtedly present differing points of view and contradictory explanations of events. You must recognize and discuss these differences. It's part of the grouping, interpreting, and synthesizing aspects of the DBQ.

   Be sure to read the source information for each document. A given writer or a date may trigger important points to include in the DBQ. Sources can also provide insight into conflicting positions since different individuals have different perspectives. Ask yourself how gender, political beliefs, race, social class, and religion may contribute to the viewpoints expressed in the documents.

Make notes as you go through each reading. List the writer, date, country/culture/region, thesis, supporting details, and any bias you detect. Consider creating a table with each document numbered across the top and what you are looking for down the left side. Use tables to analyze comparisons and contrasts and causes and effects.

4. Organize Your Information

After you have finished reading and note taking, it is time to organize your information. Review what you have written—your brainstorming and your notes—and delete repetitious or irrelevant information.

Now you are ready to create a thesis statement on the topic. Again, review your information. Ask yourself, "What do I think about the topic, and how can I support that position? What similarities and differences do I see among the documents? What is missing?" Your answers provide ideas for your thesis. Before you make a final decision, reread the question to ensure your thesis addresses all parts of the question and uses all the documents, if possible. When you begin to write, be sure to write your thesis into your first paragraph.

After you have decided on your thesis, create an outline from your brainstorming and table. Don't write an actual outline, but number the information in the order in which you plan on using it.

5. Write Your Essay

The following are helpful hints for developing the DBQ essay:

- There is no one correct answer. You can argue many different theses on a given DBQ. Choose the one that you can defend most successfully.

- Include as many documents as you can—preferably all of them but at least half plus one.

- Do not summarize individual documents. The readers are looking for a broad analysis of the documents, but you can use individual documents or groups of documents as evidence to support your thesis. Don't just summarize them.

- Remember you must include references to historical information from outside the documents if you want to score your best.

- Include references to any bias you detect.

Test-Taking Strategy

Be on the look out for comparisons and contrasts. The College Board says that comparative questions about societies in contact will be one focus of DBQ questions.

- Check the question to see if you are asked either to suggest additional documents that might round out the discussion or supply a viewpoint that is missing from the documents.

- In discussing the subject, place the documents "chronologically, culturally, and thematically," as the College Board says. This is the document's frame of reference.

- Use present tense in writing about what the document says.

- Identify documents by author or by number.

PRACTICE

Follow the directions on the next page and answer the DBQ using the suggestions that you have just read. Then read the *Steps to Answer* and review the *Points to Include* that we provide after the question. Evaluate your essay using the *Self-Evaluation Rubric* on pages 356–357.

Try to improve your essay. Revise it using your self-evaluation guide and our information points. Then evaluate it again with the rubric. Compare it with your first try to see how much your essay has improved.

When you write your next essay, consciously incorporate the strategies you used in revising this essay—focus more clearly on what the question is asking, probe each document more deeply for its meaning, analyze each document for its significance in the larger context of all the documents, group documents more innovatively, or use more evidence.

Now try *Practice DBQ Essay 2*. Repeat the evaluation and revision process.

Then write *Practice DBQ Essay 3*. Repeat the evaluation and revision process and see how much you have improved.

PRACTICE DBQ ESSAY 1

(Suggested planning and writing time—50 minutes)

Directions: The following question asks you to write a coherent essay that incorporates your interpretation of documents 1–5. Some editing of the documents has been done for this test. This question will assess your skill in working with and understanding historical documents. Cite relevant evidence from your outside knowledge of world history.

1. Analyze the similarities and the differences in the aims and the methods advocated by twentieth-century freedom and independence movements. What evaluation can you make of the short-term and the long-term effectiveness of each?

   What points of view are missing from this set of documents? How might documents written from these points of view add to your discussion?

DOCUMENT 1

SOURCE: In 1908, Mohandas Gandhi, leader of the Indian movement for independence from Great Britain, wrote *Indian Home Rule* to explain his policy of passive resistance.

Passive resistance is a method of securing rights by personal suffering; it is the reverse of resistance by arms. When I refuse to do a thing that is repugnant to my conscience, I use soul-force. For instance, the Government of the day has passed a law that is applicable to me. I do not like it. If by using violence I force the Government to repeal the law, I am employing what may be termed body-force. If I do not obey the law and accept the penalty for its breach, I use soul-force. It involves sacrifice of self.

Everybody admits that sacrifice of self is infinitely superior to sacrifice of others. Moreover, if this kind of force is used in a cause that is unjust, only the person using it suffers. He does not make others suffer for his mistakes. Men have before now done many things which were subsequently found to have been wrong. No man can claim that he is absolutely in the right or that a particular thing is wrong because he thinks so, but it is wrong for him so long as this is his deliberate judgment. It is therefore meet that he should not do that which he knows to be wrong, and suffer the consequence, whatever it may be. This is the key to the use of soul-force. . . .

. . . Passive resistance, that is, soul-force, is matchless. It is superior to the force of arms. How, then, can it be considered only a weapon of the weak? Physical-force men are strangers to the courage that is requisite in a passive resister. Do you think that a coward can ever disobey a law that he dislikes? Extremists are considered to be advocates of brute force. Why do they, then, talk about obeying the laws? I do not blame them. They can say nothing else. When they succeed in driving out the English and they themselves become governors, they will want you and me to obey their laws. And that is a fitting thing for their constitution. But a passive resister will say he will not obey a law that is against his conscience, even though he may be blown to pieces at the mouth of a cannon.

What do you think? Wherein is courage required–in blowing others to pieces from behind a cannon or with a smiling face to approach a cannon and be blown to pieces? Who is the true warrior–he who keeps death always as a bosom-friend or he who controls the death of others? Believe me that a man devoid of courage and manhood can never be a passive resister.

DOCUMENT 2

SOURCE: The following is an excerpt from a memorandum adopted by the General Syrian Congress after World War I. Syria at the time included the present-day nations of Lebanon, Jordan, and Israel.

1. We ask absolutely complete independence for Syria. . . .

2. We ask that the Government of this Syrian country should be a democratic, civil constitutional monarchy on broad centralized principles, safeguarding the rights of minorities, and that the king be Emir Feisal, who carried on a glorious struggle in the cause of our liberation and merited our full confidence and entire reliance.

3. Considering the fact that the Arabs inhabiting the Syrian area are not naturally less gifted than other more advanced races and that they are by no means less developed than the Bulgarians, Serbians, Greeks, and Romanians were at the beginning of their independence, we protest against Article of the Covenant of the League of Nations, placing us among the nations in their middle stage of development which stand in need of a mandatory power.

4. In the event of the rejection by the Peace Conference of this just protest for certain considerations that we may not understand, we, relying on the declarations of President Wilson that his object in waging war was to put an end to the ambition of conquest and colonization, can only regard the mandate mentioned in the Covenant of the League of Nations as equivalent to the rendering of economical and technical assistance that does not prejudice our complete independence. And desiring that our country should not fall a prey to colonization and believing that the American Nation is farthest from any thought of colonization and has no political ambition in our country, we will seek the technical and economical assistance from the United States of America, provided that such assistance does not exceed 20 years.

5. In the event of America not finding herself in a position to accept our desire for assistance, we will seek this assistance from Great Britain, also provided that such assistance does not infringe the complete independence and unity of our country and that the duration of such assistance does not exceed that mentioned in the previous article.

6. We do not acknowledge any right claimed by the French Government in any part whatever of our Syrian country and refuse that she should assist us or have a hand in our country under any circumstances.

DOCUMENT 3

SOURCE: The following is an excerpt from *Thoughts of Chairman Mao,* by Mao Zedong.

It is up to us to organize the people. As for the reactionaries in China, it is up to us to organize the people to overthrow them. Everything reactionary is the same; if you don't hit it, it won't fall. This is also like sweeping the floor; as a rule, where the broom does not reach, the dust will not vanish of itself.

A revolution is not a dinner party, or writing an essay, or painting a picture, or doing embroidery; it cannot be so refined, so leisurely and gentle, so . . . kind, courteous, restrained, and generous. A revolution is an insurrection, an act of violence by which one class overthrows another.

We communists are like seeds, and the people are like the soil. Wherever we go, we must unite with the people, take root and blossom among them.

Communists should set an example in study; at all times they should be pupils of the masses as well as their teachers.

We should pay close attention to the well-being of the masses, from the problems of the land and labor to those of fuel, rice, cooking oil, and salt . . . All such problems concerning the well-being of the masses should be placed on our agenda. We should discuss them, adopt them and carry out decisions, and check up on the results. We should help the masses to realize that we represent their interests; that our lives are intimately bound up with theirs.

DOCUMENT 4

SOURCE: Written six months before the French surrender in 1954, this passage by Ho Chi Minh examines Vietnamese resistance.

Our slogan during the Resistance War is, "All for the Front, All for Victory." The more the Resistance War develops, the more manpower and wealth it requires, and our peasants have contributed the greatest part of manpower and wealth it requires, and our peasants have contributed the greatest part of manpower and wealth to the Resistance. We must liberate them from the feudal yoke, foster them in order fully to mobilize this huge force for the Resistance to win victory.

The key to the victory of the Resistance lies in consolidating and enlarging the national United Front, consolidating the worker-peasant alliance and the people's power, strengthening and developing the Army, consolidating the Party and strengthening its leadership in all aspects. Only by mobilizing the masses to carry out land reform can we carry out these works satisfactorily.

The enemy actively uses Vietnamese to fight Vietnamese and feeds war by war. They are doing their utmost to deceive, divide, and exploit our people. Land reform will exert an influence on and encourage our peasant compatriots in the enemy rear to struggle more enthusiastically to support the Democratic Resistance Government; at the same time it exerts an influence on and disintegrates the puppet army because the absolute majority of the puppet soldiers are peasants in enemy-occupied areas.

The absolute majority of our people are peasants. Over the last years, thanks to their forces, the Resistance War has been successful. In the future, it is also thanks to the peasant forces that we will be able to gain complete victory and successfully build our country.

The landlord and feudal class accounts for less that 5 percent of the populations, but they and the colonists occupy about 70 percent of the arable land, live in clover, and do nothing. This situation is most unjust. Our country has been invaded, our people are backward and poor. . . . [T]he key problem which is not yet resolved is that the peasant masses do not have land or lack land. . . .

DOCUMENT 5

SOURCE: Representatives of the progressive groups in South Africa—blacks, whites, "coloureds," and Asians—signed the following Freedom Charter in June 1955.

Preamble

We, the people of South Africa, declare for all our country and the world to know:

That South Africa belongs to all who live in it, black and white, and that no government can justly claim authority unless it is based on the will of the people;

That our people have been robbed of their birthright to land, liberty, and peace by a form of government founded on injustice and equality;

That our country will never be prosperous or free until all our people live in brotherhood, enjoying equal rights and opportunities;

That only a democratic state, based on the will of all the people can secure to all their birthright without distinction of colour, race, sex or belief;

And therefore, we, the people of South Africa, black and white, together-equals, countrymen and brothers-adopt this FREEDOM CHARTER. And we pledge ourselves to strive together, sparing nothing of our strength and courage, until the democratic changes here set out have been won. . . .

Every man and woman shall have the right to vote for and stand as a candidate for all bodies which make laws. . . .

All people shall have equal rights to use their own languages and to develop their own fold culture and customs. . . .

The mineral wealth beneath the soil, the banks and monopoly industry shall be transferred to the ownership of the people as a whole;

All other industries and trade shall be controlled to assist the well-being of the people;

All people shall have equal rights to trade where they choose, to manufacture and to enter all trades, crafts and professions. . . .

Restriction of land ownership on a racial basis shall be ended, and all the land redivided amongst those who work it, to banish famine and land hunger. . . .

No one shall be imprisoned, deported or restricted without a fair trial. . . .

The privacy of the house from police raids shall be protected by law;

All shall be free to travel without restriction from countryside to town, from province to province, and from South Africa abroad. . . .

Education shall be free, compulsory, universal and equal for all children. . . .

All people shall have the right to live where they choose, to be decently housed, and to bring up their families in comfort and security.

SUGGESTIONS FOR THE PRACTICE DBQ ESSAY 1

STEPS TO THE ANSWER

1. Note that this question asks you both to compare the aims and methods of independence movements and to evaluate their effectiveness in the short term and the long term. In that case, you will need to look for data to use to set up comparisons and contrasts in aims, methods, and effectiveness—short term and long term. That will be the basic way you group documents in your discussion. But what other ways can you group them? Some possibilities are Communist and non-Communist, aggressive and nonaggressive, and Asian, African, and Middle Eastern.

2. Think about what you know about the independence movements in Asia, Africa, and the Middle East in the twentieth century. Jot down these ideas.

3. Create a table in which to write your notes. Then analyze each document for what it says. Be sure to read the source for what it tells you about the author of the document. Then consider each document in light of the others. How do they complement one another by illuminating some point, or do they? Perhaps only some do.

4. Consider the point of view or bias for each document because you will need to deal with this in your essay. Remember that point of view and bias are not the same.

5. The question asks you to indicate what point of view is missing. Did you notice that there are no documents criticizing or debating the issue of national independence? How would such documents add to the discussion?

6. Using all this information, create your thesis. The thesis must be clear, concise, and analytical. It must show how you plan on describing the aims and methods of the various independence movements and their effectiveness based on the documents and any additional information you may bring to the subject.

7. Using the organizing information and writing suggestions in this chapter and Chapter 2, write your essay. Use transition words to make your essay more cohesive. Words such as *compared to, in contrast to, balanced against, the opposite of,* and *whereas* may help you to set up comparisons and contrasts.

8. Keep checking your essay against your thesis statement. Have you gone off on a tangent, or are you sticking to relevant supporting ideas? Remember to use all the documents if you can and to use them persuasively to support your thesis.

POINTS TO INCLUDE

Study Strategy

Revise your essay using points from this list that will strengthen it.

You might have chosen the following points about Documents 1 through 5 to discuss in your essay on the similarities, differences, and effectiveness of the various nationalist movements. Consider these points as you complete your evaluation of your essay.

	Aims	Methods	Short-Term Effects	Long-Term Effects
Document 1	• Independence for India • Freedom from British rule	• Passive resistance • Soul force • Self sacrifice • Others do not suffer • Force unjust • Matchless • Passive resister courageous • Conscience determines action	• Aroused peasants • India on road to democracy • Mostly Hindu • Pakistan an Islamic republic	• Most populous democracy in world • Passive resistance used by other leaders throughout the world, e.g., Martin Luther King
Document 2	• Independent, democratic, constitutional monarchy • Rights for minorities • Feisal king • If not acceptable, U.S. to help	• Written protest • Logical argument • Presentation of acceptable alternatives	• Memorandum rejected • Embittered Arab nationalists • French less flexible than British • Armed conflict broke out	• Treaties to resolve conflicts not ratified by France • Conflict unresolved at outbreak of World War II • Contributed to conflict in the Middle East today

	Aims	Methods	Short-Term Effects	Long-Term Effects
Document 3	• Organize the people, especially the peasants • Overthrow reaction-aries • Show that Communists represent interests of masses	• Use of force; violence • Overthrow ruling party • Unite people; peasants especially important • Set an example; learn from the masses • Concern for well-being of the masses	• Peasants organized • Army raised • Long March • Rivaled Kuomin-tang • Chiang forced to flee • 1949 Mao and commu-nists in power	• Economic power • Military power • Serious human rights issues • One of few remaining Communist states
Document 4	• Independence from France • Mobilize peasants • Victory for resistance	• Enlarge United Front • Consolidate peasant alliance • Strengthen army • Unite party • Strengthen leadership • Land reform—encour-ages peasants and disintegrates puppet army	• French defeated • Civil war between northern and southern Vietnam • Long guerrilla war against U.S. • Northern Vietnam independent Commu-nist nation • Reprisals against non-Communists and southern Vietnam citizens	• Reconciliation with U.S. • One of few Communist nations remaining • Economic factor growing stronger

Document 5	Aims	Methods	Short-Term Effects	Long-Term Effects
	• End apartheid government • South African citizenship, opportunity, and equal rights for all races • A democratic state without concern for race or color • Eliminate current injustice and inequality • All citizens—regardless of gender or race—to vote and to stand for office • Opportunity for prosperity for all • Right to use own languages and develop cultures • Mineral rights and industries owned or controlled by the people • Equal rights in all economic endeavors • No ownership restrictions on land or location of residence • Unrestricted travel • Imprisonment only with fair trial • No police raids • Equal, compulsory education	• Through peaceful means • Plebiscite with all citizens regardless of gender, race, or color to vote • Boycotts • Strikes • Acts of noncooperation • ANC campaign of defiance	• 1955—charter ratified • Blueprint for emancipation from white minority • Served as draft of principles for free South Africa • PAC organized	• Sharpeville—police fired on demonstrators • ANC and PAC underground after being declared illegal • Guerilla warfare • Mandela and others jailed; Biko killed • Foreign nations invoked sanctions; refused to trade • Repeal of apartheid laws by de Klerk's government • Some unrest continues

Other points to consider:

- Bias/point of view:

    - Gandhi—passive resistance as best method of fighting oppression from anyone

    - Syrian Congress—Syrians are as capable as other nations

    - Mao Zedong—Communists as champions of the people

    - Ho Chi Minh—anti-French

    - Freedom Charter—prodemocracy and antidiscrimination

- After World War II, major powers and governments unable to retain colonies

    - Aftermath of World War II, an opportunity for independence movements to succeed

    - Different responses; some violent, others democratic

- Independence movements not new; origins in earlier intellectual movements

- Aim of nationalist movements in Africa and Asia: create new nations

You might have asked for documents suggesting other points of view:

- British government

- Muslms in India

- French government

- Chiang Kai-shek

- T.W. de Klerk

PRACTICE DBQ ESSAY 2

SECTION II

PART A

(Suggested planning and writing time–50 minutes)

Directions: The following question asks you to write a coherent essay that incorporates your interpretation of documents 1–5. (Some editing of the documents has been done for this test.) This question will assess your skill in working with and understanding historical documents. Cite relevant evidence from your outside knowledge of world history.

1. Religion and religious beliefs are major components of culture. They influence values, morals, family expectations, food, clothing, world view, and even political principles. Some nations are theocracies, in which religion determines all actions of the government. In more secular countries, religious beliefs and values also color political decisions. Throughout history, religion has been used to justify political actions, even violence. Read the documents below and determine how each belief system rewards its believers and the political implications and historical consequences of each system. Using those facts and your knowledge of world history, answer the following question: do religious beliefs and principles justify war?

What other documents might have been included?

Document 1

SOURCE: *Bhagavad-Gita,* the Hindu song of God

O Arjuna, the Atma that dwells in the body of all (beings) is eternally indestructible. Therefore, you should not mourn for any body.

Considering also your duty as a warrior you should not waver. Because there is nothing more auspicious for a warrior than a righteous war.

Only fortunate warriors, O Arjuna, get such an opportunity for an unsought war that is like an open door to heaven.

If you will not fight this righteous war, then you will fail in your duty, lose your reputation, and incur sin.

People will talk about your disgrace forever. To the honored, disgrace is worse than death.

The great warriors will think that you have retreated from the battle out of fear. Those who have greatly esteemed you will lose respect for you.

Your enemies will speak many unmentionable words and scorn your ability. What could then be more painful for you than this?

You will go to heaven if killed, or you will enjoy the kingdom of earth if victorious. Therefore, get up with a determination to fight, O Arjuna.

Treating pleasure and pain, gain and loss, and victory and defeat alike, engage yourself in your duty. By doing your duty this way you will not incur sin.

Document 2

SOURCE: *The Book of Joshua* from the Old Testament

20 When the trumpets sounded, the people shouted, and at the sound of the trumpet, when the people gave a loud shout, the wall collapsed; so every man charged straight in, and they took the city.

21 The devoted the city to the LORD and destroyed with the sword every living thing in it-men, women, young and old, cattle, sheep and donkeys.

22 Joshua said to the two men who had spied out the land, "Go into the prostitute's house and bring her out and all who belong to her, in accordance with your oath to her."

23 So the young men who had done the spying went in and brought out Rahab, her father and mother and brothers and all who belonged to her. They brought out her entire family and put them in a place outside the camp of Israel.

24 Then they burned the whole city and everything in it, but they put the silver and gold and the articles of bronze and iron into the treasury of the LORD's house.

Document 3

SOURCE: *The Art of War* by Sun Tzu, a warrior and philosopher of China in the 300s B.C.E.

Sun Tzu said:

The military is a great matter of the state.
It is the ground of death and life,
The Dao of survival or extinction
One cannot but examine it.

And so base it in the five. Compare by means of the appraisals.
Thus seek out its nature.

The first is Dao, the second is heaven, the third is earth, the fourth is the general, the fifth is the method.

And so compare by means of the appraisals
Thus seek out its nature.
Ask–
    Which ruler has Dao?
    Which general has ability?
    Which attains heaven and earth?
    Which implements method and order?
    Whose military and multitudes are strong?
    Whose officers and soldiers are trained?
    Whose rewards and punishments are clear?
By these I know victory and defeat!

The general heeds my appraisals. Employ him and he is certainly victorious.
    Retain him.
The general does not heed my appraisals. Employ him and he is certainly defeated.
    Remove him.
Having appraised the advantages, heed them.
Then make them into *shih* to aid with the external.
Shih is governing the balance according to the advantages.

The military is a Dao of deception. . . .

Document 4

SOURCE: Haji according to the Quran, 4:74–74

Those who readily fight in the cause of GOD are those who forsake this world in favor of the Hereafter. Whoever fights in the cause of GOD, then gets killed, or attains victory, we will surely grant him a great recompense. Why should you not fight in the cause of GOD when weak men, women, and children are imploring: "Our Lord, deliver us from this community whose people are oppressive, and be You our Lord and Master.

Document 5

> SOURCE: Pope Innocent III in Fourth Lateran Council, 1215
>
> ## 71. Crusade to recover the Holy Land
>
> We therefore declare, with the approval of this sacred council and on the advice of prudent men who are fully aware of the circumstances of time and place, that crusaders are to make themselves ready so that all who have arranged to go by sea shall assemble in the kingdom of Sicily on 1 June after next: some as necessary and fitting at Brindisi and others at Messina and places neighboring it on either side, where we too have arranged to be in person at that time, God willing, so that with our advice and help the Christian army may be in good order to set out with divine and apostolic blessing. . . .
>
> Let them beseech kings, dukes, princes, margraves, counts, barons and other magnates, as well as the communities of cities, vills[villages] and towns-in the name of the Father, Son, and Holy Spirit, the one, only, true and eternal God-that those who do not go in person to the aid of the Holy Land should contribute, according to their means, an appropriate number of fighting men together with their necessary expenses for three years, for the remission of their sins in accordance with what has already been explained in general letters and will be explained below for still greater assurance. We wish to share in this remission not only those who contribute ships of their own but also those who are zealous enough to build them for this purpose. To those who refuse, if there happen to be any who are so ungrateful to our lord God, we firmly declare in the name of the apostle that they should know that they will have to answer to us for this on the last day of final judgment before the fearful judge.

SUGGESTIONS FOR PRACTICE DBQ ESSAY 2

Study Strategy

Revise your essay using points from this list that will strengthen it.

Be sure that you analyzed each document. Did you notice that you are asked to discuss the meaning and implications of each document in order to answer the question? You might also have noticed that the documents are in chronological order, but you do not need to write about them in that order. You might have preferred to classify them by the methods they advocate and discuss each classification. Or you might have used them to compare and contrast points of view. The rubric for the DBQ states that documents should be grouped in one, two, or three different ways for a basic score and in additional ways for extended points.

Regardless of which forms of organization you chose, you should have incorporated references to all the documents in your essay. You should also have noted any documents that you think would present other events or other points of view that you may consider more important or that present a more balanced view than those included in the question. Be sure to mention such documentation in your essay. As you analyze your essay, consider the following points about documents 1 through 5.

Document 1

Test-Taking Strategy

Order of importance is one way to organize essays of this nature. By leaving your strongest point until last, you will leave readers with a powerful impression.

Points of View

Documents 1 through 3 are original religious texts supposedly handed down from each religion's idea of God. Document 4 is the writing of someone who is a believer in Daoism. Document 5 is the words of the head of the Roman Catholic Church calling the faithful to action and, therefore, is considered to have the force of God supporting them.

Meaning

- Duty of warrior to fight against evildoers—Hindu or not

- A just war, auspicious

- War—a door to heaven

- Refusing to fight brings

  - Failure of duty

  - Dishonor and disgrace

  - Scorn

  - Sin

- Entering the war

  - Entrance to heaven if die

  - Delights of this earth if victorious

Motivation

- Honor and esteem

- Performing *dharma* well

- Earthly delights

- Heaven

Political/Historical Consequences

- Religious beliefs as justification for violence

- Maintain cultural identity

- Battles with Buddhists

- Battles with Muslims

- Battles against the British during the colonial period

- Fight for the independence of Pakistan

- Continuing antagonism between Hindus and Muslims

Document 2

Meaning

- God on the side of Joshua

- Obey God

- Obedience to God brings rewards in this life

- City consecrated to God

- City and its gentile citizens destroyed; God's permission to kill gentiles

- All precious objects to God

- Implies that destruction and slaughter acceptable as long as victims not Jews

Motivation

- Seizure of city land and valuables for the tribe

- Those that help Israelites saved

- Knowledge that all-powerful God on the side of the Israelites

Political/Historical Consequences

- Religious beliefs as justification for force

- Hebrews extend control in western Mesopotamia

- Constant fighting in region over thousands of years

- Fighting between Jews and non-Jews in the region today

Document 3

Meaning
- Military linked with state
- Reflects duality of life—live or die
- Seek out its nature
- Appraise it by questioning
- Military—by nature deceptive
- Keep good leader for victories
- Remove poor leaders—defeats

Motivation
- Performing duty
- Victory

Political/Historical Consequences
- Religious beliefs as justification for military action
- Built powerful army
- Centuries-old teachings
- Military academies still teach writings of Sun Tzu

Document 4

Meaning
- Duty to fight for Allah
- Soldiers fighting for Allah favored in the hereafter
- If killed or victorious, greatly rewarded
- Save the weak in Allah's name

Motivations
- Rewarded in heaven
- Promote Allah's goals and plans
- Go directly to heaven if killed
- Very material rewards—food, drink, and other earthly pleasures

Political/Historical Consequences
- Religious beliefs as justification for violence
- Jihad
- Made Muslims fierce fighters
- Expanded territory

- Spread Islam throughout world

- Powerful politically; theocracies

- Conflicts with other religious groups

- Modern battles against secular governments

Document 5

Meaning

- Pope: take Holy Land back from the infidels

- Crusaders travel to fight for the Holy Land

- God's blessing on the Crusaders

- Contribute or fight

  - Money

  - Men

  - Ships

- Those that help Israelites saved

- Those unwilling to help damned

- Those participating forgiven of sin

Motivation

- Fight for beliefs

- Remission of sins

- Fame

- Wealth

- Adventure

Political/Historical Consequences

- Religious beliefs as justification of violence against not only non-Christians but also Christians of other churches

- Crusades unsuccessful

- Introduction of spices and other exotic goods to the West

- Conflict between Christians and Muslims; strife continues today

- Conflict between Roman Catholic and Orthodox churches

- Materialism of church eventually created dissent

Other points of historical importance

- Similarities in belief that not to oppose evil is to indirectly support it

- Quran: Allah loves those who battle for his cause

- Bible: Happy are those who suffer persecution because they do what God requires. The kingdom of heaven belongs to them

- Bhagavad-Gita: It is better to die for a right cause and acquire grace than to die an ordinary death. The gates of heaven open for those who stand up to vindicate justice and dharma

- Other religious wars

  - Shiite Muslims vs. Sunni Muslims

  - Protestants vs. Catholics

  - Christians vs. Jews

  - Hindus vs. Muslims

  - Buddhists vs. Hindus in India, Sri Lanka

  - Colonists/missionaries vs. indigenous peoples in the Americas, Africa, Australia, New Zealand, etc.

  - Science vs. religion

  - Inquisition vs. heretics and Jews

You might have asked for documents suggesting other important aspects of the clash between or about religions:

- Jewish pogroms

- Terrorists and non-strict Islamic states

- Northern Ireland

- Israel vs. Palestinians

- Civil wars in Bosnia, Serbia, and Kosovo

PRACTICE DBQ ESSAY 3

SECTION II

PART A

(Suggested planning and writing time–50 minutes)

> **Directions:** The following question asks you to write a coherent essay that incorporates your interpretation of documents 1–4. (Some editing of the documents has been done for this test.) This question will assess your skill in working with and understanding historical documents. Cite relevant evidence from your outside knowledge of world history.

1. The period of time between 1763 and 1914 stands as a period during which Europe was, directly or indirectly, the master of the world. In 1909, Lord Ronaldshay wrote the following:

    > Above all I wish to urge upon you once again the immense vista of difficulty and possibility of danger opened up by the newly awakened ambitions and aspirations of the Eastern races. What may be the final outcome of the collision . . . it is impossible to foretell. This, however, is certain–that contact with Western thought and Western ideals has exercised a revivifying influence upon all the races of the East. Those that have come into sharpest contact with it have exhibited most markedly its effects.

    > Consider non-Western nations, and discuss the selections in the light of Ronaldshay's statement. How applicable is this statement to non-Western nations impacted by Western culture during the latter half of the time period? Evaluate Ronaldshay's thesis in light of this analysis.

    What other documents would you include, and why?

Document 1

SOURCE: A prominent Indian, S. Banerjea, wrote this reminiscence in 1925.

Our forefathers, the firstfruits of English education, were violently pro-British. They could see no flaw in the civilization or culture of the West. They were charmed by its novelty and strangeness. The enfranchisement of the individual, the substitution of the right of private judgement in the place of traditional authority, the exaltation of duty over custom, all came with a force and suddenness of a revelation to an Oriental people who knew no more binding obligation than the mandate of immemorial usage and of venerable tradition . . . . Everything English was good–even the drinking of brandy was a virtue; everything not English was to be viewed with suspicion . . . . In due time came the reaction, and with a sudden rush. And from the adoration of all things Western, we are now in a whirlpool that would recall us beck to our ancient civilization and our time-honored ways and customs untempered by the impact of the ages that have rolled by and the forces of modern life.

Document 2

SOURCE: In 1924, Chinese leader Dr. Sun Yat-sen gave the following speech after the Japanese victory over Russia.

Thirty years ago . . . men thought and believed that European civilization was a progressive one–in science, industry, manufacture, and armament–and that Asia had nothing to compare with it. Consequently, they assumed that Asia could never resist Europe, that European oppression could never be shaken off. Such was the idea prevailing idea thirty years ago. It was a pessimistic idea. Even after Japan abolished the Unequal Treaties and attained the status of an independent country, Asia, with the exception of a few countries situated near Japan, was little influenced. Ten years later, however, the Russo-Japanese war broke out and Russia was defeatcd by Japan. For the first time in thc history of the last several hundred years, an Asiatic country has defeated a European Power. The effect of this victory immediately spread over the whole of Asia, and gave a new hope to all Asiatic peoples. In the year of the outbreak of the Russo-Japanese war I was in Europe. One day news came that Admiral Togo had defeated the Russian navy, annihilating in the Japan Sea the fleet newly despatched [sic] from Europe to Vladivostock. The population of the whole continent was taken aback. Britain was Japan's Ally, yet most of the British people were painfully surprised for in their eyes Japan's victory over Russia was certainly not a blessing for the White peoples. "Blood," after all, "is thicker than water." Later on I sailed for Asia. When the steamer passed the Suez Canal a number of natives came to see me. All of them wore smiling faces, and asked me whether I was a Japanese. I replied that I was a Chinese, and inquired what was in their minds, and why they were so happy. They said they had just heard the news that Japan had completely destroyed the Russian fleet recently despatched [sic] from Europe, and were wondering how true the story was. Some of them, living on both banks of the Canal had witnessed Russian hospital ships, with wounded on board, passing through the Canal from time to time. That was surely proof of the Russian defeat, they added.

In former days, the coloured races in Asia, suffering from the oppression of the Western peoples, thought that emancipation was impossible. We regarded the Russian defeat by Japan as the defeat of the West by the East. We regarded the Japanese victory as out own victory. It was indeed a happy event. Did not therefore this news of Russia's defeat by Japan affect the peoples of the whole of Asia? Was not its effect tremendous?

Document 3

SOURCE: An Englishman in Persia in 1906 wrote the following letter.

It seems to me that a change must be coming over the East. The victory of Japan has, it would appear, had a remarkable influence all over the East. Even here in Persia it has not been without effect. . . . Moreover, the Russian Revolution has had a most astounding effect here. Events in Russia have been watched with great attention; and a new spirit would seem to have come over the people. They are tired of their rulers, and, taking example of Russia, have come to think that it is possible to have another and better form of government . . . it almost seems that the East is stirring in its sleep. In China, there is a marked movement against foreigners, and a tendency towards the ideal of "China for the Chinese." In Persia, owing to its proximity to Russia, the awakening would appear to take the form of a movement towards democratic reform. In Egypt and North Africa it is signalized by a remarkable increase in fanaticism, coupled with the spread of the Pan-Islamic movement. The simultaneousness of these symptoms of unrest is too remarkable to be attributed solely to coincidence. Who knows? Perhaps the East is really awakening from its secular slumber, and we are about to witness the rising of these patient millions against the exploitation.

Document 4

SOURCE: The following is from an eyewitness account of turmoil in Sierra Leone.

. . . I am a Sierra Leonean. We lived at Bolian on the Mapelle River, Kassi Lake. The policemen's [indigenous people in service to the Belgians] treatment gave rise to this war. When they were sent to collect the [hut] tax, they used to ill-use the natives, and took their wives. They beat the man and assaulted the wife and daughter, and threatened his daughter with a knife if she cried out. In the place where we were (Bolian), Captain Carr [the British District Commissioner] spent three days. The police caught all the fowls in the town.

Question: did nobody complain to Captain Carr?

Answer: All the people ran away while Captain Carr was there, till he had left. Captain Carr came at 2. The people ran away. He asked for the Head Chief. He said he would burn the town if the headman did not come. Mr. smith brought the man to town, and he promised to pay the [hut] tax in a week's time. The next day a messenger, Williams, came to say he must pay in three days. . . .

We were afterwards caught by the war-boys [rebels], and I was with them for six weeks. On 29th April a sudden attack was made on Bolian. We went away in a boat, my husband, myself, a constable, and several others. I less than half an hour we got to town, and over 200 people came on us with cutlasses, sticks and guns. They rushed the policeman . . . and killed him, and took his gun, and then threw him into the sea. . . . They killed my husband at my feet. I asked them, "Why do you punish Sierra Leoneans so?" They say, "You pay the hut tax." They say, "The Sierra Leoneans with Bai Bureh had not paid the tax, so they did not kill them." . . . They say to me afterwards, "the Government say we must not keep slaves, nor have women palaver, nor pledge human beings. We say, "All right." They come, last of all, and say we must pay for these dirty huts, . . .The Government look on us as a lazy people, but the whole of us will die before we pay this tax. We will kill Captain Carr, and then the Governor will come; we will kill the Governor, and then the Queen will come herself.

SUGGESTIONS FOR PRACTICE DBQ ESSAY 3

Study Strategy

Revise your essay using points from this list that will strengthen it.

Be sure that you analyzed each document. Did you notice that you must first find the similarities and differences in how non-Western peoples reacted to Westernization? Then you are to evaluate how true Ronaldshay's assertion is in relation to various world regions. You might have noticed that his documents are not in chronological order, but you do not need to write about them in the order they appear. You may prefer to deal with it chronologically or by similarities and differences. The rubric for the DBQ states that documents should be grouped in one, two, or three different ways for a basic score and in additional ways for extended points.

Regardless of which forms of organization you chose, you should have incorporated references to all the documents in your essay. You should also have noted any documents that you think would present other events or other points of view that you may consider more important or that present a more balanced view than those included in the question. Be sure to mention such documentation in your essay. As you analyze your essay, consider the following points about documents 1 through 4.

Document 1

Test-Taking Strategy

Identify the point of view of each writer, his message, and the circumstances surrounding it.

Point of View: ambivalence

Message: switching from traditional ways to Western ways and back again so quickly is problematic

- British dominance
  - New ways of thinking
  - New way of life
- Initially pro-British
  - Civilization and culture "perfect" to Indians
  - Attracted to its novelty
  - Enfranchisement of individual
  - Right of private judgment, not traditional authority
- Intellectual change
  - Primarily small upper classes in India
  - Knew Western languages
  - Read Western newspapers and books
  - Familiar with Western history and politics
  - Not affecting peasant masses

- Later reaction

- Return to ancient customs and way of life

- Skepticism about European civilization

Relevant Historical Facts

- Under British rule

- Material growth

- Literacy rate improved

- Miles of railroads, telegraph wires

- Universities, hospitals, factories, seaports

- Native ruling class extraordinarily rich

- Peasants at subsistence level

- Middle class developing

- Debate: social revolution or stagnation

- Racism

- British view

  - Indians working way to greater responsibility gradually

  - Opposed move toward independence

- Gandhi beginning to mobilize Indians at return in 1913

Document 2

Point of View: strongly pro-Asian

Message • Asians not inferior to Westerners
  • Asian nations can defeat the West

- European civilization thought to be superior

  - Science

  - Industry

  - Manufacture

  - Armament

- Asia unable to resist the West

  - Accept Western oppression

  - Few Asian nations influenced by Japan's rejection of treaties

- Russo-Japanese War victory

  - Demolished Russian navy

  - Asian sense of pride

  - Shattered belief that European powers are invincible

  - Demonstrated that independence is possible

  - Success of resistance by adaptation

  - Westerners surprised, even though Britain Japan's ally

Relevant Historical Facts
- Adaptation of Western technology by Japan

- Industrial growth modeled on Western nations

- Expansion into Liaodong peninsula of Korea

- Forbidden use of Port Arthur because of treaties with Russia

  - Result—war

    - Russian army defeated

    - Russian navy virtually destroyed

- Turning point in recent history

  - Hope and excitement ripples through colonial world

  - Seen as East's victory over West

  - Indicated change coming in Asia

Document 3

Point of View: Westerner sympathetic with colonial people's desire for independence

  - Eyewitness observer, personal opinion

Message: aroused emotions and expectations in colonial lands is a sign of coming independence movements

- Independence movements to come

- Victory of Japan in Russo-Japanese War and Russian Revolution

  - Influence all of Asia

  - Eagerly watched

  - Forge a new desire for independence

  - Feeling that a battle for independence can be won

- Different types of independence movements
  - China
    - Anti-foreign feelings
- Persia
  - Movement toward democratic reform
- Egypt and North Africa
  - Growing fanaticism

Relevant Historical Facts
- Summary of the situation

- Prophetic since all countries mentioned experienced revolutions

- Only when native people begin to adopt Western ideas and technology to use against Europeans will success be possible

- Success of Russian Revolution encouraged others fighting for independence

- Birth of twentieth-century nationalist movements

- Consequences persist today

Document 4

Point of View: eyewitness to the violence and brutality of the English and the Sierra Leonean rebels

Message: rebels determined that no one pay the brutal hut tax

- Police mistreatment of native population is the cause of rebellion
  - Assaulted wives and daughters
  - Beat men
  - Threatened people with knives
  - Stole livestock
- Villagers in hiding to avoid the tax
  - Threatened to burn village if head man did not return
  - Promised to pay in one week
- Europeans revised time to three days
- Rebels attacked village
  - To prevent tax collection
  - Village refugees massacred because of tax
  - Those refusing to pay were spared

- Point out natives accepted many demands that run contrary to their culture

    - No slaves

    - No women's talks

    - No indentured servants

- Declaration of "war"

    - Not lazy

    - Fight and kill all the British administrators

    - Force Queen Victoria to come and negotiate

Relevant Historical Facts
- By the turn of the twentieth century, Europeans directly or indirectly controlled virtually all of Africa

    - Division of Africa without consideration of clan and language groups

    - Reliance of natives for civil service and other lower-status jobs

- Taxes imposed

    - Had to be paid in currency

    - Men forced to cities and mines to make money

    - Deeply resented Europeans

    - Revolt suppressed in 1898

Other Historical Points for Essay
- The statement is very applicable; although is some cases, ironic because the reaction was anti-Western

- Initial response to Western culture

    - Enthusiastic

    - Uncritical admiration for all things Western

    - Reaction against the West then follows

- "White Man's Burden"

    - Europeans assumed their primacy resulted from superiority of Western civilization and of white race

    - Belief God created people unequal

    - Whites more intelligent

    - Intended to direct labor of inferior indigenous races

- Guide their development
- Superiority an aspect of "survival of the fittest": social Darwinism
  - Attempt to preserve and foster the traditional culture
    - Ineffective when using traditional ways
      - Boxer Rebellion
      - Hut Tax War
      - Indian Mutiny
    - Effective when using Western technology in fight for independence
      - Young Turk Revolution in 1908
      - Chinese Revolution in 1911

You might have asked for documents suggesting other important aspects of the clash between East and West:

- Young Turk Revolution in 1908
- Chinese Revolution in 1911
- Unrest and terrorism in India
- Fundamentalist Islamic view of the West

Chapter 4

WRITING THE CHANGE-OVER-TIME ESSAY

Red Alert!

Remember that all three essays are worth the same percentage of your Section II score.

Part B of the free-response section of the AP World History Test is the change-over-time essay question. It is scored on a scale of 1 to 9 using a holistic rubric similar to the ones for the DBQ and the comparative essay. On the day of the test, Part B will begin immediately after the DBQ, and you will have 40 minutes to plan and write your essay. The directions suggest that you spend the first 5 minutes of the time reading the question and planning your essay.

DEFINING THE CHANGE-OVER-TIME ESSAY QUESTION

Study Strategy

Use the table in Chapter 2, p. 101, to refresh your memory about question types and clue words.

There is no single correct answer for the change-over-time essay. Two students could take opposing points of view and still earn 9s if their arguments are supported by the evidence. You will be graded on how clearly you state your point of view on a topic and then how logically and effectively you develop and support your thesis. All the information you use to illustrate your points and how you interpret the evidence must be grounded in your knowledge and understanding of world history.

The change-over-time essay question

- will ask you about change over time,

- will involve one or more periods as designated in the course description (Foundations, 1000 to 1450, 1450 to 1750, 1750 to 1914, and 1914 to the Present), and

- will highlight the broad issues in world history

- in one cultural area

    OR

- in several.

You may be told which cultural areas to write about, or you may be given a list and told to choose a specific number from the list to describe.

For example, you might be asked to describe the continuities and changes in the status of women in Chinese society from the adoption of Confucian principles to the present. The time span is from the early Foundation era to modern times, so all the time periods in the course are to be included. The big issue is culture, and the specifics are the Chinese gender system and how developments in various eras did or did not change the attitudes about, and the role of, women in Chinese society.

Or you might be given a list that includes China, the Middle East, Africa, and Europe and asked to choose one (or two) culture regions and describe how migrations affected the political, cultural, and social structures of the regions from the Foundations era through 1450. The time periods are Foundations and 1000 to 1450. The issue is migrations, and the specifics are whether and how migrations caused change within certain culture regions and what those changes were.

Suppose the question told you to choose two regions. You would have to decide which two of the five you know most about in the context of the question. Note the phrase "in the context of the question." It doesn't matter if you can write five pages about African kingdoms, can you write a well-reasoned and well-supported essay about migrations in Africa between 200 and 1450 C.E.? If not, then look for another region in the list whose migratory patterns you know more about.

It is important that you know specific information that you can use to illustrate the points in your essay because the directions for the change-over-time essay tell you that you are to "use specific examples to support your answer." You must cite relevant historical facts, events, and theories as evidence.

The sample rubric that the College Board provides for the change-over-time essay notes that students must address each part of the question with equal emphasis and provide "links with relevant ideas, events, and trends in an innovative way." You need to take the reader through each period listed in the question, circa 200 as appropriate to 1000, 1000 to 1450, and so on, making sure to provide equal information for each period.

In showing continuity and change over time,

1. start by stating what the condition or situation was at the beginning of the spans you are to address,

2. then show how the condition or circumstance changed from then until the end point of the time span you are writing about, and

3. if you have to write about more than one time period, note how the circumstance or condition was different (or the same) in each intervening time period.

For example, in an essay discussing African migrations, you would start by stating where the Bantu were in 200 C.E. and what their political, cultural, and social structures were. Then, you would note how they moved out from these areas between 200 and 1000 and what the effects of these movements were on their political, cultural, and social structures, being sure to include how their interaction with their new environments changed some culture traits while not affecting others. Then, you would provide the same information for the period 1000 to 1450, clearly stating that you are now discussing the continuities and changes between 1000 and 1450. In essence, you are creating a long cause-and-effect chain while also keeping track of what did not change—the similarities and differences between circumstances—in subsequent time periods.

THE GAME PLAN FOR THE CHANGE-OVER-TIME ESSAY

Chapter 2 describes general strategies for writing "9" essays. The following are the basic steps for structuring an AP essay as they relate to the change-over-time essay:

1. Analyze the question to determine what is really being asked. Circle, underline, and use brackets to highlight the key words that list the time periods and the actors in the cause-and-effect chain. Look for the specific details on which you are to build your essay.

2. Be sure you know if the question is asking you to do something in addition to describing the outcome of events over time, such as explaining or interpreting what you are describing.

3. Make a quick list of ideas that relate to the topic and how you will write about it. In the case of change-over-time, you should note each period listed in the question, the original condition, what changed about it over the time period, what did not change, how you would interpret the significance of the change or continuity.

4. Create a table to list each time period; original circumstance or condition; what changed in the period, why, how; what did not change, why, how.

5. Evaluate your notes, and develop a thesis.

6. Organize your information in a logical way in an information outline. Number the items in your quick list or table in the order in which you expect to use them. Don't rewrite them in an actual outline form.

7. Write your essay. Be sure as you go along that you are using examples to illustrate each time period and each culture region within each time period, if you are to write about more than one world area.

PRACTICAL ADVICE

Reread Chapter 2 to review the suggestions for good writing and question types. Here are a few suggestions that are repeated in Chapter 5 that will give your essays a final polish, so you will score all the points you can. We repeat them because they are very important for you to remember.

- Some essays may combine several question types.

- Plan your time well, so you spend about 5 minutes reading and planning, 33 writing, and 2 reading, revising, and checking for spelling and grammar. Pace yourself.

- Your introduction is one of the most important paragraphs in your essay. Make sure you state the topic and your opinion. If you do not, the evaluator may be confused. Do not write "In my opinion" or "I believe" in your opening paragraph. Just state your opinion or position clearly.

- Remember that you can argue many different theses on a given question. Choose the one that **you** can defend most successfully.

- Include as many facts and as much historical evidence as you can to support your essay. The directions tell you to do this.

- Remember that you must answer all parts of a given question.

- Write an essay that clearly, logically, and coherently answers the question with special insight or a unique point of view.

- Write clearly and neatly. If your writing is difficult to read, print.

PRACTICE

Now it's time to practice writing a change-over-time essay question. Follow the directions, and write the essay using the suggestions you have just read. Then read the *Steps to the Answer,* and review the *Points to Include* that we provide after the question. Evaluate your essay using the *Self-Evaluation Rubric* on pages 356–357.

How could you improve your essay? Revise it once using your self-evaluation and our information points. Evaluate it again with the rubric, and see how much your essay has improved. When you write your next essay, consciously incorporate the techniques that you used in revising this practice essay—focus more clearly on what the question is asking, write a stronger thesis, or use more evidence.

Now answer *Practice Change-Over-Time Essay 2.* Evaluate and revise it. Then write *Practice Change-Over-Time Essay 3.* Evaluate and revise it to see how much you have improved.

PRACTICE CHANGE-OVER-TIME ESSAY 1

(Suggested planning and writing time—40 minutes)

Directions: You are to answer the following question. In writing your essay, you should <u>use</u> <u>specific examples to support your answer.</u>

2. Trace and evaluate the evolution of racism from 1750 to the present in two of the regions listed below. Include the relationship among imperialism, nationalism, and racism in showing the continuities and changes over time.

Europe
North America (United States)
South Africa

SUGGESTIONS FOR THE PRACTICE CHANGE-OVER-TIME ESSAY 2

STEPS TO THE ANSWER

1. Note that this question asks you both to trace (describe over time) and to evaluate how racism has developed over time. You must provide information on two time periods, 1750 to 1914 and 1914 to the present, and you have to choose two cultural regions from a list of three.

2. Think about what you know about racism in the periods 1750 to 1914 and 1914 to 1750. Begin your brainstorming. First, define racism in 1750 in each world region. Then, define racism in 1914 in each world region. Note changes in the intervening years. Note continuities. Ask yourself what caused each change. Don't forget that the change-over-time essay requires that your answer fit into historical context, making links—showing trends—across time.

3. Your answer also has to give equal emphasis to each region you discuss. In choosing which two culture regions to write about, consider which two you know the history of racism of in some depth. List specific examples from each region's development to illustrate your description of the evolution of racism and your evaluation of its development.

4. Using the ideas you brainstormed in steps 3 and 4, choose the two regions that you will describe and create a thesis. The thesis must be clear, concise, and analytical. It must show how you plan on describing the evolution of racism in the two culture regions you chose and how you will evaluate its impact.

5. Using the organizing and writing suggestions in this chapter and Chapter 2, write your essay. Use transition words to make your essay more cohesive. Words like *then, afterward, as a result of, because,* and *whereas* help convey the idea of change and movement over time.

6. As you write, more ideas and facts may come to mind. If the new idea is a better fit with what you have to say, don't be afraid to use it just because it is not in your quick list or table. But don't get carried away and ignore your brainstorming ideas. Go back and check your thesis as you finish writing each idea to make sure that you stick to your main idea and develop a cohesive and coherent essay.

POINTS TO INCLUDE

Study Strategy

Be sure to complete the "Self-Evaluation Rubric" for each essay.

You might have chosen the following information to include in your essay on the development of racism between 1750 and the present. Consider these points as you complete your self-evaluation of your essay.

Europe

- Anti-Semitism well-established in Europe by 1800s
- Dreyfus case in France
- Jews as scapegoats for Germany's defeat in World War I, other socioeconomic problems
- Under Hitler, Aryans as superior race; genocide of Jews, Gypsies, Poles, Slavs, disabled
- World War II stops German expansionism, stops genocide, restores human rights
- Contemporary racism, prejudice, discrimination: jobs, marriage, politics, education, housing

North America (United States)

- Africans enslaved from 1600s through mid-1800s
- Trace beginnings of racism to slave trade; Africans inferior, not human; justification for buying, selling, enslaving
- Protests against but continued under Constitution
- Importation banned after 1808
- Flourishing of internal slave trade
- Civil War: slavery prohibited (1865), Universal Male Suffrage (1870)
- Nonenforcement of civil rights and human rights until 1950s and 1960s
- Affirmative action
- Discrimination against and denial of rights of Native Americans from mid-1800s into the 1920s; federal government's paternalism as a form of prejudice
- Prejudice and discrimination in present; paternalism
- Quotas against immigration of Chinese, Japanese, Southern Europeans in 1800s, 1920s
- Inferior to white Americans: cultural and religious stereotypes
- Denial of civil rights: Mexicans, 1920s; Japanese Americans, 1940s

- Protests for civil rights, 1960s

- Affirmative action

- Civil rights legislation prohibits some forms of discrimination (1960s)

- Post-Vietnam War, Asian immigration, renewed racism (1970s)

- Racism, prejudice, discrimination: jobs, marriage, politics, education, housing (2001)

South Africa
- Dutch colony in 1600s; Afrikaners

- British control in 1800s

- Transplanting of European racism to African colonies

- British, Afrikaners: White supremacists, oppress nonwhites economically, politically

- Afrikaner control of South African politics, society after British leave

- Legalize racism as apartheid (1960s), set up Bantustans

- Apartheid abolished (1991), whites in control of 75 percent of land

- Racism, prejudice, discrimination: jobs, politics, education, housing (2001)

Other Points to Include

- Imperialism, expression of nationalism

- Imperialism, oppression in "colonial possessions"

- Imperialism fostered by racism; Social Darwinism

PRACTICE CHANGE-OVER-TIME ESSAY 2

SECTION II

PART B

(Suggested planning and writing time—40 minutes)

> **Directions:** You are to answer the following question. In writing your essay, you should <u>use</u> <u>specific examples to support your answer.</u>

2. Karl Marx wrote in the *Communist Manifesto,*

> The history of all hitherto existing society is the history of class struggles. Freeman and slave, patrician and plebeian, lord and serf, guildmaster and journeyman, in a world, oppressor and oppressed . . . carried on an uninterrupted . . . fight that each time ended, either in revolutionary re-constitution of society at large, or in the common ruin of the contending classes.

Evaluate the historical accuracy of Marx's thesis using examples from two of the following twentieth-century revolutions. Consider purpose, methods, and short-term and long-term success.

- China

- Cuba

- Iran

- Philippines

- Russia (1917)

SUGGESTIONS FOR PRACTICE CHANGE-OVER-TIME ESSAY 2

Test-Taking Strategy

Be sure to support your thesis and major points with examples, explanations, and relevant facts.

You might have chosen the following points to include in your essay on class struggles and revolution—what has changed over time and what continues today.

China

- Ycars of civil war interrupted by World War II

- Defeated Nationalists Chinese, democratic or at least non-Communist government

- 1949 takeover of mainland China by Mao Zedong and Communists

  - People rebel against

  - Confucian ideals

  - Land ownership by a few

  - Government corruption

- Desire to end

  - Disease

  - Hunger

  - Illiteracy

  - Excessive taxation

  - Conscription

- Changes

  - End of Confucian ideals

  - Land held in common

  - Intellectuals disgraced

  - Everyone on equal footing

  - High level of literacy

- Continuities

- Economic problems

- Human rights violations

- Low standard of living

- Ruling elite

Test-Taking Strategy

In a change-over-time essay, you need to explain what the state or condition of the region was in relation to the topic at the beginning of the time period you are discussing, how it changed during that time, and what it was at the end of the period you are addressing.

Cuba

- Fulgencio Batista as dictator, foreign domination of industry
- Small wealthy elite, great poverty among workers and especially farmers
- 1959 Communist takeover by Fidel Castro
- Publicly espoused communism only afterwards
- People rebel against
  - Corruption
  - Foreign domination
- Desire to end
  - Disease
  - Hunger
  - Illiteracy
  - Land ownership by foreigners and the upper class
- Changes
  - Government ownership of land
  - Nationalization of businesses
  - Reduced trade
  - Increased literacy
- Continuities
  - Economic problems
  - Human rights violations
  - Low standard of living

Iran

- Western-style society, not democratic
- 1979 overthrow of Reza Pahlavi by Shi'ite Muslims
- People rebel against
  - Westernization
  - Violations of Islamic law
  - Repression
  - Wealthy elite

- Changes
  - Women's rights abolished
  - Western culture banned
  - Religion as law
- Continuities
  - Poverty
  - Corruption
  - Unemployment
  - Illiteracy
  - Economic problems
- Current fundamentalist Islamic government less restrictive

Philippines
- 1986 ousting of dictator Ferdinand Marcos by democratic election, massive demonstrations
- People rebel against
  - Corruption
  - Oppression
  - Hunger
  - Poverty
  - Land ownership by a few
- Changes
  - Democracy
  - Islamic fundamentalist rebels
- Continuities
  - Poverty
  - Unemployment
  - Illiteracy
  - Economic problems

Russia

- 1917, Czar Nicholas II abdicates under force

- Provisional Government takes control

- People rebel against

  - Poverty, law standard of living, bad working conditions

  - Corruption

  - Illiteracy

  - Excessive taxation

  - Political repression

- Changes

  - Russian Orthodox Church outlawed

  - Capitalism replaced with socialism

  - Land held in common

  - All businesses nationalized

- Continuities

  - Poverty, low standard of living, bad working conditions

  - Corruption

  - Illiteracy

  - Excessive taxation

  - Political repression

PRACTICE CHANGE-OVER-TIME ESSAY 3

SECTION II

PART B

(Suggested planning and writing time—40 minutes)

Directions: You are to answer the following question. In writing your essay, you should use specific examples to support your answer.

2. Discuss changes over time in the Pacific Rim economy from 1945 to the present. Include world or local events or conditions that you believe are important in shaping these changes.

SUGGESTIONS FOR PRACTICE CHANGE-OVER-TIME ESSAY 3

You may wish to include some of the following points in your essay on the economy of the Pacific Rim. Although you will probably be using generalizations for the most part, be sure to cite specific countries to illustrate your points.

Location

- The Pacific Rim includes but is not limited to
  - North America
    - Canada: British Columbia
    - United States: Alaska, Washington, Oregon, California, Hawaii
  - Central and South America
    - Mexico
    - Peru
    - Chile
    - Ecuador
    - Panama
    - Costa Rica
    - Columbia
  - Asia, Southeast Asia, and Oceania
    - Japan
    - Korea
    - Taiwan
    - China
    - Singapore
    - Hong Kong
    - Malaysia
    - Thailand
    - Philippines
    - Indonesia
    - Brunei
    - Vietnam
    - Cambodia
    - Laos
    - Australia
    - New Zealand

Economic Growth in the Pacific Rim Requires

- Access to raw materials

- Large labor pool

- Mineral resources, especially oil

- Political climate amenable to supporting trade

- High degree of urbanization, industrialization

- Some degree of literacy

Common Reasons for Growth

- Abundant human resources

- High skills, low wages

- High capacity for production

- Desire for economic development

Common Problems

- Pollution

- Urban problems of overcrowding, crime, health and sanitation

- Overtaxed infrastructure

- Economic downturns

Selected Countries

- Japan

    - Destruction of economic infrastructure during World War II

    - 1950–1975, economic miracle

        - No monies for defense means more investment in economy

    - Cheap labor

    - Cheap hydroelectric power

    - Good location

    - Good work ethic

    - Global industrial giant

    - Global investor

    - Economic downturn since the late 1990s: global competition, bloated work force

- South Korea
  - Before 1945, economically undeveloped
  - After World War II, infusion of aid from U.S. and Japan
  - By 1980, had become one of top 10 trading powers in world
- Taiwan
  - During World War II, used for source of food, raw materials for Japan
  - After 1945, infusion of monies from U.S.
  - Now potent economic power in Pacific Rim
  - Invests hundreds of billions of dollars in research and development
- Hong Kong
  - Before 1945, busy trading port
  - Korean War cuts off Chinese control
  - Became center of banking and trade
  - Returned to China by British in 1997
    - Limitations on civil and political rights
    - Continues to be important financial and trade center
- Singapore
  - Before 1945, busy trading port
  - Low worker education limits technical capabilities
  - Now partnering with Malaysia, Indonesia
- Australia
  - Before 1945 exported
    - Livestock
    - Raw materials
    - Wheat
  - Mid to late twentieth century, economic growth
  - Late twentieth century, economic decline

- China

  - Before 1945

    - Busy urban trading centers

    - Rural areas undeveloped

  - Communism, collectivism, economy declines

  - Now extensive global trading partner

  - Huge market for Western investment

  - Still difficult to maneuver Communist bureaucracy

- Southeast Asia

  - Each country very different

    - Geographically

    - Politically

    - Educationally

    - Human resources

    - Mineral resources

    - Raw materials

    - Effects of Vietnam War in several nations

- United States

  - Before 1945, most urban centers in Northeast and Midwest

  - After 1945, highly urbanized, industrial centers on West Coast

    - Seattle

    - San Francisco

    - Los Angeles

    - San Diego

  - Labor costs high compared to others in Pacific Rim

  - Global economic power

  - Negative balance of trade

Chapter 5

WRITING THE COMPARATIVE ESSAY

Red Alert!

All three essays are worth the same percentage of your Section II score.

The comparative essay is Part C, the final part of the AP World History Test. Like the DBQ and change-over-time essay, the comparative essay is scored on a scale of 1 to 9. On the day of the test, you will begin Part C after you have finished the DBQ and Part B essays. You will have 40 minutes to plan and write your comparative essay. As you will see, the directions recommend that you spend the first 5 minutes reading the question and planning your essay.

DEFINING THE COMPARATIVE ESSAY QUESTION

Study Strategy

Use the table in Chapter 2, page 101, to refresh your memory about question types and clue words.

Like the other essays, the comparative essay question has no single correct answer. All the information and interpretation must come from your knowledge and understanding of world history.

The comparative essay question

- will ask you about broad issues in world history

- in relation to at least two societies

- interacting

  - with each other

    OR

- with major themes or events.

For example, you might be asked to compare the caste system of India with the Confucian social structure of China to assess the effects of each on the dynamics of societal development. The broad issue is what are the effects of various types of social organization, the two societies are India and China, and the question relates the two to the major theme of the systems of social structure.

A comparative essay question might also focus on the interactions between two societies. For example, you might be asked to discuss how cultural differences between the Chinese and the British led to hostilities in the late 1800s. The broad issue is how differences in cultural developments can lead to misunderstandings, prejudices, and violence between societies, in this case the Chinese and the British.

In reading the directions, you will see that they tell you that you are to "use specific examples to support your answer." You must cite relevant historical facts, events, and theories as evidence.

In making comparisons, it is best to have the same number of differences or similarities as examples for Subject A as you have for Subject B. The examples should also correlate to each another. That is, if you're comparing how Buddhism and Islam spread, you might have a statement that monasticism played an important role in the spread of Buddhism. You should also state the role of monasticism in the spread of Islam. In the case of the latter, you would say that Islam did not have the same tradition of monasticism, but you could mention the role of the Sufi, Islamic mystics. The sample rubric that the College Board provides for the comparative essay notes that students should provide similarities as well as differences and make "direct comparisons consistently between or among societies."

THE GAME PLAN FOR THE COMPARATIVE ESSAY

You have already read a great deal about writing "9" essays in Chapters 2, 3, and 4. The following are the basic steps for structuring an AP essay as they relate to the comparative essay:

1. Analyze the question to determine what it is really asking. Circle, underline, and use brackets to highlight the key words that describe what you are to compare.

2. Be sure you know if the question is asking you to do something in addition to comparing information, such as explaining or interpreting what you are comparing.

3. Make a quick list of ideas that relate to the topic and how you will write about it. For the comparative question, you will want to list differences and similarities.

4. Create a table to list those differences and similarities. Try to list the same number for each culture region.

5. Evaluate your notes, and develop a thesis.

6. Organize your information in a logical way in an information outline. Number the items in the order in which you expect to use them. Don't rewrite them in an actual outline form.

7. Write your essay. Be sure as you go along that you are using examples to illustrate differences and similarities.

PRACTICAL ADVICE

Reread Chapter 2 to review the suggestions for good writing and question types. Here are a few suggestions repeated from Chapter 4 that will give your essays a final polish, so you will score all the points you can. We repeat them because they are very important for you to remember.

- Some essays may combine several question types.

- Plan your time well, so you spend about 5 minutes reading and planning, 33 writing, and 2 reading, revising, and checking for spelling and grammar. Pace yourself.

- Your introduction is one of the most important paragraphs in your essay. Make sure you state the topic and your opinion. If you do not, the evaluator may be confused. You do not need to write "In my opinion" or "I believe" in your opening paragraph. Just state your opinion or position clearly.

- Remember that you can argue many different theses on a given question. Choose the one that **you** can defend most successfully.

- Include as many facts and as much historical evidence as you can to support your essay. The directions tell you to do this.

- Remember that you must answer all parts of a given question.

- Write an essay that clearly, logically, and coherently answers the question with special insight or a unique point of view.

- Write clearly and neatly. If your writing is difficult to read, print.

PRACTICE

Let's look at an example of a comparative essay question, Part C of the test. Follow the directions and write the essay using the suggestions you have just read. Then read the *Steps to the Answer* and review the *Points to Include* that we provide after the question. Evaluate your essay using the *Self-Evaluation Rubric* on pages 356–357.

How could you improve your essay? Revise it once using your self-evaluation and our points. Evaluate it again and see how much your essay has improved. When you write your next essay, incorporate those techniques as you plan and write—focus better on what the question was asking, write a stronger thesis, use more evidence, or whatever.

Now answer *Practice Comparative Essay 1*. Evaluate and revise it. Then write *Practice Comparative Essay 2*. Evaluate and revise it to see how much you have improved.

PRACTICE COMPARATIVE ESSAY 1

3. Interregional networks of trade characterized the period 1000 to 1450. As these trade networks expanded, urban populations grew and major trading centers developed. Describe the part played by trade in the development of trading centers by comparing three of the following urban centers:

    - Cairo

    - Guangzhou (Canton)

    - Samarkand

    - Timbuktu

    - Venice

SUGGESTIONS FOR PRACTICE COMPARATIVE ESSAY 1

STEPS TO THE ANSWER

Test-Taking Strategy

Create a thesis that shows that you understand the concept in the question. Then support your main idea with examples, facts, and details.

1. Note that this question combines description with comparison and contrast. The question is asking for an account of the role of trade in the development of urban centers and how its role was similar and different in different places.

2. Think about what you know of the period 1000 to 1450 and interregional trade networks. Begin your brainstorming. Ask yourself how the development of trading centers and trade routes and the movement of products along those routes were important to the development of urban centers. Don't forget that the comparative question requires that your answer fit into the global picture of the time.

3. In choosing which three cities to write about, consider which three cities you know this information about in some depth, so you can set up comparisons and contrasts. Choose specific examples from each city's development to illustrate your description and the similarities and differences between and among these cities.

4. Using the ideas that you developed in Steps 3 and 4, choose the three cities that you will describe and create a thesis. The thesis must be clear, concise, and analytical. It must show how you plan on using the cities to describe the impact of trade on the development of major population centers and how you will compare these cities.

5. Using the organizing and writing suggestions in this chapter and Chapter 2, write your essay. Use transition words to make your essay more cohesive. Words like compared to, in contrast to, however, on the other hand, similarly convey comparison and contrast.

6. Keep in mind that every fact and every event that you jotted down may not support your thesis. Don't ignore these differing elements. Deal with counterpoints, acknowledging them and the issues that they raise while showing that support for your position is stronger. By doing so, you confirm that you understand the complexities of history.

POINTS TO INCLUDE

You might have chosen the following information to include in your discussion regarding a city's role in the development of political systems. Consider them as you complete the self-evaluation of your essay.

CAIRO

- Cairo was a center for intellectual life and commerce between Europe, the Middle East, Africa, and Asia.

- Founded in 969 by the Fatimid general Gawhar, this capital city was located at the mouth of the Nile River.

- The first Fatimid emperor, Al-Aziz, built bridges, canals, palaces, and mosques.

- Seljuk Turks overran the city in 1168, but under Salah-el-Din (Saladin) a few years later, Cairo once again prospered with new mosques, universities, hospitals, and a new fortress, the Citadel.

GUANGZHOU (CANTON)

- Guangzhou was an important center of trade, cultural diffusion, and intellectual development.

- A principal city in southern China, Guangzhou has been an important link to the outside world for centuries.

- Trade contacts were developed between Roman traders seeking tea, silk, and spices and Arab and Persian merchants.

- Hindu and Islamic traders were regularly conducting trade in the city by the tenth century.

SAMARKAND

- Samarkand is an ancient city located within the Zarafshan River Valley and along many Central Asian trade routes.

- It was an important city along the Silk Road from China to the Middle East.

- The city came under Muslim control by the middle of the eighth century and was later invaded by Chingis Khan in 1220.

- Ibn Battuta commented that Samarkand was the most beautiful of cities when he traveled there in the early 1300s.

- Tamerlane made the city his imperial capital in the 1370s, rebuilding most of the city and expanding its streets, markets, and mosques.

- Samarkand's power as a trading center declined with the declining power of Tamerlane and his followers, the Tatars.

TIMBUKTU

- Timbuktu was founded in the 1000s by Tuareg nomads and later incorporated into the empire of Mali and later Songhay.

- The city sat astride the main trade routes across the Sahara in what is today Mali and close to the flood plain of the Niger River.

- Timbuktu became an important city in the trans-Saharan trading network of salt and gold.

- The city also flourished as the starting point for African pilgrims going on the *hajj* to Mecca.

- Timbuktu was also an important center of Islamic culture with mosques, palaces, and a university.

VENICE

- Settled at first by people being pushed south by Germanic invaders, Gauls, Venice is located on islands in a lagoon at the head of the Adriatic Sea.

- A treaty with the Saracens gave Venice nearly complete control over European trade with the Arabs and Asia beyond.

- Venetian merchants used the Crusades to their advantage, gaining profits from ferrying men, supplies, and arms to the Holy Land.

- Venetian merchants continued their voyages after the crusades and cut out overland intermediaries on trade routes.

- Venetian government encouraged ventures to increase tax revenues.

PRACTICE COMPARATIVE ESSAY 2

SECTION II

PART C

(Suggested planning and writing time—40 minutes)

> **Directions:** You are to answer the following question. In writing your essay, use specific examples to support your answer.

3. Missionary activity flourished in the period from 700 to 1000 as societies expanded beyond their traditional boundaries. Explain the major similarities and differences of missionary activity between two of the following:

- Buddhism
- Christianity
- Islam

SUGGESTIONS FOR PRACTICE COMPARATIVE ESSAY 2

You might have chosen the following information to include in your discussion about missionary activity by Buddhists, Christians, or Muslims.

Buddhism

- Siddhartha Gautama (563–483 B.C.E.)

  - Preached a philosophical system, known as Buddhism, in the fifth century B.C.E. in northern India

  - Eightfold Path to Four Noble Truths considered the Middle Way

- Two main sects developed after the death of the Buddha: Hinayana, or Theravada, and Mahayana

  - Hinayana (lesser vehicle), very strict form of Buddhism: practiced mainly in southern India and Southeast Asia

  - Mahayana (greater vehicle), more flexible form of Buddhism that encourages enlightenment for all believers

    - Spread rapidly through India and then to Central Asia, China, Korea, Japan, and Vietnam

    - Believe that *bodhisattvas* are beings of enlightenment who postponed their own nirvana in order to help others become enlightened

- Ashoka, Mauryan Empire attempt to solidify Buddhism in India through state sponsorship

  - Sent Buddhist missionaries to Sri Lanka, Burma, Kashmir, Nepal, Syria, Egypt, and Greece

- Buddhism spread into China through the merchant trade from Central Asia along the Silk Road beginning around the first century C.E.

  - Easily absorbed elements of Chinese life and thought

  - Warlords quickly accept many Buddhist ideas as counter to traditional Confucian and Daoist court teachings

  - Fa-hsien, a Chinese scholar who traveled widely in India, 399–414, and returned with hundreds of Buddhist texts

  - Buddhism reached a zenith during the Tang period, adopted and patronized by the emperors, which created backlash from scholar-gentry

- Chinese missionaries, merchants, and imperial edict spread Buddhism to Korea, Japan, and Vietnam.

Test-Taking Strategy

Did you notice that the question asks you to explain and to compare and contrast information? You have to provide details about how and why the groups sent out missionaries as well as differences and similarities.

Christianity

- Jesus of Nazareth (c. 4 B.C.E.–30 C.E.) expanded upon the Judaic belief in a messiah, promoting a vision of spiritual salvation and eternal life

  - Would become known as Christianity.

- Jesus' apostles and disciples spread his teachings, proselytizing zeal

  - Peter and Paul, most important apostles

  - Peter as the lead apostle

  - Paul who preached to non-Jews

- Belief system appealing to people in the Roman Empire

  - Monotheism

  - Moral teachings

  - Brotherhood

  - Promise of salvation

- Roman emperor Constantine (324–337) converted to Christianity

  - Church, semi-official status

  - Emperor Theodosius (379–395), banning of all non-Christian religions.

- Church councils, attempts to formalize doctrine, practice, and theology

- Schism between the two main branches of Christianity, the Roman Catholic and Eastern Orthodox, first in 867 and final one in 1054

- Missionary activity

  - Originally within the Roman Empire

  - Quickly began to expand beyond the borders of the Empire

  - Conversion of large numbers of Germanic and Celtic peoples

- Monasticism, preservation of Christian ideas, culture, and literature after the fall of Rome

- Religious leaders, confidantes to Germanic kings, because of their education and organizational abilities

- Conversion of Clovis, king of the Franks, to Roman Catholicism in 496 solidified place of Church in western Europe

- Later kings, such as Charlemagne, use missionary zeal and military force to convert most western European peoples to Roman Catholicism

- Early foothold in Ethiopia after King Ezana of Axum adopted it as the official religion in 350

- Expanded to Egypt and Nubia

Islam

- Muhammad (570–622), preached a message from God, later called the Quran, that was revealed to him by the angel Gabriel after meditating in the mountains near Mecca.

- Fled to Medina, the *hijra*, in 622 where he founded a religious community based on the Quran

- Arabian Peninsula converted to Islam by the time of his death in 632 through military action and religious zeal

  - Brought rival Bedoiun tribes together

- A succession crisis after Muhammad's death, between the followers of Abu Bakr, Muhammad's closest friend, known as Sunnis, and Ali, Muhammad's adopted brother, cousin, and brother-in-law, known as Shi'ites

  - Sunnis, dominant branch of Islam, encouraging consensus among the majority of believers

  - Shi'ites, centered mostly in Iran, following the teachings of a line of divinely inspired successors to Muhammad

- Islam accepts the traditions of Judaism and Christianity

- Views itself as the last true revelation from God and Muhammad as the last and greatest of the prophets

- Sunni as successors to Muhammad conquered Syria, Palestine, Jerusalem, Egypt, Mesopotamia, and Iran by 642

- From 647 to 732, Islamic troops captured North Africa, Turkistan, Spain, and parts of the Indus River Valley.

  - Religious conversion followed military troops

  - No coercion to convert

  - Mawali, later converts had same status as original converts under Muhammad himself

- Penetrates into sub-Saharan Africa in the 1100s

  - Follows the major trade route

  - Some earlier contact with West Africa by scholars and traders in the ninth century

- Mahmud of Ghazni, a warlord over most of Afghanistan and Iran, had several campaigns into northern India beginning in 1000

  - Weakened Buddhist hold throughout this region

PRACTICE COMPARATIVE ESSAY 3

SECTION II
PART C

(Suggested planning and writing time–40 minutes)

Directions: You are to answer the following question. In writing your essay, use specific examples to support your answer.

3. World history from 1750 onward is considered one of Western domination. Compare and discuss changes in the functions and structures of states brought about by European involvement from 1750–1920. Choose two of the regions listed below.

    - China

    - India

    - Mexico

    - South Africa

SUGGESTIONS FOR PRACTICE COMPARATIVE ESSAY 3

Review Strategy

Check Chapters 9 and 10 to review content you are not sure about.

You might have chosen the following points to include in your essay on political changes brought about by European involvement. Consider these points as you complete your self-evaluation.

China

- Imperial system

    - Well-entrenched bureaucracy of scholar-gentry

    - Grounded in Confucian principles

- European presence in China by mid-1700s (Portuguese, Dutch, French, British)

- Competition for trade, control of ports, European interference, extraterritoriality

- Opium Wars, weakening of China's power

    - Foreign spheres of influence after 1840s

- Boxer Uprising, further weakening of imperial control

    - Dowager Empress initial support of uprising

    - Foreign military put down uprising

    - Increase in foreign influence

- Continued unrest in China, especially among Western-educated Chinese

    - Provinces seceded

    - Emperor abdicates, end of Imperial era in 1911

- Republic established, internal rivalries

India

- Indian kingdoms, large and small, ruled by kings, traditional Hindu system

- Past history of invasions and control by outside forces: Persians, Afghans, Turks, Mongols

- Portuguese, Dutch, British, French compete for trade

    - British and French outlast rivals, fight for control

- British win and British East India Company slowly comes to dominate subcontinent

    - Seesaw policy of nonintervention, reforms, acquisition of territory

    - Plays rival Indian states off against one another

- Indian Mutiny of 1857

  - British government removes British East India Company in 1858

  - Takes over direct supervision of India

- Indians demand greater participation in government (1885)

  - Indian nationalism, civil unrest, reforms, self-government, dyarchy (1919)

Mexico

- Pre-Columbian Mexico, three great civilizations: Toltec, Maya, Aztec

- Spanish conquistadores conquer Aztecs

  - Spanish Crown rules through viceroys

  - Class system with mass of people poor mestizos and Native Americans at bottom of society

- Uprisings against Spanish rule begun in 1810 by El Grito de Dolores! Movement

  - Mestizo and Native American insurgents

  - Continues for next 10 years

- Mexico declares independence from Spain (1821)

  - Independent Republic of Mexico (1824)

  - Lack of political stability: Dictatorship, democratic republic, French empire, republic, dictatorship

  - Little in the way of reform to help the poorest people

- Mexican Revolution of 1910

  - Lasts until 1917

  - New constitution: democratic republic with elected president

South Africa

- Early African small kingdoms and city-states

  - Bushmen, Khoikhoi, Bantu speakers

  - Noncentralized societies ruled by kings, chiefs and councils

- Dutch establish Cape Colony in 1652

  - At first peaceful coexistence

  - Dutch known as Boers move inland

  - Clash with settled, agricultural peoples

- Series of Xhosa Wars in late 1800s
- British establish colonial rule from 1806 to 1910
  - Clash with black Africans and Boers
- British defeat Boers
  - Establish Union of South Africa in 1910
  - Dominion status
  - Dominated by white minority
  - Lack of civil and human rights for black Africans

Chapter 6

FOUNDATIONS OF WORLD HISTORY

"Foundations," the first section of the AP World History course description, sets the stage for the world in 1000 C.E,* the jumping-off point for the majority of the year's work. "Foundations" deals with the crises of late antiquity; the basic cultural, social, and economic systems in existence by 1000; and the principal international connections that were in place by 1000. A major focus, according to the course description, should be knowledge of the "basic features of world geography."

Before turning to the geography review, it is important to look at the kind of information the test appears to assess. Each chronological boundary as outlined in the Acorn book has a section listed as "Examples of types of information students are expected to know contrasted with examples of those things students are not expected to know." If you analyze that list, you will see that the items that you are expected to know are broad categories of information, concepts, or generalizations; for example, the political heritage of classical China but not how the Qin dynasty ended and the Han came to power. As you read, ask yourself what the significance is of this event, person's actions, or place. How does it fit into the broader picture? What is the broader picture? Focus on the concepts and not the specific details.

---

* The College Board uses B.C.E (Before Common Era) and C.E. (Common Era) rather than B.C. and A.D.

SECTION 1. SETTING THE STAGE: GEOGRAPHIC KNOWLEDGE

You probably looked at the listing in the Acorn Book and said to yourself, "I know where the continents are and the oceans, seas, and major rivers. I don't have to study that stuff. Besides, nobody is going to ask me to find the Indian Ocean on a map."

It is undoubtedly true that you will not be given a map and asked to identify the Indian Ocean, but you might be asked, What was the primary reason that the east coast of Africa developed a thriving trade with South Asia? The correct answer is the monsoons that blow across the Indian Ocean. While this is a history question, if you did not know the answer immediately, it would have been helpful to know that the Indian Ocean lies between the east coast cities of Africa and the Indian subcontinent, part of South Asia.

While you can't second-guess the test writers, you can read and study every map that you come across in your textbook—not just glance at it but *study* it.

QUICK GUIDE TO STUDYING MAPS

FAST FACTS

- These are the basic things to look for when you read a map:
  - Title
  - Scale
  - Compass, if there is one, to orient the area to the rest of the region and/or world
  - Locator map, if there is one, to see where the map area is in relation to the rest of the region and/or world
  - The map key to determine what is shown on the map and by what symbols or colors
  - The information on the map represented by the symbols, arrows, and colors
  - Mountains, rivers, and bodies of water
  - Any political boundaries, such as kingdoms or nation-states
  - The relationship of political boundaries to physical features

- Maps are an easy way to visualize and remember concepts. For example, special-purpose maps can illustrate important themes in world history: trade, migration, and conquest. Study who or what is moving from where to where. Note any geographic factors that influence these movements, such as the monsoons across the Indian Ocean—and much of Asia. Remember not just that monsoons exist, but also that they blow in different directions at different times of the year, which allows for ease of two-way ocean trade.

- The previous item is a way of saying don't just read the map for what it shows, but make connections between the map data and what you know about the era, place, people, or movement of which the map is a snapshot. Besides telling you about the goods that made up each leg of the trade, a map of the eighteenth-century Triangle Trade should trigger information about the effects of the slave trade on West African kingdoms.

- The boundaries of civilizations and empires may not be the same as modern political boundaries. For example, the Han empire in China between 206 B.C.E. and 220 C.E. was in the eastern half of modern China.

- Earlier empires and civilizations may be smaller than later empires in an area. This is true of the Qin empire that preceded the Han from 221 B.C.E to 210 B.C.E.

- However, when large empires and civilizations break apart, the successors may be a number of smaller states. For example, the end of the Roman Empire resulted in many small fiefdoms across western Europe.

FIVE THEMES OF GEOGRAPHY

- Remembering the five themes of geography can help you to understand some of the factors that influenced how, why, and where certain groups developed. As you study, observe how these themes interact with the six themes of the AP World History course, especially the impact of interactions among major societies through trade and war and the impact of technology on people and the environment.

- **Location: Absolute location** is where a place is on the globe. It is identified by latitude and longitude. **Relative location** is where a place is in relation to other places.

- **Place:** A place has **physical characteristics,** such as vegetation and climate, and **human characteristics,** those ways, such as cultural traits, economic system, and governmental structure, that distinguish its people from people in other places. Each place is unique in the way it combines physical and human characteristics.

- **Human-Environment Interaction:** This theme studies how people have interacted with and changed the environment. This covers everything from the Bantu spreading agriculture as they moved north, east, and south through Africa to the smokestacks of the Industrial Revolution blackening the skies in London.

- **Movement:** This theme studies how geography affects the movement of people, goods, and ideas between and among groups. It is also a central theme underlying the study of world history.

- **Regions:** A region is a group of places with at least one characteristic in common. Latin America is so called because the majority of the people speak either Spanish or Portuguese, both Latin-based languages. However, Ecuador, Peru, Bolivia, and Chile are also known as Andean countries, because they are in the Andes Mountains and have been heavily influenced by their place. Regional designations are fluid and depend on what a geographer, historian, demographer, or other social scientist is studying.

KEY POLITICAL UNITS OF THE PRE-1000 C.E. WORLD

- The AP World History course description lists the following political units as ones whose locations students should know.

  Roman Empire at its height
  Abbasid caliphate
  Sudanic kingdom of Ghana
  Sudanic kingdom of Nubia
  Han dynasty
  Tang dynasty
  Byzantine Empire
  Mayan civilization

Read the descriptions in the following table, and write in the correct name of the empire or civilization in the first column. (Answers are at the bottom of the next page.)

LOCATING IMPORTANT POLITICAL UNITS

Political Unit	Dates	Location
	202 B.C.E. to 220 C.E.	It began in the southeast corner and spread westward in what is modern China. By circa 100 C.E., it had reached northward to what is modern Mongolia, as far west as the western boundary of Mongolia, and eastward into what is now the Korean peninsula.
	330–1453 C.E.	At its height in the sixth century C.E., it ruled southern Spain, Italy, Sicily, North Africa (parts of modern Algeria, Tunisia, Libya, and Egypt), Jordan, Israel, Lebanon, Syria, Turkey, the Balkans, Cyprus, and the Aegean islands.
	300s–1076 C.E.	It extended into Mauritania, Mali, Senegal, and Guinea.
	750–1258 C.E.	It extended across the top of North Africa through the entire Arabian Peninsula and what are modern Iran and Iraq into Afghanistan, Pakistan, and northwest India. It also included what are today Jordan, Syria, Israel, and Lebanon.
	200 to late 1300s C.E.	It extended along both banks of the Nile River from Aswan nearly to Khartoum in an area that is now mostly modern Sudan.
	31 B.C.E. to 476 C.E.	By 117 C.E. at its height, it extended completely around the Mediterranean Sea and included present-day England, Scotland, and Wales as well
	618–906 C.E.	It began in the southeast corner of what is modern China and spread westward into what is now Turkestan. On the south, it ran around the Plateau of Tibet. To the southeast, its authority spread into what is modern Southeast Asia. To the north, it spread up to Mongolia and into what is the modern Korean Peninsula.
	2400 B.C.E. to 1200s C.E.	It extended through Central America to include what is now the Yucatan Peninsula in southeastern Mexico, Belize, and Guatemala and parts of El Salvador and Honduras.

Take a map of the world, and see if you can place each empire or kingdom on the map based on its geographic description. Then find a historical map that shows the same empire or kingdom. How well did you do?

Answer Key

(Han dynasty, Byzantine Empire, Ghana, Abbasid caliphate, Nubia, Roman Empire, Tang dynasty, Mayan civilization)

Be sure you know the meaning of these geographical or geopolitical terms. While you probably won't be asked to identify them, your ability to answer a question may depend on knowing where one of them is and what countries comprise it.

- Asia Minor
- Balkans
- Central Asia
- Crimea
- Eurasia
- Horn of Africa
- Near East
- Scandinavia
- South Asia
- Southeast Asia
- the Caucasus

SECTION 2. SETTING THE STAGE: DIVERSE INTERPRETATIONS AND DEMOGRAPHY

As you study for the AP World History Test, remember that each section has a set of questions related to what is called **diverse interpretations.** For "Foundations," the questions relate to the definition of the term *civilization* and the issue of which factor—diffusion or independent invention—is the most common source of change.

FAST FACTS

Diverse Interpretations

- The question of what constitutes a **civilization** is a central issue in the debate about which cultures or groups to study. For many years, the term *civilization* had a distinctly Westerncentric meaning. Groups that were considered civilizations had certain characteristics in common: (1) a food-producing base that generated surpluses, which, in turn, made possible (2) an increase in population, (3) specialization of labor, (4) a social hierarchy, (5) growth of trade, (6) centralization of political and religious authority, (7) monumental building, and (8) often, but not always, the development of writing and written records. Other factors that might be included are a high level of technological innovation and the development of the arts.

World historians take a less parochial view and recognize that civilization, in the words of one historian, is "the interaction of human beings in a very creative way, when . . . a critical mass of cultural potential and material resources has been built up, and human capacities are released for development." Recognizing the primacy of human creativity recognizes the significance of non-Western civilizations that have emphasized certain aspects of development over others. This viewpoint would base the study of human societies on the social developments common to them rather than on whether or not they had developed certain levels of technology.

Idea Bank Strategy

As you review for the test, begin a table of cultural changes. Label one column "Cultural Diffusion" and the other "Independent Invention." The information on this table might come in handy when you need to think of examples for the essays.

- **Cultural diffusion** is the transmittal of culture traits from one culture, society, or civilization to another. The spread of ironworking from the Assyrians of the Middle East to the Kushites of what is now Sudan in Africa is such an example. **Independent invention** is the development of a culture trait separate from any other group. It is thought that the Nok people of what is now central Nigeria learned to smelt iron independently of other groups in Africa.

BASIC UNITS OF SOCIETY

- The **Neolithic Revolution** marked the change from **hunting and gathering** to **settled agriculture** as a way of life. The **domestication of plants and animals** made possible this change. However, hunting and gathering did not necessarily disappear in an area when some groups turned to settled agriculture. Within any given area, some groups may have cultivated fields around their villages, which over time became cities, while other groups continued to practice **shifting cultivation** as **migratory farmers,** to **forage,** or to hunt and fish. In time, **nomadic pastoralism,** the herding of animals, developed in areas that were inhospitable to farming.

- The Neolithic Revolution occurred in different parts of the world at different times and involved different types of plants and animals, but it is generally believed that by 8000 B.C.E., many groups in the Middle East had turned to agriculture to secure their food. Between 8000 B.C.E. and 5000 B.C.E., farming of certain crops spread from the Middle East to India and Europe and south along the Nile. However, **farming developed independently** in sub-Saharan Africa, Southeast Asia, China, and the Americas.

- Along with the development of settled agriculture came (1) differentiation of labor, including the development of artisans who made their living from work other than farming; (2) the development of a political hierarchy, often with a basis in religion, to run the settlements; and thus (3) the development of social classes.

- **Nomadic societies** lived on the plains of Asia, Africa, and the Americas. Those in Asia and Africa played important roles in the development and sometimes fall of civilizations. One example is the Mongols under Tamerlane who established an empire that included Persia, northern India, Syria, and the Ottoman Turks. Unlike Tamerlane, whose empire collapsed rapidly after his death, some nomadic bands were able to establish long-lasting states, such as the Luba in what are modern Democratic Republic of the Congo and Zambia. Note that both these examples are from late in world history—1364 to 1405 C.E. and the 1500s to mid-1800s C.E.

- By 1000 C.E., there was still little difference in how people earned their livings. They practiced **sedentary agriculture, shifting cultivation, pastoral nomadism,** or **foraging. Trade** in foodstuffs, raw materials, and handcrafted goods played a role to a greater or lesser degree in any given society.

SECTION 3. CRISES OF LATE ANTIQUITY

KEY TERMS/IDEAS

Study Strategy

See if you can relate these terms and ideas to their correct context in the "Fast Facts" section.

- ethnocentrism

- slash-and-burn agriculture

- social structures: extended family, nuclear family, matrilineal, patrilineal

According to the Acorn book, the focus of the AP World History Test is post-1000 C.E., and the "Foundations" section provides background beginning only around the third century C.E. While your course probably provides a unit on developments—cultures, civilizations, and peoples—from as early as the emergence of *homo sapiens,* this review begins with the crises of late antiquity as outlined in the AP course description.

MOVEMENT OF PEOPLES

FAST FACTS

Geography Study

Be sure to locate these groups and trace their movements on maps in your textbook.

- A word about the word *barbarian.* It is of Latin origin, meaning alien or foreigner. It has come to mean a person of a culture or civilization that is primitive or inferior, a cruel or savage person. This viewpoint has colored people's, including historians', attitude toward the Germans and other groups that overran Europe. As a result, the period that followed the fall of Rome in the West has been referred to as the Dark Ages. One of the reasons for the study of world history is to put these cultures in perspective. In employing the term *barbarian,* use it to mean "other" and not savage or primitive.

- The major agents of movement in Europe in the 300s and 400s C.E. were the **Huns,** also known as **Hsing-Nu**, who originated south of the Gobi Desert and were driven north to the **steppes** of Mongolia during the Han dynasty. In the late 300s C.E., the Huns were driving the **Visigoths** from their homeland near the Black Sea into the Roman Empire. From their seat of power on the Hungarian Plain, they pushed the **Vandals** and other Germanic bands west and south as well. In 451 under their chief **Attila,** the Huns invaded Gaul but were repulsed. In 453, they threatened Rome, but their Italian invasion ended when Attila died. The Hunnic empire quickly collapsed because of internal rivalries and rebellion by conquered people.

- The **Germanic people** crowded along the Roman frontier from the Black Sea to the Rhine. In places, the frontier was an actual boundary line marked by the Rhine and Danube Rivers and patrolled from forts manned by Roman legions. By the 200s C.E., the Germanic peoples were being pushed south and west by groups farther east who were being pushed by the Huns.

Idea Bank Strategy

Begin a list of important concepts or generalizations like this one, and then look for examples as you read that illustrate each one. These examples could come in handy when you are writing your essays.

- An important concept to remember is that the empires created by the **warrior cultures**—Huns, Visigoths, and Vandals, for example—were short-lived. This is true of the **Zhou dynasty** in China as well. Jealousies among rivals after the death of the strong central leader and the resentment of conquered peoples combined to undermine states built on war and fear.

MOVEMENT OF GERMANIC PEOPLES ACROSS EUROPE

People	Dates	Original Location	Movement
Visigoths	Late 300s	Danube Delta and western Black Sea	• Moved into the eastern Roman Empire to flee the Huns • Defeated the Romans in 378 near Constantinople and received a subsidy from the emperor • Eventually moved into southern Gaul and then Spain • Under Alaric sacked Rome in 410 • Defeated by **Moorish invaders** in Spain between 711 and 718
Ostrogoths	400s	Northern Black Sea	• As vassals of the Huns, besieged Rome in 451 but were defeated • In 491 under Theodoric the Great took Italy and ruled until 552
Vandals	400s	Originally from south of the Baltic, moved into Balkans by 300s	• Driven west by the Huns • Driven from Gaul and Spain by the Visigoths • Sailed to North Africa and set up kingdom that included Sicily • Sacked Rome in 455 • Defeated in 534 by the **Byzantine Emperor Justinian**
Lombards	Late 500s	Danube area	• Series of wars with Byzantine Empire • Carved up Italy with Byzantine Empire • United Lombardy dukedoms in 584 to resist the Franks • Defeated by the Franks by end of the 700s
Jutes, Anglos, Saxons	Mid 400s	Scandinavia, North Sea	• Raiders • Came as **mercenaries** at the end of Roman occupation • Stayed after withdrawal of Roman army in 420 • Set up independent kingdoms • Combined to become England • Overthrown in 1066 by William the Conqueror

Franks	200s to 400s	East of the Rhine	• Invaded Gaul
			• Clovis I
			  • Defeated Romans
			  • Defeated Burgundians
			  • Drove out Visigoths
			  • United Gaul into a single Frankish kingdom
			• By 500s strongest and largest of Germanic states; predecessor of modern **Germany** and **France**

Connections Strategy

Note the connection between the Zhou revolutionary principle and later Confucian thought.

- There are two other facts about the **Zhou dynasty** (c. 1122–249 B.C.E) to remember. When the Zhou overthrew the **Shang dynasty,** they invoked the principle that the people could overthrow a ruler who was not a good ruler. The Zhou emperor also introduced a system of **feudalism** in which **vassal lords** paid **tribute**—money or goods—to the ruler.

- Other continents also saw movements of people. From its beginning in 632 C.E. on the Arabian Peninsula under **Muhammad,** the **Muslim Empire** by 750 reached west across North Africa and north and east through the Middle East and into what are now modern Turkey, Afghanistan, Pakistan, and Turkmenistan. While some consider this a result of **Islam's** belief in the *jihad,* or holy war, the fact that **Arabs** were desert nomads, **bedouins,** used to fighting to gain and protect their territory, is more to the point. They were more interested in gaining riches and power than converts.

- As noted in the table, **Moors, Muslim invaders** from North Africa, captured Spain. In 732 at Tours, they were pushed back by Charles Martel and his Frankish army when they tried to invade France. The Moors retreated to Spain and ruled for more than 750 years until 1492 when Granada, their last kingdom, fell to the Catholic monarchs Ferdinand and Isabella.

- On the African continent, the **Bantu** represent the major migratory force. Some experts believe the Bantu may have begun moving out of their homeland in what is modern Nigeria around 2500 B.C.E. as people coming from the drying Sahara pushed the Bantu in front of them. Other experts believe the first Bantu began moving sometime after 2000 B.C.E.

Connections Strategy

Add this to your list of similarities and differences among groups of peoples. See Section 5 for more on the Bantu as a force for interconnectedness.

- There is an important distinction between the movement of the Germanic peoples and the Bantu. The Bantu generally did not come as armed invaders. Small groups moved into an area, took up herding in the grasslands and farming in the rain forest, and when the population grew too large to feed, a new group would break off and move on. This movement of Bantu continued into the 1800s C.E. until the Bantu had spread from their original home throughout Central Africa to the east coast and down and across southern Africa.

COLLAPSE OF EMPIRES

Connection Strategy

Note the mention of trade in this "Fast Fact." Trade as an example of the interaction among groups is one of the six themes of the AP World History course.

Connection Strategy

Look for similarities and differences among similar topics, such as the collapse of empires. This information could be helpful to you in answering a comparative free-response essay.

- With the exception of a few years, the **Han** ruled a united China from around 206 B.C.E. to 220 C.E. During this period, (1) the arts and technology flourished, (2) a trading network linked China to the Roman Empire, (3) **Confucianism** became the basis of government and **ethical conduct,** and (4) a **civil service** was introduced. The empire collapsed because of pressures from within and without. Internally, (1) innovation and creativity in government, arts, and technology declined; (2) peasants rebelled in the face of huge tax burdens from greedy warlords; (3) court factions fought for imperial power; and (4) warlords fought among themselves for regional power. The internal problems put the empire at risk from nomadic invaders from Central Asia. In 221, the last Han emperor resigned.

- After the death of Caesar Augustus (63 B.C.E –14 C.E), the first emperor, the **Roman Empire** endured 400 years of infighting, murder, cruelty, corruption, and the occasional brilliant emperor. One of these was **Diocletian** (284–305) who divided the empire into a western portion—Gaul, Spain, Britain, North Africa, and Italy—and an eastern portion—Greece and Greek-speaking areas in the Middle East. A successor, **Constantine** (307–337), reunited the Empire and built a new capital at **Constantinople, Byzantium.** Constantine's other major act was recognizing and legalizing the practice of **Christianity.**

- The Roman Empire was divided again in 395 by the Emperor Theodosius for his two sons. The western portion of the **Roman Empire** collapsed because of (1) a decline in tax revenue resulting from an end to territorial expansion; (2) which, in turn, resulted in a decline in the ability to pay for government services, including feeding the poor and financing a vast and widespread army; (3) disease; (4) the movement of people to the countryside to avoid the ever-increasing tax burden and thus the beginning of agricultural units that could support themselves; and (5) invasions by Germanic peoples. The year 476 is generally considered the end of the Roman Empire in the West. In that year, Odoacer, a Visigoth, removed the emperor and placed himself in power. However, there was little left to govern.

EMERGENCE OF NEW EMPIRES AND POLITICAL SYSTEMS

Study Strategy

See "Major Developments in the Arts and Sciences," p. 194, for more on the Tang.

- The **Tang dynasty** (618–906) is important for several reasons. (1) Under the Tang, the Chinese empire spread westward into Central Asia and southward into Southeast Asia. (2) The period was a golden age in Chinese arts and sciences. (3) The **imperial bureaucracy,** or **civil service,** became the chief administrative arm of the government and reached down to the local level. (4) Entrance into and promotion through the bureaucracy depended on passing examinations in the Confucian classics—philosophy and law—and Chinese literature. As a Chinese man moved up the ladder of appointments in the civil service, his wealth and status increased. An important concept to remember about the almost total reliance of the Chinese on a single set of ethical principles is the uniformity of the values and ideals of China's governing class of **scholar-gentry.**

- In the twenty-nine years after **Muhammad's** death in 632 C.E., various factions fought for the title of **caliph** and leader of Islam. In 661, **Muawiyah** became caliph and established the **Umayyad (Ommaid)** dynasty. In doing so, the split between his followers and those of **Ali,** the son-in-law of Muhammad, became institutionalized as the two sects of Islam, **Sunni** and **Shi'is.**

Geography Study

See Section 1 of this chapter for more information on the territorial growth of the Abbasid dynasty and the other empires discussed in this section.

- Muawiyah set up a central government for the conquered territories but allowed **provincial leaders** to appoint their own officials. This had the effect of diluting the central authority of the caliph, which in the end proved fatal to the dynasty. In 750, **Shi'ite Muslims** in Iran and Iraq rebelled, drove out the Umayyad, and installed the **Abbasid dynasty,** which was to rule for 500 years, until the **Mongols** sacked Baghdad and killed the last caliph. However, before the actual end of their rule, the Abbasids had let their power slip away to their Iranian prime ministers and Turkish mercenaries. Slowly the Abbasid empire broke apart, and regional leaders set up their own states, such as the caliphate of Cordova in Spain and the Fatmid dynasty in Egypt.

- A major significance of these dynasties and the history of Islam is the place of **sacred law, Sharia.** This is the body of Muhammad's teachings, the Quran, and the interpretations of it by *ulama,* holy men. Once set down, this sacred law was considered immutable and the model by which every Muslim should live and the state should govern. Issues that might be considered proper for a secular government to deal with became religious concerns.

Connections Strategy

*Note the comparison
between the Chinese and
Byzantine governments.*

- The **Byzantine Empire,** the eastern portion of the former Roman Empire, continued until 1453 when **Byzantium** fell to **the Ottoman Turks.** For a thousand years, the Empire served as a buffer between Christian Europe and Islamic and other invaders, such as the Bulgars. Like the **Tang,** the Byzantine Empire instituted a highly structured bureaucracy to administer its centralized government. In addition to highly educated officials, the Byzantine Empire employed a network of spies to report perceived disloyalty.

- In time, a **feudal system** developed in the Byzantine Empire. In return for service in the military, men were granted tracts of land. Over time, some of these warrior-landowning families assumed power over their area and were as apt to use their power against one another or the emperor as against Arab invaders.

KEY TERMS/IDEAS

Study Strategy

*See if you can relate these
terms and ideas to their
correct context in the "Fast
Facts" section.*

- **caliph (successor)**
- **codification of Roman law, Justinian**
- **Great Wall of China**
- **Gupta dynasty, Huns**
- **Han empire: eunuchs, concubines, scholar-gentry**
- **Islamic fundamentalism**
- **Silk Road**

SECTION 4. KEY CULTURAL, SOCIAL, AND ECONOMIC SYSTEMS BY 1000 C.E.

This section describes the major cultural, social, and economic ideas listed under "Foundations" in the course description. An important concept to remember is the interplay between belief systems—whether a code of ethical behavior or a formal religion—and social and economic developments. Note, for example, how Hinduism's concept of the cycle of rebirths gave rise to the caste system.

FAST FACTS

Major Belief Systems

- As you review the table, look for change and continuity over time. For example, while Buddhism changed as it spread through Asia and Southeast Asia, many of its principal tenets remained the same. Look also for comparisons. Buddhism arose as a protest against some of the practices of the Hindu priests. What similarities do you see between the two religions? What similarities and differences can you find between Buddhism and Christianity or Christianity and Islam?

MAJOR BELIEF SYSTEMS BY 1000 C.E.

Belief System	Origin/Date	Spread	Tenets	Significance
Hinduism	Origins with **Aryan** invaders between 1700 and 1500 B.C.E.; later groups added ideas	Originally spread throughout India (and modern Pakistan)	• One **Ultimate Reality, Brahma,** which is formless and nameless • Rebirth (**reincarnation**) for spiritual progress, determined by **karma** • Release from cycle of rebirth (**moshka**) of the soul (**Atman**) through oneness with the Ultimate Reality • Four stages of life: student, householder, anchorite, **sannyasi (holy one)** • **Dharma,** duties and rules of conduct to be followed to achieve salvation	• No founder and no date of founding • Tolerant of other religions • Little in the way of formal beliefs • Adaptable; offers both meditation and ritual • **Varna,** division of people into four classes, beginnings of **caste,** as a measure of one's spiritual progress
Buddhism	Grew out of protest of practices of **Brahmans,** Hindu priests; **Gautama Buddha**/500s B.C.E.	From northern India spread throughout Asia and Southeast Asia as far as Japan in 700s C.E.	**Four Noble Truths** • Universality of suffering • Desire as the cause of suffering • **Nirvana** as the cessation of desire • **Eightfold Path** as the guide to entering nirvana: rightness of • knowledge of the cause and ending of suffering • thought • speech • conduct • livelihood • effort • mind, and • meditation	• Strong **monastic tradition** • Monks carried Buddhism beyond India • Revival of Hinduism and Islamic invasions wiped out Buddhism in India by 1000 C.E. • In first century C.E. split into **Mahayana** (northern Asia) and **Theravada** • **Mahayana:** delay entrance into nirvana to help others find enlightenment; use of additional texts • **Theravada:** emphasis on seeking individual enlightenment; based more closely on teachings of Gautama Buddha • **Zen Buddhism:** 700s in China and by 1200s in Japan, sudden enlightenment through meditation

MAJOR BELIEF SYSTEMS BY 1000 C.E.

Belief System	Origin/Date	Spread	Tenets	Significance
Confucianism	China/Confucius, 500s B.C.E. and Mencius, 300s B.C.E.	China	• Based on *jen,* the quality that relates all people to one another, sympathy • Humaneness • Filial piety; family as the teacher of social roles; family as extension of the state; five relationships • Superior man; only the educated should govern	• Philosophical and ethical system of conduct • Dominant influence in Chinese government, education, and scholarship for 2,000 years • Knowledge of Confucianism basis of **civil service** • **Conservative influence,** acceptance of the status quo • But the right to overthrow a ruler who did not govern for the good of the ruled, **mandate from heaven** • **Ancestor worship**
Daoism	Traditionally attributed to Lao-tzu/400s and 300s B.C.E.	China, second most influential system after Confucianism	• **Tao** meaning **"The Way"**; indefinable but like nature, naturalness • Live in accord with one's nature • Oneness with everything through the tao; meditation • Interaction of **yin** and **yang,** passive and active principles, as influences on everything that happens	• Social conventions such as Confucian rituals unnatural • Became mixed with peasant belief in spirits and over time became polytheistic religion • Interest in nature greatly influenced Chinese arts
Judaism	Hebrews, ancient Israelites/first historical writings between 1000 and 800 B.C.E.	Land of Canaan, ancient Israel; **Diaspora** 130s C.E. by the Romans; Middle East, North Africa, and Europe	• One God • Chosen people through a special relationship with God • **Messiah** to come • Beliefs set forth in the **Torah,** Mosaic Law, and **Talmud,** collection of oral laws	• First **monotheistic** religion • Greatly influenced Christianity and Islam • No widespread hierarchical structure

MAJOR BELIEF SYSTEMS BY 1000 C.E.

Belief System	Origin/Date	Spread	Tenets	Significance
Christianity	Teachings of Jesus/ 30s C.E.	From Palestine throughout the Roman world, including the Byzantine Empire and northern Europe	• One God • Jesus as the **Messiah** • Through God's grace people are saved through the gift of faith in Jesus Christ • Through this faith sins are forgiven; receive new and eternal life • **Gospels** as main source of early teachings of Jesus • Large body of later writings developed to interpret and build on original teachings	• Persecuted by Romans • Legalized by **Constantine** in late 300s • Strong **monastic** element; **monks** preserved much of ancient Greek and Roman learning after the breakup of the Roman Empire • Strong missionary outreach • Strong, universal hierarchial structure and discipline • As **Roman Catholic Church** power of the **papacy** came to rival that of European emperors and kings
Islam	Muhammad/ Early 600s C.E.	From Arabian Peninsula spread through Middle East to western India, western China, sub-Saharan Africa, and Moorish enclaves in Spain	• One God, **Allah** • Muhammad as the **Seal of the Prophets** (Jewish Abraham and Moses; Christian Jesus; Muhammad) • **Five Basic Pillars:** • **"There is no God but Allah and Muhammad is His Prophet."** • Prayer five times a day facing Mecca • Charity • Fasting during **Ramadan** • Pilgrimage to **Kaaba,** shrine in Mecca • Original teachings recorded in the **Quran**	• Split into **Sunni** and **Shi'is** sects • **Sunni:** modern majority, originally adherents of the Ymayyad • **Shi'is:** originally followers of Ali • Development of the **Sharia,** legal code for many Islamic nations • Lack of hierarchial structure
Polytheism	Earliest religions across all culture regions	Continued in areas that had not been evangelized by Christianity and Islam	• Belief in many gods/spirits • Gods as personifications of nature • **Animism**	• Examples: Sumerian, Shang, Greek, Roman, Germanic, Mayan, Aztec, and African religions • Modern religion: Hinduism

Major Developments in the Arts and Sciences

- The purpose of the following table is not to provide exhaustive information on developments in the arts and sciences across all world regions circa 1000 C.E., but rather to provide information on the civilizations that the "Foundations" section has highlighted as key political units in 1000 C.E.

Connection Strategy

This is a good three-way example of the theme of cultural and intellectual developments and interactions among and within cultures.

- **Arab Muslim scholars** preserved past learning. Rather than destroy the manuscripts of the ancient Greeks, such as Aristotle and Plato, they translated them into Arabic and used them as texts from which to learn and extend that learning. Non-Arabic scholars such as the **Sephardim, Jews in Spain,** were also writing and working in Arabic and served as a "cultural bridge" between the Middle East and Europe. **Christian monks** in Europe took these Arabic texts and translated them into Latin, thus preserving this knowledge again and making it available to later Europeans.

Social Structures by 1000

- The **caste system** as the basic social structure of Hindu society began as early as the 3000s B.C.E. with the division of people into four graded classes, the **Varna,** as an indication of where a soul is on its path to salvation, the release from the cycle of rebirth. The classes are the (1) **Brahmans,** or priestly class; (2) warrior class; (3) farmer and merchant class; and (4) laborers. There is also what is now called the **scheduled class** but was formerly the outcaste or untouchable. These people are outside the class structure and are assigned the most menial of jobs. The caste system establishes a rigid societal structure in which one's birth dictates occupation, traditions, and the social strata from which one may select a marriage partner.

- **Slavery** had been known from centuries beginning whenever one warring group decided to turn the survivors of their opponents into workers for life. For example, the Sumerians took slaves in battle, Egyptians enslaved the Hebrews, and the Romans had slaves from Nubia. Slavery was known in the Americas as well. How rigid it was depended on the culture.

- By 1000 C.E., a prosperous business in selling black Africans had developed in the Islamic East Coast of Africa as part of the **trans-Saharan trade.** Only non-Muslims could be enslaved. The children of a non-Muslim slave who converted would be freed but not the convert. However, if a female slave married her owner, she was freed. Wherever Muslims established their authority, they took slaves from among the conquered peoples—Spain, Greece, India, Africa, and Central Asia.

ARTS AND SCIENCES OF REPRESENTATIVE CIVILIZATIONS CIRCA 1000 C.E.

Political Unit	The Arts	Science and Technology
Mayan civilization, 2400 B.C.E to 1200s C.E.	• Murals, sculptures, ornamentation • Elaborate detail on buildings, such as carved pillars	• **Ideographic** writing system • Accurately predict eclipses • Accurate calendar • Created monumental buildings such as temples without use of metal tools or wheeled vehicles
Byzantine Empire, 330–1453	• Religious **icons** • Illustrated manuscripts • Works in gold and silver valued as trade goods	• **Cyrillic alphabet** • Monumental buildings such as Hagia Sofia
Tang Dynasty, 618–906 C.E. "Golden Age of Chinese Art and Poetry"	• Nature as subject matter for paintings; any humans were insignificant in relation to the landscape • Poetry • Dictionaries • Family histories	• **Woodblock printing** • Fine pottery as both artistic and technological achievements
Abbasid Caliphate, 750–1258	• **Arabesque,** use of Arabic script and geometric and floral patterns instead of human and animal figures in art • **Miniature painting** in Persia (and later India under the Moguls) • Poetry	• Knew earth rotates on axis and revolved around the sun • More accurate calendar than current European Western calendar • Improved on Greek **astrolabe** • Wrote medical treatises translated into Latin and used in Europe • Use of steel for swords • Chinese inventions such as paper, printing, and compass transmitted through Arabs • **Arabic numerals, decimal system,** concept of **zero** • Developed **mosque** with **minarets, a dome, pillars** • Other monumental buildings such as forts and palaces
Europe, Circa 1000 C.E.	• Development of **vernacular languages** • Mystery plays • Few literary works except stories about the lives of the saints • Development of **polyphonic music,** chants, for example, for religious ceremonies	• **Romanesque,** imitation of Roman architectural styles • Return to stone for building

Study Strategy

See Chapter 7 under feudal-ism for more on serfdom.

- **Serfdom** was another form of enforced service and existed throughout eastern and western Europe beginning in the European Middle Ages. A peasant had the use of a plot of land belonging to his lord and was protected from bandits and raiders by the lord's troops in exchange for crops grown on the plot or service working the lord's fields.

- Integral to Confucianism was a **social hierarchy.** According to Confucius, there were five basic social relationships in life: (1) between ruler and subject, (2) between father and son, (3) between elder brother and younger brother, (4) between husband and wife, and (5) between friend and friend. With the exception of friend to friend, each relationship involved a set of duties and responsibilities between a **superior** and a **subordinate.** The relationship between friends was between equals, but each person still had a set of duties and responsibilities. Harmony within the state, as an extension of the family, and within families was the result of **right conduct** on the part of each person involved.

Key People

Study Strategy

See if you can relate these people to their correct context in the "Fast Facts" section.

- **Asoka, Maurya dynasty**

- **Avicenna, Al Razi (Rhazes), Al Khwarizmi**

- **bodhisattva, Buddhas**

- **Christian saints**

- **imam**

- **Moses Maimonides,** *Guide to the Perplexed,* **attempt to reconcile Aristotle and the Bible**

- **Omar Khayyam,** *Rubaiyat* **in Persian**

- **poets: Li Tai-po, Tu Fu, Po Chu-i**

- **rabbi**

- **Thomas Aquinas,** *Summa Theologica,* **attempt to use reason, Aristotelian logic, to support the truths of Catholicism**

KEY TERMS/IDEAS

Study Strategy

See if you can relate these terms and ideas to their correct context in the "Fast Facts" section.

- Ch'an Buddhism
- *Confucian Analects*
- Conservative, Orthodox, and Reform Judaism
- Eastern or Greek Orthodox Church, patriarch, Great Schism
- Hadith, Sunna
- Legalism
- Scholasticism
- Shinto: Sect Shinto, State Shinto
- *Tao Te Ching*
- *Thousand and One Nights* in Arabic

SECTION 5. INTERNATIONAL CONNECTIONS

This section focuses on the impact of interactions among major societies. As you review the material, look for the results of contacts but also look for similarities and differences among the forces that initiated the changes.

FAST FACTS

Missionary Outreach

Study Strategy

See the table Major Belief Systems by 1000 C.E. on pp. 191–193 to see where each religion had spread by 1000.

- In discussing the spread of religions, it is necessary to discuss why missionaries were successful. What conditions created a willingness on the part of people to convert to one of the new belief systems? How did the new religions address those conditions?

1. After the fall of the Roman Empire and the incursion of Germanic peoples from the east, Europeans looked for stability in their lives and an answer to their material sufferings. The **Roman Catholic Church** provided both. It had a strong, well-ordered structure that reached from Rome down into the local manor, and its emphasis on the soul and life after death gave meaning to one's trials on earth.

2. The traditional date for the arrival of Buddhism in China is 61 C.E. during the Han dynasty, but it made little headway until the collapse of the Han. During the next 400 years, China was enveloped in chaos—wars among local warlords and invasions by outsiders, including the Huns. The spiritual comfort that **Buddhism** offered became very appealing to many Chinese. In time, it mixed with native Confucianism and Daoism and became distinctly Chinese in many ways. Once stable dynasties were established, Buddhism lost much of its importance as the bureaucracy, educated in Confucian philosophy, worked to limit its influence—and that of other non-Chinese religions.

3. Originally, **Islam** had offered the peoples of the Arabian Peninsula the same stability as the Catholic Church had offered Europeans. The Peninsula was home to many rival groups that engaged in constant skirmishing. Islam provided a way to unite these competing groups under a new religion that was both monotheistic—a single God and a single body of thought—and Arabic in origin. The reliance on a single voice along with the great discipline of Islam provided the force that turned the power of the **Bedouins** of the Arabian Peninsula into an army of conquerors that in time ruled an empire that extended beyond the Middle East. The Muslims did not impose their religion on those they conquered. Islam spread through contact and the efforts of **Sufis,** Islamic mystics who stressed one's personal connection to God.

4. Like Christianity and Buddhism, people were attracted to Islam because it answered their need for some supernatural or greater power outside themselves. All three religions developed rich ritual and ceremonial traditions that appealed to people as well.

Trading Patterns

• A major force that initiated change among all cultures was trade. Traders brought not only goods like salt and iron with them but also ideas and cultural practices. Along with trade goods, Muslim traders imported Islam across the trans-Saharan network and the Indian Ocean. Centuries before, Buddhism had traveled with traders into Southeast Asia. The following table summarizes the major trading influences by 1000 C.E.

MAJOR TRADE ROUTES CIRCA 1000 C.E.

Civilization/ Area	Representative Trade Goods	Trade Routes	Significance
Chinese	• First silks from China; later porcelain • Woolen and linen cloth, glass, horses, ivory from other trading partners	Silk Road from Han dynasty onward: Northern Route across Central Asia; Southern Route, westward toward the Mediterranean to Syria and southward to India	• Spread Buddhism and Christianity into China • Spurred European interest in finding a water route to China to eliminate intermediaries in getting silks and other goods to European markets
Muslim	• Carpets, linen, brocade, ceramics from the Abbasid Empire • Silk and porcelain from China • Rubies, silver, ebony, and dyestuffs from India • Trinkets and slaves from the Byzantine Empire • See also trans-Saharan and Indian Ocean trade.	• On the main trade routes between Asia and Europe • See also trans-Saharan and Indian Ocean trade.	• Spread of Islam • Assimilating and adapting artistic styles, scientific, and intellectual achievements • See also trans-Saharan and Indian Ocean trade.
East European	• Furs, wood, amber, grain from Kievan Russia • Wine, perfume, glass, silk from the Byzantine Empire	Waterways of Kievan Russia between Western Europe and the Byzantine Empire	• Safe route away from Muslim raiders in Mediterranean and Black Seas • Heavy Byzantine influence on development of Russian religion, art, architecture • **Eastern Orthodox Christianity** became official religion, strengthened power of the czars

MAJOR TRADE ROUTES CIRCA 1000 C.E.

Trans-Saharan	• Gold, ivory, slaves, and spices from below the Sahara • Salt, cloth, and metalware from the Sahara	• Across the Sahara between North Africa and Europe beyond to West Africa	• Aided the rise of African empires and kingdoms in West Africa • Spread Islam through West Africa
Indian Ocean	• Slaves, ivory, gold, iron from Africa • Porcelain from China • Pottery from Burma • Cloth from India	• Major route between East Africa and Asia • Made possible by the action of **monsoons**, which blew northnortheast from December to February and south-southwest from April to September • Traded with China through intermediary merchants (Arab, Indian, Malayan, Indonesian) until around 1400s when direct trade began	• Brought prosperity to East Africa through the development of trading networks into the interior of the continent • Set stage for the rise of African trading cities such as **Sofala** and **Kilwa** • **Swahili**, mix of Arabic and Bantu languages • Brought Islam to coastal Bantu speakers

Nomadic Groups in Central Asia

- Central Asia spawned several nomadic groups that would play roles in the development of China, India, the Middle East, and Europe after 1000—the Turks, Mongols, and Moguls among them. The Turks, both **Seljuk Turks** and **Ottoman Turks,** originated in the Central Asian steppes. By the 500s, the Turks had taken a vast area from Mongolia to the Caspian Sea. In the 700s, the Abbasids had invaded and conquered a part of their territory, and many Turks converted to Islam.

- In the 1000s, when the **Abbasid Empire** began to disintegrate, Turks, under their leader **Seljuk,** captured the Abbasid capital of Baghdad and replaced the political power of the caliph with their own leader, whom they called **sultan.** The caliph retained religious authority over Islam. The Seljuk Turks moved westward and fought the Byzantine Empire for territory, capturing much of Asia Minor and then moving into Palestine. Their capture of Jerusalem precipitated the first **Crusade.**

Bantu Migrations

> **Study Strategy**
>
> *See Section 3 for more on the Bantu movements.*

- The **Bantu** were another force of peoples on the move during the 1000s C.E. Many of their kingdoms and states were founded after the 1000s, but **Zimbabwe** became an important center of the gold trade for **Shona Bantu-speakers** between 1000 and 1100.

- A major significance of the Bantu is their **transmission of cultural features** as they moved through the African subcontinent. They adopted and adapted foods, such as cereal grains; agricultural methods, such as terracing crops; and cattle herding as they came in contact with peoples already living in areas in which the Bantu settled. When a Bantu group would move on, they would take what they had learned with them.

KEY TERMS/IDEAS

> **Study Strategy**
>
> *See if you can relate these terms and ideas to their correct context in the "Fast Facts" section.*

- **assimilation**
- **culture trait**
- **Ottoman Turks**
- **Turkistan**

Chapter 7

FROM 1000 TO 1450

Idea Bank

As you read this chapter, look for examples of continuity and change for your change-over-time essay.

The period from 1000 to 1450 saw the development of more connections within parts of the world and among parts of the world. As you study this period, be aware of (1) how each culture region in 1450 was different from what it had been in 1000 and (2) how events in a culture region appeared to flow in an unbroken series until the accumulation of events produced change or (3) how sudden outside intervention could change the course of events. The economic revolution of the Song and the growth of European feudalism are examples of the first type of change, item 2, whereas the Mongol invasions and the Crusades are examples of the second type of change, item 3.

By 1450, the West—western Europe—was on the verge of becoming the most powerful region in the world. For the most part, (1) it had coalesced into several large political units, (2) there was a uniformity of religious practice, (3) the mass movements of people had ended, and (4) trade was becoming the basis of economic activity and growth. The Byzantine Empire in the East was teetering on the verge of collapse and would fall to the Ottomans in 1453. The political power of Islamic states was in decline and with it the vast Islamic trading network. China turned its back on direct trade contacts beyond Asia and invested its energies and resources on internal developments.

MANAGING THE INFORMATION OVERLOAD

As you study your world history course and use this study guide, don't be overwhelmed by all the facts you are learning.

- Look for the big ideas—the major concepts, or generalizations, and trends.

- Look for examples of change over time within culture areas and also between culture areas.

- Look for ways to compare and contrast information between culture areas.

The Acorn book itself lists examples of information that you are expected to know and information you are not expected to know. If you analyze the list for this period in history, you will see that the course designers expect a broad understanding of the era—knowledge of the important ideas. For example, the list says "Mamluks but not Almohads."

The difference between the two is that the Mamluks had a long-lasting effect on the development of Islamic history. The Mamluks were non-Arab slaves and bodyguards to the Egyptian caliphs and sultans who overthrew the Egyptian sultanate and ruled from 1250 to 1517 when the Ottomans overthrew them. The Mamluks then joined the Turkish army and continued in importance until 1811 when the Egyptian ruler decided to eliminate them. Some fled, but most were murdered.

The Almohads' importance was less long-term and less significant. The Almohads were an Islamic dynasty that ruled Spain and North Africa from 1130 to 1269. The Almohads were Berbers who sought to purge Islam of practices they considered corrupting. The dynasty could not withstand Spanish forces intent on recapturing control of Spain from its Islamic invaders.

If you look at the rest of the list, you will see similar examples of the broad picture, not the small detail. For example,

- the concept of feudalism but not specific feudal monarchs,

- the impact (the effects) of the Crusades in general but not information about each crusade or even the most important ones, and

- the rise in importance of the papacy of the Roman Catholic Church but not the actions of specific popes.

Connections Strategy

Throughout this chapter, look for differences and similarities between and among cultures. Besides the ones directly stated, what comparisons and contrasts can you make for yourself? Be sure to make notes for your Idea Bank for the essays.

This does not mean that to illustrate some idea in an essay you shouldn't use the actions of a specific person or the effects of a minor dynasty, but don't memorize them all. Prepare yourself to develop your viewpoints in the essays by choosing a few actors and events for each major concept and by learning pertinent facts that you can use to support your viewpoint in an essay.

DIVERSE INTERPRETATIONS

The Acorn book lists several questions as the basis for viewing the history of the period from 1000 to 1450. The questions ask you to consider

- the issues involved in using cultural areas rather than states as the units of analysis,

- whether nomadic migration or urban growth was the source of change,

- if there was a world economic network in this period, and

- if yes, how it compares with the economic system of the period from 1450 to 1750.

Here are some "Fast Facts" to help you think about these ideas.

FAST FACTS

The dictionary defines a state as (1) the political organization constituting the basis of civil government and as (2) the power and authority represented by a body of people politically organized under one government. As you study the events of the period from 1000 to 1450, you will see that even in western Europe, which boasted kingdoms, duchies, and empires, the state was a loosely organized political entity. In Africa, Asia, and Central America, the extent of an empire was often in the spread of its influence more than in its control of an area. Certain characteristics, such as whether the predominant religion was Catholicism or Islam or whether the basic unit of economic enterprise was agriculture or a growing mercantile trade, bound certain areas together more than the still somewhat artificial notion of statehood.

Study Strategy

See Sections 1, 4, and 5 of this chapter for the specifics of each culture.

- The economic growth of China during the Song period is an argument for urbanization as the source of change rather than nomadic migrations. An example of nomadic migrations as the source of change could be the invasions of the Mongols, Turks, and Arabs across Europe and Asia in this period or the movement of the Toltec and Aztec peoples in Central America.

Study Strategy

See Sections 1, 3, 4, and 5 of this chapter for more on interregional trade.

- To determine whether there was a world economic network, it is necessary to define what is meant by *world*. In the sense of a network between Eastern and Western Hemispheres, the answer is no, because there was no contact between them. If the term is meant "world as known to Europeans, Asians, and Africans," the answer is yes. Goods flowed between Europe and Asia, between Africa and Europe, and between Africa and Asia, often through Arab intermediaries. Within the Americas, there is evidence of trade within Central America and between Central America and the U.S. Southwest and possibly the Southeast.

SECTION 1. EXPANSION OF CHINESE TERRITORY

This section provides an opportunity to make connections between and among regions of the world as they begin to have more contact with each other. Much of this contact continues to be spurred through trade and invasions in this period.

FAST FACTS

Song Dynasty

Study Strategy

For more on the Mongols, see Section 5, p. 223.

- The **Song dynasty** came to power in 960 and was ousted in 1279 by Mongols who established the **Yuan dynasty.** The Song reign followed a period of chaos and warfare after the collapse of the **Tang dynasty** in 907. Initially, the Song commanded an area that covered most of China, but by 1127, because of a weak military, the Song were restricted to the southern part of China, below the Huai River, where two thirds of China's population lived.

- A variety of reasons made it possible for China to support ten cities with populations of more than a million each by 1100. The reasons were also the source of change: (1) new strains of **rice** that made it possible to support larger populations, (2) the opening of more land to agriculture by terracing hillsides and draining swamps, (3) the end to government-controlled markets and the introduction of privately owned shops, (4) a **currency-based economy,** (5) iron manufacturing, which gave rise to (6) industrialization, and (7) the development of **oceangoing vessels** that carried Chinese trade goods to ports throughout East Asia.

Connections Strategy

See Chapter 6, Section 4, for information on the philosophy of scholasticism in Europe during this period. See also the earlier discussion of the principles of Confucianism in Chapter 6, Section 4.

- A counterpoint to this economic revolution was the development of **Neo-Confucianism.** During the Song dynasty, Confucianists, most notably **Zhu Xi**, reasserted the dominance of Confucianism. While the ordinary people may have continued to practice Dao and Buddhism, Neo-Confucianim became the practice of those in the upper classes. According to Neo-Confucianism, (1) human nature is good, but (2) men must use education to improve themselves, and (3) even rulers need the advice of well-educated advisers.

- The results were (1) the reemergence of the scholar-gentry class as an important force in Chinese government, (2) the weakening of the military's influence at the urging of the **scholar-gentry** (as a way to control a rival force), (3) the restrictions on the merchant class at the urging of the scholar-gentry (as a way to control a rival force), (4) the institutionalizing of the **civil service examination system,** which resulted in (5) a large and often idle bureaucracy, (6) the hardening of the **Five Relationships** (7) with its rank and **gender distinctions,** and (8) an insistence on **tradition.** Neo-Confucianism influenced Chinese thought and practice well into the twentieth century. J.M. Roberts has stated that the Chinese civilization seems to have pursued goals that resulted in the "assurance of continuity and the prevention of fundamental change."

Connections Strategy

Here are some facts about art and science during the Song dynasty in case you need to compare and contrast Chinese dynasties across time or with other societies. See Chapter 6, Section 4, for additional information on arts and science in other cultures.

- During the Song dynasty, the Chinese (1) learned how to use the **compass** for navigation; (2) built ocean-going ships for trade; (3) developed military uses for explosives (gunpowder), such as missiles; (4) developed **movable type;** and (5) invented the **abacus.**

- **Landscape painting** became the dominant art form. Artists painted their **impression** of nature rather than the view before them.

THE MAJOR TRADING CITIES OF THE PERIOD

One of the major concepts of this chronological boundary for the AP world history course is interregional networks and how they facilitated the exchange of technology, trade goods, culture traits, and communication. The following table compares and contrasts five major trading centers of the period from 1000 to 1450.

- The **Silk Road** is also an example of how **culture** traits flow along with commerce. In addition to trade goods, the Chinese imported to its trading partners knowledge of silk-worm breeding, papermaking, iron smelting, and irrigation systems. In return, Buddhism found its way to China.

CONTRASTING THE MAJOR TRADING CITIES OF THE PERIOD

City/Dates	Location	Economic Importance	Political/Social Structures	Significance
• Guangzhou (Canton), 200s C.E. as a trading center	• Southern China, near the mouth of the Xi River	• Trade with Roman Empire through Arab and Persian intermediaries • Trade goods included tea, silk, spices • Trade with Hindu and Islamic merchants by the 1000s • In the 1500s, the first Chinese seaport to trade with Europeans	• Part of various Chinese dynasties • Neo-Confucian class system • Scholar-gentry • Aristocracy • Merchants (invested in land to become landed gentry) • Military • Gender distinctions that severely limited the role of women; women as mothers; women as subservient	• Example of a major Chinese city of this period • Large population • Cultural center
• Samarkand—built around 3000 B.C.E.	• In the Zarafshan River Valley in what is modern Uzbekistan along caravan routes (Silk Road) from China to the Middle East	• Major city on Silk Road • Trade goods included silk from China and from trading partners, grapes, cotton, pomegranates	• Part of various Islamic empires in this period • Islamic social system • Acceptance of **mawali** as equals • Somewhat diminished role of upper-class women in relation to early Islamic practices • Property, inheritance, divorce, remarriage rights continued • Female literacy	• Muslim city from mid-700s C.E. • **Abbasid** capital in the 800s to 900s • Center of Islamic culture • **Tamerlane's** capital in late 1300s and early 1400s • Declined with declining power of Tamerlane and the Tartars
• Timbuktu—founded in 1000s	• In what is today central Mali near the Niger River	• On **trans-Saharan** route exhanging gold from the south for salt from the desert • Other trade goods included ivory and slaves	• Part of various African-Islamic empires • Islamic social structure	• By 1300s, a major cultural and commercial center of the **Mali Empire** • In 1400s and 1500s, a major center of the **Songhay Empire** • Center of Islamic learning; site of University of Sankore • Starting point for pilgrimages (**hajj**) to Mecca

CONTRASTING THE MAJOR TRADING CITIES OF THE PERIOD

City/Dates	Location	Economic Importance	Political/Social Structures	Significance
• Cairo—founded in 969 C.E. as Al-Qahira	• At the mouth of the Nile River in what is today Egypt	• Commercial center between Europe, the Middle East, and Africa	• Part of Islamic caliphates • Islamic social structure	• Founded by the Fatmid dynasty • Overrun by Seljuk Turks in 1168 • Salah-el-din (Saladin) regained city • Became part of the Ottoman Empire in 1517 • Site of early Islamic university, al-Azhar • Center of intellectual life
• Venice—800s C.E. as the Republic of St. Mark	• Located on islands in a lagoon at the head of the Adriatic Sea	• Grew through trade, first with Byzantium • Made treaty with Saracens (Muslims) to control European trade with Arabs and Asia beyond • Major trade goods included spices and silk	• Independent city-state • Ruled by **oligarchy** of wealthy merchant families • City of independent merchants and craftworkers • Roman Catholic • Upper-class women more limited in roles than lower class but gender distinctions for all women; women as assistants and helpmates	• Originally settled by Veneti who were being pushed by Gauls • Too marshy to farm • Used Crusades to advantage by ferrying men, supplies, and arms to Holy Land • Important producer of fine glass

CHINESE INFLUENCE ON JAPAN

- Around 552, Buddhism had been introduced into Japan from China. In 607, **Prince Shotoku** of the ruling **Yamato clan** sent a mission to China to study Chinese culture, thus beginning a dialogue that lasted for almost 300 years. The Japanese borrowed and adapted to their own culture such Chinese developments as their (1) system of writing, (2) organization of the government into departments or ministries, (3) law codes, (4) tax system, (5) calendar, and (6) art, literature, and music styles.

- Modifications were made based on the **practicality** of adopting certain traits (the Chinese system of writing did not completely work with the structure of Japanese one) and the **compatibility** of Chinese values and traditions with Japan's own system (Japanese nobles ran the government rather than China's class of scholar-gentry). In the Confucian system of relationships, the emperor could be overthrown if he did not serve the people. In Japan, the emperor held his position by virtue of being a descendant of the founder of the clan, the sun goddess.

Idea Bank

China's influence on Japan is not only an example of interregional networks but also of comparison and contrast.

KEY PEOPLE

Review Strategy

See if you can relate these people to their correct context in "Fast Facts."

- Ibn Battuta, historian, observer, traveler
- Mansa Musa, ruler of Mali, responsible for growth of Timbuktu
- Sunni Ali, Askia Mohammed: ruler of Songhay, latter centralized government

KEY TERMS/IDEAS

Review Strategy

See if you can relate these terms and ideas to their correct context in "Fast Facts."

- calligraphy, monochrome
- footbinding as a metaphor for the role of women in Neo-Confucianist China
- interregnum
- shogun, shogunate, pupper emperor, rise of military
- Taika reforms, Reform Edict
- uji
- warlordism

SECTION 2. RESTRUCTURING OF EUROPE

Study Strategy

See Chapter 6, Section 3, on the fall of the Roman Empire and the aftermath.

Three factors helped to stabilize Europe after the collapse of the Roman Empire: (1) the Roman Catholic Church, (2) feudalism, and (3) manorialism. By 1450, only the Roman Catholic Church remained important. While only 30 percent of the AP world history course should deal with developments in Europe, this section provides an opportunity to set up several comparisons and contrasts that may be useful for answering the comparative essay question.

FAST FACTS

Feudalism

Idea Bank

In discussing periodization, point out that by 1000, the shape of modern Europe was becoming apparent in the establishment of various political units: England, Scotland, Denmark, Norway, Sweden, France, Portugal, and Spain.

- **Feudalism** was the political and military system of the European Middle Ages, whereas **manorialism** was an administrative and economic system. Feudalism began as a means of **local self-defense.** Under feudalism, plots of land called **fiefs** were distributed by **lords**, who could be women as well as men, to **vassals** who owed the grantor allegiance. The land could be a huge area encompassing hundreds of square miles, such as the Duchy of Normandy, granted by the monarch or a small estate granted in turn by the duke to a lesser noble. Even the Roman Catholic Church was part of the feudal system holding certain lands as fiefs. In time, fiefs became hereditary and usually it was the eldest son who inherited.

COMPARING EUROPEAN AND JAPANESE FEUDALISM

	European Political Units	Japan
Date Established	By 800s after the division of Charlemagne's Holy Roman Empire	Mid-800s in opposition to the power of the Fujiwara
Title of Main Ruler	King, queen, emperor	• Emperor as puppet ruler or figurehead • **Shogun** as real power between 1100s and 1945
Length of Office of Ruler	Hereditary unless deposed	• Emperor: hereditary unless deposed • Shogun, by force and intrigue
Ranks	• Ruler • Vassal as lord • Vassal (lesser noble) as lord • Knight who had no vassal under him	• Emperor • Provincial aristocrat as lord • Vassal (warrior chief) as lord • **Samurai**
Economic Base	• Large population engaged in agriculture • Change over time as trade and cities grew	Small agricultural population

- Feudalism set up a **reciprocal relationship** between lords and vassals. Lords were to protect vassals from enemies in return for the vassals' loyalty and aid, which included equipping knights to fight for the lord and payment of certain fees.

MANORIALISM

Russian serfs were bound to the land until the 1861, when they were emancipated, given civil rights, and allotted small pieces of land they had to buy.

- The economy of medieval Europe was based on farming. The basic agricultural unit was called a **manor,** which was self-sufficient. **Serfs,** who might be free or bound to the land, lived on the manor and farmed plots "rented" from the lord. In return for the right to farm, serfs paid the lord in produce, money, or work. They also paid the lord for the use of the manor's mill, blacksmith shop, and so on. The manor was also an administrative unit that included a court, which was presided over by the lord.

A CHANGING EUROPE

- Among the factors that led to the practical end of the manorial system were (1) the rise of towns, (2) the use of money rather than barter, (3) the labor shortage resulting from the plague in the 1300s, (4) enclosures of open fields, and (5) peasant rebellions.

- Around the 1100s, trade became an increasingly important factor in the development of Europe. With increasing commerce came (1) the rise of towns and cities, (2) the development of a banking system, and (3) the growth of a middle class whose livelihood came from commerce, not farming.

THE CRUSADES AS CHANGE AGENT

- One of the factors that created the impetus for increased trade—and with it political, social, and cultural changes—was the Crusades. Initially meant to free the Holy Land from Muslim hands, the eight Crusades mounted between 1096 and 1270 did not achieve their goal. The Crusades, however, (1) enhanced the power of European monarchs who won the right to collect taxes to support their armies; (2) introduced many Europeans to the riches of the Middle East and Asia, such as spices, silk, perfumes, and medicines; (3) thus encouraged the growth of a merchant and artisan middle class; (4) gave Europeans a better sense of geography; (5) exposed Europeans to the arts, science, technology, and learning of Islamic scholars; (6) resulted in the development of a number of wealthy trading cities, such as Venice and Genoa, that capitalized on supplying the Crusades themselves and then on controlling the new trade routes to the Middle East; and (7) led to the development of internal European trading routes, such as those on the North and Baltic Seas and between England and France.

- Among the negative effects of the Crusades were (1) the creation of hostility between Muslims and Christians; (2) the undermining of the Byzantine Empire with the capture of Constantinople in 1204 and the establishment of a temporary state; (3) thus further souring relations between Eastern and Western Christendom; and (4) the encouragement of anti-Semitism by the Crusaders' killing of Jews in Europe on their way to the Holy Land.

The Development of Central Monarchies

- Two areas to coalesce as **nation-states** were England and France. England's monarchy developed somewhat differently from the **absolute despotism** of the Continent. **William the Conqueror,** Duke of Normandy, confiscated the fiefs of his new Anglo-Saxon subjects and distributed them to his Norman vassals. Over the years, his successors established (1) a paid bureaucracy to administer the government, (2) a royal court system, (3) a single system of law for all subjects, (4) the system of circuit court hearings in the countryside, and (5) the **jury system.**

- As counterpoint to the weakening of their power, the English barons rebelled against **King John** and forced him to sign the **Magna Carta,** which among its 61 clauses promised (1) no taxation without the consent of the Great Council and the Church, (2) no arbitrary arrest or imprisonment of a free person without a hearing before a jury of peers, and (3) a guarantee of justice to all. The major significance of the document is in its recognition that the monarch is not above the law.

- Another step in limiting the rights of the English monarch was the development of **Parliament.** In 1265, representatives of towns for the first time were summoned to the national assembly along with nobles, clergymen, and knights, the representatives of rural counties. In the 1300s and 1400s, Parliament learned to use the **power of the purse** to get what it wanted from the royal government, which needed money for its many wars.

COMPARING THE DEVELOPMENT OF FRANCE AND MALI BETWEEN 1100 AND 1450

	France	Mali
Founding/Date	• **Hugh Capets** king in 987 over a greatly fragmented empire of strong feudal lords • Monarchy made hereditary	**Sundiata** conquered what was left of the Empire of Ghana around 1240 C.E.
Economic System	• Mix of agriculture, trade, and manufacture by hand and simple machinery	• Most Malians farmers, herders, hunters • Trans-Saharan salt and gold trade; tax revenue • Major trading centers at **Timbuktu** and Gao • Antipathy between Islamic merchants and traditional rural farmers

Political Organization	Various Capetian kings, most notably **Louis IX,** strengthened the monarchy by
	  • levying and collecting taxes
	  • imposing royal law
	  • establishing a bureaucracy with appointed officials from the middle class rather than nobles
	  • increasing the extent of royal lands at the expense of vassal lords
	  • organizing a standing army
	  • chartering new towns
	  • ending serfdom
	  • outlawing private wars between nobles
		System of dependent, or vassal, states
		• Within the central region, administered by governors who were members of the royal family
		• Conquered states kept their own rulers whose families lived as hostages in the capital

Future Development	By 1270 when Louis IX died, France a **centralized monarchy** that would last until the French Revolution of 1789	• Rebellion in 1335 by Songhay, a vassal state, that eventually took control of Mali and built its own empire • Lack of cohesion between urban and rural groups created inability to fuse lasting empires in region

RENAISSANCE

Study Strategy

See Chapter 6, Section 5, for more on Arab contributions to the Renaissance.

- The **Renaissance** began in Italy in the 1300s and around 1500 spread outward to the rest of Europe. The Renaissance, meaning rebirth, was characterized by a revival of interest in the classical eras of Greece and Rome. The recovery of the works of **Aristotle, Plato,** and other Greek thinkers as well as the works of Roman authors such as **Cicero,** which had been preserved by Islamic scholars and Catholic monks, sparked an interest in classical themes and classical styles. The Roman ruins throughout Italy provided inspiration for artistic expression.

- One outcome of the Renaissance was the development of **humanism,** a philosophy focusing on humans and human values. Because of studying the classics, humanists began to seek an answer for human life in the here and now, not in eternity—or religious dogma. People needed to exercise their own free will. Humanists replaced the medieval **scholasticism** of the universities with the study of the Greek and Latin classics, which deeply affected the cultural attitude of Europeans.

DIVISION OF CHRISTENDOM—ROLE OF THE PAPACY

- After the collapse of the Roman Empire in the West, the Eastern branch known as the **Byzantine Empire** continued for another thousand years. While people in the West struggled to make a new way of life, members of the Byzantine Empire enjoyed a high degree of stability, which enabled them to develop political, economic, cultural, religious, and social organizations that differed from those of the West. While the **Roman Catholic Church** came to be the most powerful single authority—both in spiritual and secular matters—in the West, the emperor in the East wielded more power than the **patriarch** of Constantinople who had authority over church matters in the empire. Over time, the emperor and the Roman pope clashed over various issues, such as the **iconoclastic controversy,** that called into question the authority of the emperor over church affairs. A meeting called in 1054 to discuss various doctrinal issues resulted in a lack of agreement and the beginning of the **east-west schism** that continues to the present between the Roman Catholic Church and the **Eastern, or Greek, Orthodox Church.**

- As noted above, the Roman Catholic Church enjoyed great authority and prestige in the West. Chief among the church's **clergy** was the bishop of Rome who as the **pope** presided over the Church's organization. Rome had become the principal **see** of the Church because of its connection to early church history. Over time, the pope's influence and power grew as that of the Holy Roman Emperor, successor to Charlemagne, declined and ultimately collapsed by 1254. The pope was left as the single most powerful ruler in the former Holy Roman Empire. However, the pope was not able to hold off the assault on his authority by the new monarchies in England and France. In 1307, a French cleric became pope and the papacy moved to **Avignon** where the popes were closely aligned with the political interests of France for seventy years. After a period of rival popes, the papacy returned to Rome, greatly weakened.

- Papal power was enhanced by the papacy's (1) insistence on being the sole authority over clergy and Church property, (2) refusal to pay taxes on church property to secular governments, and (3) insistence on naming bishops without consulting the temporal authority. Popes found that they could not always enforce the last element.

- In the meantime, lesser clerics, powerful in their own right because of their positions as sons of noble families with wealth and influence of their own, were spending more energy on political intrigue than in tending to the spiritual needs of the faithful. This environment set the stage for a number of heresies in the 1300s and the later developments of the **Reformation** and **Counter-reformation.**

Idea Bank

Note this example as an idea for your change-over-time essay.

KEY PEOPLE

Review Strategy

See if you can relate these people to their correct context in "Fast Facts."

- **Charlemagne, Frank, united large area as Holy Roman Empire, redivided**

- **Eleanor of Aquitaine as feudal lord**

- **Humanists: Petrarch, Bocaccio, Erasmus, Machiavelli**

- **Mansa Musa**

- **Vikings: movement, areas of settlement, cultural adaptability, Normans, Crusades**

KEY TERMS/IDEAS

Review Strategy

See if you can relate these terms and ideas to their correct context in "Fast Facts."

- **code of chivalry, code of the samurai**
- **demesne land**
- **guilds, skilled craftworkers, women as guild members**
- **Gothic style in architecture**
- **Hanseatic League**
- **Hundred Years' War**
- **interdict, excommunication as punishments of the Roman Catholic Church**
- **Inquisition**
- **Monasticism, role in preserving learning in the Middle Ages in Europe, role in deepening and containing spirituality, monastic orders for men and women, opportunities for women**
- **Northern Renaissance, High Renaissance**
- **Papal States**
- **Russian Orthodox Church**
- **perspective in art**
- **villein**

SECTION 3. NON-ISLAMIC AFRICA

African history south of the Sahara is very complex because of the size of the subcontinent and the number of kingdoms, states, and empires that rose and fell there. As you read in Section 2, much of West Africa and the East African coast converted to Islam, which greatly influenced the development of these political units. However, other empires and kingdoms rose in Central Africa, the highlands, and southern Africa. One of the most notable is Zimbabwe.

FAST FACTS

Zimbabwe

Geography Study

Zimbabwe was located in what is now modern Zimbabwe and Mozambique between the Limpopo and Zambezi Rivers.

- The **Shona** word *zimbabwe* means stone houses, and **Great Zimbabwe** is the largest city of the stone structures that have marked the region since around 1000 C.E. or earlier. The earliest Bantu-speakers, probably ancestors of the **Sotho,** arrived in the area around 400 to 500 C.E. They brought with them their iron-making, farming, and herding culture. In time, they began to mine the rich deposits of gold and copper.

Connections Strategy

One of the topics for the time period from 1000 to 1450 is interregional networks, one of which is trade. Zimbabwe is an example of trade between black Africa and the Arabian Peninsula.

- Many experts believe that **trade** was the major force in the development of Zimbabwe. Possibly as early as 700 C.E., the people of the Zimbabwe culture traded gold and other goods with their neighbors. In time, their gold reached the east coast trading center of **Sofala** in what is now Mozambique and from there to the **Arabs.**

- There are various opinions about when **Great Zimbabwe,** the major ruins and largest city of the culture region, was built. Some scholars date it to around 1000 C.E. and some to the early 500s C.E. The city has massive walls for enclosures, large buildings, rounded gateways, and enclosed passages. All are made of stone held without the use of mortar. Scholars believe that one particular section is the ruins of the king's residence.

Connections Strategy

Compare Mutota's tax strategy with that of the Sudanic empires of West Africa.

- In the early 1400s, the Sotho people were pushed out by the **Shona,** another group of Bantu-speakers who were moving into the area. They were divided into clans, as were most Bantu-speakers. A **clan** is a group of families who claim a common ancestry through either the male or female line and who recognize the authority of a single ruler. Around 1440, the **Karanga** clan began to build their own empire in Zimbabwe. First, the gold mines fell to the Karanga under their king, **Mutota,** and then the trade routes to the east coast. Mutota imposed taxes on all imports and exports. His son, **Matope,** continued the Karanga conquests and took control of much of Mozambique and east coast trading centers such as **Sofala.** He founded what has become known as the **Monomotapa Empire,** which was a **feudal society.**

KEY PEOPLE

Review Strategy

See if you can relate these people to their correct context in "Fast Facts."

- **Changamire, emir as honorific, Changamire Kingdom**
- **Ngoni, Zulu**
- **Portuguese, policy of playing rivals off against each other**

KEY PLACES

Review Strategy

See if you can relate these places to their correct context in "Fast Facts." Can you locate them on historical maps?

- **Ethiopia**
- **Kingdom of the Kongo**

KEY TERMS/IDEAS

Review Strategy

See if you can relate these terms and ideas to their correct context in "Fast Facts."

- **ancestor worship**

- **divinity of kings**

- *mfecane* **(Time of Troubles)**

- **vassals, rebel vassals**

SECTION 4. DEMOGRAPHIC CHANGES

The impact of nomadic migrations is an important concept in world history. If you remember, one of the diverse interpretations that was a point for study in the period to 1000 C.E. was whether the most common source of change was cultural diffusion or independent invention. Nomads played a major role in cultural diffusion. This section provides another opportunity for you to examine this argument but from another viewpoint. How much did each group of nomadic invaders affect the culture of those they conquered and settled among, and how much did the native culture affect the conquerors?

FAST FACTS

New Waves of Migrations

Geography Study

Be sure you can locate these peoples on historical maps to help you visualize their locations.

- The following table provides information to help you set up comparisons and contrasts among and between the major migratory groups of the years between approximately 1000 and 1450. See Chapter 6, Sections 4 and 5, for more on the movement and history of the Arabs under Islam. Note especially that once the **Abbasid dynasty** declined and the empire broke into smaller caliphates, (1) Islamic culture was spread and reinforced by contact with traders along the caravan and sea routes (2) by scholars going from Islamic university to university, and by (3) pilgrims on the way to and from Mecca.

COMPARING THE IMPACT OF NOMADIC INVADERS BETWEEN 1000 AND 1450

Nomadic Peoples	Date/Location	Route	Impact/Significance
Arabs, nomadic Bedouin tribes, Semites	Originally the **Arabian Peninsula;** moved out in a series of conquests between 600s and 700s	• Through the entire Arabian Peninsula west across North Africa into Spain and into West Africa; east through what are now Iran and Iraq, into Afghanistan, Pakistan, and northwest India; north and east through what are now Jordan, Syria, Israel, and Lebanon • Muslims in East African port cities as traders, not conquerors	• Rise of the **Abbasid dynasty,** the peak of Islamic power • Power of the caliphs supplanted by sultans • Rival caliphates in Egypt (**Fatmid**) and Spain (**Moors**) in 800s and 900s • Egypt ruled by Islamic **Mamluks, Ottomans** • Last Moorish stronghold in Spain defeated in 1504 by Christians • Allowed Jews and Christians to practice religions • Gave **mawali** (converts to Islam) equal status with original Muslims • Preserved and contributed to Greek learning • Religious influence on art, architecture • Influence of universal Arabic language and Islamic law

Turkic peoples: **Tatars, Khazaks (Khazars),** Uzbeks, Turkmens, and Uighurs, among others	**Turkistan** area of central Asia; by 500s C.E. territory stretched from Mongolia to Caspian Sea	Began moving out of Central Asia in the 500s; increasing migration through Middle East to what are now Armenia, Georgia, Syria, Turkey **(Asia Minor)**	• Converted to Islam in 900s
			• Seljuk Turks
			  • Adopted Islamic culture
			  • Invaded Byzantine Empire; took **Jerusalem**
			  • Broke up into small dynasties
			  • Weakened by **Crusades**
			  • Defeated by Genghiz Khan and **Golden Horde** in 1200s
			• Ottoman Turks 1300s to 1923
			  • Extended Turkish territory
			  • Took Constantinope in 1453; end of the Byzantine Empirc
			  • Continued to expand under later sultans
			• **Khazars,** empire in southern Russia
			  • Controlled trade between Slavs, **Byzantium,** Asia
			  • Defeated by Russians, Byzantium in late 900s and early 1000s

COMPARING THE IMPACT OF NOMADIC INVADERS BETWEEN 1000 AND 1450

Nomadic Peoples	Date/Location	Route	Impact/Significance
Mongols: loosely related nomadic tribes	Moved out of northeastern steppes of Asia, Mongolia	Moved into what are now China; central Russia, Poland, Hungary, Bulgaria, Romania; later movement into Iran **(Persia)**	• United under **Genghiz Khan** in 1200s • 1260, four **khanates** • Khanate in China known as **Yuan dynasty;** 1368, driven out by Chinese • 1480, end of Mongol control in Russia; rise of Moscow and the tsars

Slavs
• Eastern Slavs: Russians, Ukrainians, Bylorussians
• Western Slavs: Czechs, Poles, Slovaks
• Southern Slavs: Serbs, Croats, Slovenes, Macedonians, Montenegrins, Bulgarians
 	
Varangians, related to the Vikings
	Slavs
	• Originally north of the Black Sea around 2000 B.C.E.
	
	Varangians
	• Originally from what is now Sweden
		Slavs
		• Agricultural people
		• Around 100 C.E. began to move north and northeast into the Russian forests and **steppes,** west toward the Vistula River Basin, and south into the **Balkan Peninsula**
		
		Varangians
		• Crossed the Baltic Sea and began to move down the rivers into Slav territory
			• Varangians conquered Eastern Slavs and established basis of **Kievan Russia,** confederation of **city-states**
			  • Extensive river-based trading network
			  • Influenced by Byzantine religion, art, architecture
			  • Cultural and religious ties strengthened trade and vice versa
			  • Beginning of sense of **national identity**
			• Western and Southern Slavs:
			  • Merging with local peoples and cultures
			  • Wresting political power from earlier settlers
			  • Spur to political unity
			  • Set up trading networks
			  • Converted to Roman Catholic or Byzantine Church

THE PLAGUE

- The **plague,** caused by germ-infested fleas who live on rodents, is an example of an environmental factor that greatly affected the demographics of the period. The spread of the **bubonic plague,** known as the **Black Death,** between 1346 and 1348 in Europe caused the loss of an estimated 25 to 50 percent of the population. England may have lost as much as half its population. The one benefit was the severe labor shortage that it created, thus raising wages for workers. The plague also affected central Asia and the Middle East. It is possible that the plague began in south China and central Asia and was transmitted by herds of Mongol cattle or in goods transported along trading routes in the Mongol empire and then to the Middle East and Europe.

KEY PEOPLE

Review Strategy

See if you can relate these people to their correct context in "Fast Facts."

- Delhi sultanate, north and central India, Ganges plain; Persian, Afghan, Turkic rulers as sultans; large military force

- Golden Horde

- Magyars, Central Asian people, basis of Hungarian state

- Mughal dynasty, mixed Turkic and Mongol peoples, India

- Rurik, Varangian prince, founder of Novgorod

- Tamerlane, Tatars

KEY PLACES

Review Strategy

See if you can relate these places to their correct context in "Fast Facts." Can you locate them on historical maps?

- Bosporus

- Dardanelles

SECTION 5. AMERINDIAN CIVILIZATIONS

Idea Bank

List these pairs in your notebook as potential comparisons:

Settled agriculture: Mayans and serfs of France

Traders: Toltecs and the Kingdom of the Kongo

Nomads: Aztecs and the Bedouins of the Arabian Peninsula

The Americas were home to millions of people divided into hundreds of clans, cultures, and language groups long before Columbus "discovered" the West Indies. Like groups in other parts of the world, some Amerindians lived in **settled agricultural communities** while others were **nomadic hunters, gathers,** and **fishers.** Some Native Americans lived in small groups that moved often, others lived in small permanent farming villages, while still others lived in large cities. Some Native Americans found just enough berries, cereal grasses, and wild animals to **subsist** on, while other groups built elaborate **irrigation systems** (Inca) to water their crops. With a permanent food supply came **surpluses,** which, in turn, generated large populations, complex social structures, and **differentiated labor** that supported trade. Large **ceremonial centers,** often dotted with stone **pyramids** or dirt-packed **mounds,** are characteristic of certain culture regions.

COMPARING MAJOR NATIVE AMERICAN CIVILIZATIONS

FAST FACTS

Connections Strategy

To compare and contrast groups, it is necessary to list the same type of information for each group. Note the column headings for the table on page 226 and how each column is filled in for each group.

Study Strategy

Take the information in these paragraphs and create your own table that shows when and why the various Amerindian cultures ended.

- The civilizations of **Mesoamerica** highlighted in the AP course description illustrate an important concept about cultural change. Conquerors and conquered often share their cultures, each marking the other's religious, artistic, social, and political systems. For example, the strong militaristic influence of the Toltecs appears in the art of the Maya in the Yucatan after 1200 C.E. The Toltec influence can also be seen in the emphasis on human sacrifice among the later Aztecs.

- At their height, the **Maya** numbered an estimated 16 million people. The reasons for their decline are still unknown. It is possible that an earthquake, volcanic eruption, or epidemic caused the abandonment of various Mayan sites beginning in the 900s C.E. It could also have been overpopulation and overcultivation of the rain forest. Or it might have been warfare—internal and external. The **Toltecs** from northern Mexico began moving into Mayan territory and fighting the inhabitants for control around that time. Whatever the cause, the Maya were a vastly diminished group by the coming of the Spanish in the 1500s, and their last center was captured by the Spanish in the late 1600s.

- About 1200 C.E., the **Toltecs** in the Yucatan lost their power to an re-emerging Mayan force. In central Mexico, **Tula,** the Toltec capital, was conquered by nomadic peoples known as the **Chichimecs.**

- The **Aztec Empire** fell to the Spanish under **Hernán Cortés** in 1519, although they were far outnumbered by the Aztecs. (1) The Spanish had guns and horses, which the Aztec did not. (2) **Moctezuma,** the Chief of the Aztecs, and his advisers were not sure if Cortés was the white god whom the Aztecs were expecting one day to return. (3) The subjugated peoples from whom the Aztecs had exacted tribute and victims for sacrifice to their deities were only too willing to turn on them and join the Spanish.

FOUR MAJOR MESOAMERICAN CIVILIZATIONS

Culture/Date	Location	Political Structure	Economic System	Arts/Science
Mayan; possibly as early as the 2000s B.C.E; peaked between 300 and 900 C.E.	Rain forests; from the Yucatan Peninsula spread into what are now Guatemala, Honduras, Belize, El Salvador	Ruled by noble class of warriors and hereditary priests (**priest-scholars**)	• Based on farming • Also artisans and traders • Trade goods included carved jade objects	• Hieroglyphic writing on stele and manuscripts • Very accurate calendar • Knew the movement of the planets • Knowledge of sophisticated mathematical concepts • Ceremonial centers with temples, pyramids, and monuments of limestone blocks • Used bricks, mortar, stucco • Frescoes • Lacked knowledge of the arch, metal working, and the wheel
Toltec; possibly c. 750 C.E.; peaked between 900s and 1100s	Central Mexican highlands; invaded Mayan territory and took control of large areas; influence also widespread through its trade network	Jointly ruled by a military and a religious leader; in time the religious leader lost a power struggle and left, giving rise to the legend of **Quetzalcoatl**	• Originally nomads who conquered farming peoples • Extensive trading network that reached from central plateau of Mexico south and north to what is now the U.S. Southwest • Trade goods included copper bells, turquoise	• Massive buildings, pyramids, ceremonial ball courts of stone • Painted ceramics • Metalwork in gold and copper

FOUR MAJOR MESOAMERICAN CIVILIZATIONS

Culture/Date	Location	Political Structure	Economic System	Arts/Science
Aztec (Mexica); late 1100s C.E. appeared in the Valley of Mexico from northern Mexico	Built empire that covered most of what is today central and southern Mexico	• Chief of Men (emperor to the Spanish), both civil and religious leader • Rigid class system, including slaves • Exacted **tribute** from conquered peoples	• Originally, nomads who conquered farming peoples as they moved south • Maize as main crop • Extensive trade network • Trade goods included metalwork and textiles	• Manuscripts • Elaborate irrigation systems • Hillside terracing for agriculture • Artificial lakes, causeways, island cities • Featherwork, textiles • Metalwork in gold, silver • Jade objects • Semiprecious stones as jewelry
Inca; c. 1200 C.E., began to move out from the central Andes in the 1400s	What is now Peru and parts of Ecuador, Chile, Bolivia, and Argentina	• **Inca** as ruler, descended from the Sun god, founder of the **dynasty** • Rigid class system • Inca owned all land and the people worked it for the ruler	• Farming • Potato, quinoa (berry), maize	• **Quipu** for recordkeeping • **Hillside terracing** for farming • Extensive system of roads • Suspension bridges • Ceramics, textiles • Metalwork • Lacked system of writing and knowledge of the wheel

- By the time of the Spanish arrival under **Francisco Pizarro,** the Inca were involved in a **civil war,** with two brothers fighting for control of the empire. Pizarro promised to help **Atahualpa,** ruler of the northern part, but after Atahualpa had **Huascar,** his rival and ruler of the southern part, murdered, Pizarro executed him for the murder in 1533. **Cuzco,** the Inca capital, fell to the Spanish, and by 1537, most of the empire was in Spanish hands.

KEY PLACES

Review Strategy

See if you can relate these places to their correct context in Fast Facts. *Can you locate them on historical maps?*

- pre-Incan civilizations: Chavin, Nazca, Mochica
- Chichén Itzá
- Mesoamerica
- Teotihuacán: Pyramids of the Sun and the Moon, vast trading network from Guatemala to the Southwest United States
- Tenochtitlán

KEY TERMS/IDEAS

Review Strategy

See if you can relate these terms and ideas to their correct context in Fast Facts.

- acculturation
- calpulli, Aztec clans
- despotism
- Olmec Civilization: base culture of Mesoamerica, ceremonial centers, culture traits

Chapter 8

FROM 1450 TO 1750

Idea Bank

Be sure to continue listing Change-Over-Time and Cause-and-Effect ideas in your "Idea Bank" for essays.

The year 1450 is a significant benchmark for a number of reasons. In European history, 1450 is often used to mark the end of the **Middle Ages** and the beginning of the **Northern Renaissance** when the classical revival moved out from the Italian city-states to the rest of Europe. In 1453, the English were evicted from France and a unified France began to exercise its power. The mid-1400s are also a convenient date from which to view the **globalization of trade.** The fifteenth century marks the beginning of direct contact between Europe and sub-Saharan Africa and the Americas. The Americas were no longer isolated from the rest of the world. The mid-1400s (1453) also mark the end of the **Byzantine Empire** and the ascendancy of the **Ottoman Turks** to dominance in that part of the world. Within 30 years Moscow would declare itself free of Mongol control and begin to expand its territory and authority. This period also saw the rise of large-scale international conflicts. Where once England and France fought over territory on the European continent, they now fought in Europe and their overseas territories.

As you study this period, be sure to keep track of the causes—for example, conflict over territory, direct contact between different cultures, advances in shipbuilding, and the like—that brought about change. Not all the causal relationships may be limited to the period between 1450 and 1750. You may need to look back in time to see change building. For example, in the case of the introduction of the **Americas** to the global stage, the **Crusades** played a long-term role. They were a similar stimulus in the growth of trade. Be sure to refer back to Sections 1, 2, 3, and 5 in Chapter 7 to make connections with the discussion of trade in this chapter.

DIVERSE INTERPRETATIONS

There are a number of theories supported by a variety of arguments that can be advanced to explain why Europe came to dominate the world economy at this particular time in history.

- One is based on the **"great man (or woman) theory"** that posits that it was the visionary thinking of a few extraordinary people like Prince Henry the Navigator or Sir Isaac Newton who spurred people on to new endeavors. The counterargument is that, in reality, these people influenced very few others.

- There are also those who believe that **culture** played the central role in European expansion. One argument to support the theory is that the Middle Age's view of life on earth as a burden to be borne in order to enter heaven was giving way to a new belief that life on earth had a value of its own—and that life was getting better. The idea of continual progress was developing and owed much to the influence of the Renaissance.

- A third theory sees **economics** as the major causal factor for the dominance of Europe on the world stage. It was the desire of these nations and their citizens for wealth and the power that could be bought with it that spurred the surge outward.

- The same arguments could be used to support a **political theory.** European monarchs needed the money supplied by new colonies and new trade networks to finance their wars and add to their power.

SECTION 1. MAJOR EMPIRES AND POLITICAL UNITS

This period in world history provides an opportunity to compare and contrast the development of political units around the world. Note the similar methods of governing that developed. Note also that no single government practiced democracy. The most common traits were (1) a single ruler who may or may not have had **absolute** and **divine** power and (2) the use to a greater or lesser degree of the **nobility** as counselors and a **civil service.**

For earlier developments among the Mongols and the Ottomans, see Chapter 7, Section 4. Although the Aztec and Inca were unknown to the Eastern Hemisphere before this period, their civilizations were highly developed by this period. See Chapter 7, Section 5 for information on their empires on the eve of contact with Europeans.

Fast Facts

Asian Empires and States

Connections Strategy

See the discussion of feudalism in Europe and Japan in Chapter 7, pp. 212-213.

- In comparing and contrasting governments, look for subtle differences. For example, while both Europe in the Middle Ages and Japan during the same period had a political structure that was **feudal** in general outline, there was a major difference. European feudalism was **decentralized.** The feudal aristocracy owed allegiance upward to the monarch but ruled vast territories as lords. It was necessary for the monarch to rein in the nobles as the former tried to build a single nation and assert authority over it.

- In Japan, on the other hand, feudalism became **centralized.** The nation enjoyed several centuries of peace compared to the constant warfare in Europe. This occurred because of the strong control exerted by the **Tokugawa Shogunate.** Under previous shoguns, the second layer in Japanese feudalism had been made up of many large landowners, known as **daimyo.** Under the Tokogawa, (1) their number was reduced, (2) potential rivals were relocated, (3) restrictions were placed on what they could and could not do, and (4) strict loyalty to the shogun was required.

- In Europe the growth of trade (and with it the growth of towns and the bourgeoisie) as well as the deliberate actions of central monarchies robbed nobles of their power. In Japan the countervailing forces of trade with its attendant growth in urban life and the merchant class were beginning to cause problems, but it was the end of Japan's isolation in the mid-1800s that finally brought change to Japan.

COMPARING ASIAN EMPIRES BETWEEN 1450 AND 1750

Empire/State/Location	Political System/Date	Economic System	Significance
Ottoman Empire, spread from Anatolia (Asian Turkey) to include Balkan Peninsula and what are today Greece; parts of Austria, Poland, Hungary, Georgia, Armenia, and southern Russia; North Africa; and a large area of the Arabian Peninsual	**Sultan** as ruler of the **dynastic empire;** 1300s–1923 • Initially sultan as secular ruler; over time also claimed title of **caliph** • **Grand Vizier,** second most powerful person • **Ottoman Ruling Institution** • Trained officials, **civil service** • Military officers: standing army, bodyguard	• Agriculture • Little local manufacturing • Commerce—trade, banking—not worthy occupation; as a result controlled by foreigners	• Muslim empire of Turks • **Capitulation agreements** with European nations to ensure rights of each nation's merchants; benefitted Europeans more • Toleration of other religions • Captured **Constantinople** in 1453; end of **Byzantine Empire** • **Siege of Vienna** (central Europe) failed; end of invasion threat in Europe • Succession of military defeats in 1700s and 1800s; loss of territory; slow decline of empire
Ming, China	**Dynastic empire** with emperor; 1368–1644, post-Yuan dynasty • **Civil service** examination system; basis in Confucianism • Established **tribute system** with dependent states	Agriculture	• Had turned inward during Song dynasty • Explored as far as Persian Gulf and east coast of Africa in 1400s but did not establish own external trading network with the West • Contact with Europe established in 1500s; trading privileges to **Portuguese** in limited areas • Few Christian converts who continued to adhere to Confucianism • Numerous peasant rebellions • Overrun by Manchu, north of Great Wall

COMPARING ASIAN EMPIRES BETWEEN 1450 AND 1750

Empire/State/ Location	Political System/Date	Economic System	Significance

Qing (Manchu), **pastoral nomadic Manchus moved into** China; area expanded to include Manchuria, Taiwan, Tibet, Mongolia, and Turkistan	**Dynastic empire with emperor;** 1644–1912
	 • **Civil service examination** system; basis in Confucianism
		• Agriculture
		   • Introduction of sweet potatoes and corn from **Americas**
		   • Introduction of peanuts from **Africa**
		 • Export of porcelain, silk, and tea
		 • **Money economy**
			• Segregation of Manchu from Chinese
			 • "Other" considered barbarian
			 • Confined Europeans and later Americans to **foreign treaty ports**
			 • Trade drain on silver of trading partners
			 • British importation of **opium** to relieve silver drain; cause of nineteenth-century problems of China with West

Tokugawa Shogunate, Japan	**Centralized feudalism;** 1603– 1868 • **Sankin kotai, daimyos** to live in capital of Edo for part of year and with families all the time • Rise of **samurai** administrators	• Agriculture • Almost no foreign trade • Diverse internal trade • Local manufacturing • Rise of urban merchant class • From barter to money economy	• Adopted policy of **isolation/ seclusion,** 1633–1639, which was not broken until **Perry's** arrival in 1853 • Limited foreign trade contact; no large-scale trading empire built • No travel abroad by Japanese • Banned **Christianity** • Lack of dissemination of science and technology from West • Saved Japan from consequences of Western interference or colonial exploitation

COMPARING ASIAN EMPIRES BETWEEN 1450 AND 1750

Empire/State/Location	Political System/Date	Economic System	Significance
Mughal (Mongol), invaded from what is today Afghanistan, took all but southern tip of India (Portuguese)	Emperor of a **dynastic empire;** • 1526–1803, fall of **Delhi** to **British East India Company** • 1803–1857, **British** allow "king" to rule Delhi; exile of last king • Centralized government, civil service • Divided empire into 12 provinces with appointed governor aided by tax collector and religious official Used Hindu administrators to gain allegiance of conquered Indians	• Agriculture • Trade	• Muslim dynasty of Turks and Mongols • Introduction of **Urdu,** Persian language, as official language • Initial toleration of Hindu majority • Erosion of support over end of religious tolerance; rise of Hindu group, **Marathas** • Rivalry among dependent provinces causes of internal division • Attempts to limit Portuguese influence and trade • Arrival of British, imposition of colonial control on declining empire

- One of the characteristics that is common to these empires is their disdain for westerners. They felt that these people were inferior—barbarians—and could be controlled by keeping them to trading centers. However, by cutting themselves off from the scientific and technological advances of the West, these rulers and their advisers cut themselves off from advancing their own societies. Because they did not know their enemies, they had difficulty in fighting them—whether it was the appetite for wealth of the British in the nineteenth century or the philosophy of Marxist communism in the twentieth century.

European Empires and Nation-States

Study Strategy

For the beginnings of the political development of Russia, France, and England, see Chapter 7, Sections 2 and 4.

Connections Strategy

Jot this information down in your Idea Bank. It might be useful for a change-over-time essay.

- As you study the table, look for comparisons and contrasts and change over time. Note, for example, that while the tactics of the French monarchs and economic conditions in France were undermining the power of French feudal nobility in this period, the Russian tsars were encouraging the rise of feudal-style landholders. There is a parallel to Russia in Japanese policies of the period. Note also the difference in the development of the English monarchy.

- The contact among the Spanish, native peoples, and African slaves in the Americas resulted in a new **social structure**, or **class system,** peculiar to the colonies. (1) At the top were the native-born Spanish, known as **peninsulares,** who were the government officials sent out from Spain; (2) next came the **creoles,** descendants of the original Spanish colonists who were born in the colonies; (3) below them were the **mestizos,** who were part Spanish and part Native American; (4) then came **mulattoes** of Spanish and African descent; (5) below them were the Native Americans; (6) and at the bottom, slaves. In the nineteenth century it was the creoles, wealthy ranchers and merchants, who would fuel the movement for independence in Latin America. Tired of having little say in the government and sometimes educated in Europe, they were aware of the principles of the **Enlightenment** and of the **American** and **French Revolutions.**

COMPARING EUROPEAN EMPIRES AND KINGDOMS BETWEEN 1450 AND 1750

Empire/Kingdom/ Location	Political Organization/Date	Economic System	Significance
Portugal, western part of the Iberian Peninsula	• Became independent in 1143 • Had retaken all of country from **Moors** by 1249 • Administered **overseas empire** beginning in 1400s • Seized by Spain in 1580 but regained independence in 1600 • Used Portuguese officials to run colonies	• Vast international trading network • Colonies • Restricted to trading centers in China and Japan	• Major trading partners are Asian and African • Brazil as colony in South America • Worked sea lanes to Africa, Sri Lanka, Malaysia, Indonesia, China, and Japan • Sent Catholic missionaries to convert peoples, **Kingdom of Kongo** as an example • Portuguese trade as a government **monopoly** at a disadvantage against other European traders; lost advantage as earliest explorers to British and French private companies
Spain, eastern part of the Iberian Peninsula	• Reconquered lands lost to **Moors** by 1504 • Became part of the **Holy Roman Empire** under Charles V • Under **Philip II**, son of Charles, united Spain, European holdings (Milan, Naples, Sicily, and the Netherlands), and colonies into the **Spanish empire** • Used Spanish-born officials to run far-flung empire • **Viceroyalty system** in Americas	Vast international network based on colonial holdings in the Americas, North Africa, and the Philippines • Wealth secured through seizing of land and resources • Trade	• Importance to Spain of explorers' voyages: Columbus—laid basis for claim to territory in the Americas; Magellan—Philippines • Rather than simply trade, took land and sources of wealth; imposed Spanish rule through force; enslaved Native Americans • Sent Catholic missionaries to convert peoples; soldiers as disciplinary force; **mission system** • Introduced Africans as slaves • Spanish, Native American, and African cultures mixed in Americas; new culture resulted

COMPARING EUROPEAN EMPIRES AND KINGDOMS BETWEEN 1450 AND 1750

Empire/Kingdom/ Location	Political Organization/Date	Economic System	Significance
Russia, united and expanded from Moscovy north and east along the Baltic and west into Siberia to Pacific	• 1480 marks beginning of Russia; end of Mongol control; rise of Muscovy • **Centralized government** under the **tsar** (emperor); **autocrat; ruled through divine authority** • **Dynastic empire** • Late 1500s, taking on characteristics of **feudal system**	Agriculture, basis of economy • 1649, peasants become **serfs; bound to land**	• Shift of allegiance by **Eastern Orthodox Church** from authority of collapsed Byzantine Empire to Russian tsar; mutually beneficial alliance • Under Ivan IV (the Terrible) new class of **military-service landholders** to replace power of old nobility; land in return for service to the tsar • **Europeanization** policies of **Peter the Great** • Prior to Peter, segregation of foreigners in Russia • **St. Petersburg, "window to the West"**; exchange of Western and Russian ideas
France, Outline of modern nation	• Ousted England in 1453, ending **Hundred Years' War** • Unified France as **dynastic empire** • Worldwide colonial and trading empire • Used French officials to run colonies • Evolution of France's **centralized monarchy** into a **divine right monarchy**; monarch ruled because God had planned it; subjects must obey • **Estates-General** rarely used (for example, convoked in 1614, not again until 1788)	• Agriculture • Trade, commerce becoming larger parts of economic mix • International network of colonies and trading centers • French East India Company	• Importance to France of early explorers in North America—lay claim to territory • Holdings in India and North America; later, colonies in North Africa • Did not impose control on Native Americans as Spanish had; fewer native peoples, not the wealth of Central and South America • Sent **missionaries** to convert peoples • Over time build up of anger (over policies of a weak government, series of costly wars, financial burdens on subjects, discontent of the bourgeoisie over the continued dominance of the aristocracy, role of the Catholic church) leading to the **French Revolution** in 1789

COMPARING EUROPEAN EMPIRES AND KINGDOMS BETWEEN 1450 AND 1750

Empire/Kingdom/Location	Political Organization/Date	Economic System	Significance
England, on island of Britain	• Incorporated Wales and Scotland; Union of 1707 • Acquired worldwide empire through exploration and wars • Period of fight between Henry VIII and the Roman Catholic Church • Split with Church; enhanced power of the monarch and supporters • **Petition of Right**, limit on monarch's power to tax • Civil war, **Puritan** victory • **Glorious Revolution**, monarch's role further limited • Continued evolution of **Parliament**	• Vast international trading network • Colonies • Trading centers • **Hudson's Bay Company** in Canada • **British East India Company** in India • **Royal African Company** for the slave trade	• **Mercantilism** to control trade within colonial empire • Where colonies set up, took land and imposed government • Little interest on government level in converting native peoples to Christianity • Further limits on monarchy after the **Restoration: Bill of Rights, Act of Settlement** • Rise of political parties • Among Parliament's powers: levy taxes, declare war

Comparing European Monarchies and Asian Empires

- One of the topics listed under comparisons for this time period in the Acorn book is a comparison of a European monarchy to that of a land-based Asian empire. As you can see from the table above, you will reach very different conclusions if you use France or England for your comparison. **France** in this period hardened into a (1) **centralized government** ruled (2) without the benefit of a legislative body (Estates-General) (3) by a monarchy surrounded by advisers (4) who believed in the **divine right of kings. England,** on the other hand, evolved into a (1) **constitutional monarchy** with a (2) **cabinet** chosen from the **majority political party** (3) who debated in a **legislative** body, **Parliament,** regularly called to meet. In addition, the **Act of Settlement** stated that Parliament, not the monarch, was the superior power.

- Using either the **Ming** or **Qing** empires will provide a somewhat similar set of facts. Both were (1) **dynastic empires** based on (2) **Confucian principles** and (3) the use of a rigid system of **civil service examinations.** (4) Each had difficulty in keeping outlying regions, rival warlords, and peasants under the control of a centralized government.

Sub-Saharan African Empires and States Between 1450 and 1750

- The period between 1450 and 1750 saw the rise of a number of empires and states in West Africa. **Songhay** rose in the general area where first **Ghana** and then **Mali** rose and fell. As in the two previous empires, **Islam** was an important force.

- A characteristic common to the decline of the Kongo, the Yoruba city-states, and the Ashanti is the devastating effect of the slave trade. The desire for more and more wealth corrupted their rulers and escalated the trade in captured humans.

COMPARING AFRICAN KINGDOMS, EMPIRES, AND STATES BETWEEN 1450 AND 1750

Empire/State/ Location	Political Organization/Date	Economic System	Result
Kingdom of the Kongo in what are today the Democratic Republic of Congo and Angola	**Manikongo** (king); king and followers married into important families of conquered peoples to legitimize rule; king as **absolute** and **divine**; expansion began before 1400	• Trade in pottery, cloth, iron goods • Agriculture • **Maize** introduced in 1600s from the Americas • With coming of the Portuguese in 1500s, growth of trade in **slaves**	• Civil war over conversion of part of royal family to Christianity • **Europeanization** effort by **King Afonso** in early 1500s • Portuguese influence and interference • Corrupting influence of the slave trade • Division into small states by 1600s • Importance of merchants offset ruling families • Kingdom gone by 1800s
Songhay Empire in what are today Niger, Mali, Nigeria, Mauritania, Senegal, and Guinea	**Empire** of conquered territories (later four regions subdivided into provinces) with governors appointed by the emperor and **civil service (bureaucracy)** to administer it; local rulers not allowed to keep power; expansion began in 1464	• Control of gold and salt trade • Tax revenue from gold and salt trade	• Supported **Islam** over local religions **(ancestor worship, animism)** • Invaded by Moroccans armed with guns in 1591–1592 • Revolts by subject peoples • Empire gone by early 1600s

COMPARING AFRICAN KINGDOMS, EMPIRES, AND STATES BETWEEN 1450 AND 1750

Empire/State/ Location	Political Organization/Date	Economic System	Result
Oyo and Benin in what is present-day Nigeria	**Independent city-states** of the Yoruba people; grew up around 1000 C.E.; controlled surrounding areas	• **Slave trade** with Europeans • Exchanged slaves for guns	• Disintegrated in the 1700s as a result of civil wars and rulers' greed over the slave trade
Ashanti Union of Akan States in what are today Ivory Coast and Ghana	Union of **Akan-speaking** states with an elected chief who took his authority from the **Golden Stool of Kumasi** (capital city); 1695	• Gold trade (known as the **Gold Coast States**) • Expanding south became a major **slave-trading state** • Exchanged slaves for guns • Power declined with end of the slave trade in the 1800s	• Use of the slave trade to feed rulers' desire for increasing wealth led to conflict with Europeans and Ashanti downfall • Fell to the British in 1901 after a long, bloody war

European Exploration

Study Strategy

In studying about European explorations, remember that it is the broad overview that you should be learning and not specific explorers. For example, the impact of Portuguese explorations on Portugal's economy is the important idea to remember, not the specific significance of Vasco da Gama's voyage around Africa to India.

• Several factors spurred European interest in exploration: (1) The **Crusades** of the eleventh, twelfth, and thirteenth centuries had interested Europeans in trade with Asia for luxury goods, such as spices and silk. (2) European merchants, especially in trading cities such as Genoa and Venice and the Hanseatic League, a confederation of cities on the North and Baltic Seas, wanted to develop their own **trade routes** to Asia to cut out Middle Eastern intermediaries. (3) Technological advances introduced to the West from Asia, such as the **astrolabe** and **compass,** and new ship designs made it possible for sailors to try new and dangerous water routes. (4) The rise of **nation-states** encouraged economic development and also rivalry among European nations for new territories and new wealth. (5) The **Renaissance** engendered a sense of curiosity and adventure among Europeans.

• The impact of European explorations depends on which world region is being studied.

1. In China and India, the Portuguese in the 1500s and later the Dutch in the 1600s wrangled **trade concessions** from local rulers and established trading centers and regular **trade routes.**

2. The Spanish in the Caribbean, Central America, and South America subdued the native peoples, subjugated them, looted them of their wealth, and exploited their labor. In so doing, the Spanish destroyed the native cultures.

3. In North America in the 1600s and 1700s, the English and to a lesser extent the French usurped the land and rights of the native peoples, killed those who fought back, and reproduced as best they could their home countries in the wilderness. Where Europeans claimed the land, they also claimed dominion over the people who were already living there. European weaponry and horses enforced this claim.

Study Strategy

See page 251 for more on the crosscultural transmission of crops and diseases.

4. In Europe, the fruits of exploration included the following: an influx of gold and silver, which resulted in drastic increases in prices that caused **inflation;** the shifting of economic power from Italian city-states to England, France, and the Netherlands; the rise of **capitalism;** the consolidation of power among the new middle class **(bourgeoisie);** the loss of power by the **feudal aristocracy,** which led to the rise of **absolute monarchs;** the introduction of new foodstuffs; and the spread of diseases.

Examples of Continuity and Change

Connections Strategy

Besides providing ideas for a change-over-time essay, this paragraph and the next offer examples for comparative essays.

- Note the **continuity and change** apparent in the interactions described above. For example, while Europeans in this period controlled external trade routes with China and India, Chinese and Indian societies did not change because the Europeans did not seek to exert political control over these groups. Amerindian civilizations, on the other hand, were destroyed by the Spanish, who were intent on seizing the sources of wealth of these peoples. What rose in their place was a new society that was Spanish in organization but influenced by Amerindian and African cultural characteristics.

Connections Strategy

Did you notice that these three factors were examples of continuity and change when you read about them in the paragraph on the significance of European explorations? As you study, look for how situations developed slowly within a period until the weight of events created change.

- In European society, this period saw a continuation of the rise to power of the **middle class,** which had begun in the late Middle Ages. With this rise came the eclipse of **feudal nobility.** At the same time, power was being consolidated in a single government ruled by a **central monarch** who in this period would become an **absolute monarch**—except in England.

Empire Building in Asia, Africa, and Europe

- To set up this comparison on a table, think of appropriate categories— Motivation, Means, Impediments, and Advantages—and then fill them in.

    1. The motivation for Asian, African, and European rulers was the same: the desire to increase wealth and power. For Africans and Europeans, there was also a desire to convert nonbelievers to Islam and Christianity respectively.

    2. The means for each was also similar, force. For Europeans and Asians, this meant firearms and for Africans after the advent of the European slave trade, also guns.

    3. An impediment for Europeans was the lack of available territory on the European continent that was rich in resources and that would offer new markets that were not already settled and ruled over by a powerful government. Impediments for Africans and Asians were distance, ability to set up stable and strong organizations to govern conquered people, and rivals who worked against the rulers to gain either local or imperial power.

    4. Advantages for Europeans were their superior technology (including weaponry) and their navies (which could secure supply lines). An advantage for some African empires and states for a time was their access to European weapons as part of the slave trade. The regular pattern of Chinese dynasties alternating with periods that saw warring states made the stability of being part of an empire appealing to the Chinese at times.

Looking at the West

- The reaction of **Peter the Great** was very different from that of the Ottoman sultans, Ming and Qing Chinese emperors, the Tokugawa shoguns, and the Mughal kings. Until the time of Peter in the early 1600s, Russian reaction to Europeans had been mistrust, and Europeans doing business in Russia had been kept away from ordinary Russians. Peter embarked on a **Europeanization** effort that was meant to **modernize** his nation.

- The **Ottomans** took a military approach. Although they traded with the West, they also desired to enlarge their empire at the expense of these same nations. They struck westward several times in an effort to enlarge their domain. They captured Constantinople in 1453 and brought down the already teetering **Byzantine Empire.** The Ottomans farthest foray west was to the gates of **Vienna**, but their siege failed. They continued their fight against the **Holy Roman Empire** in the Mediterranean and won control of its eastern portion.

Connections Strategy

See Chapter 7, Section 1, for more on cultural diffusion of Chinese culture to Japan.

- The **Chinese** turned their backs on the Europeans, considering themselves superior to them. Contacts with European traders were limited to certain **treaty ports.** The **Japanese,** too, banned Europeans except for limited trade. Where once the Japanese had sent missions to China to learn about its culture, the Japanese **seclusion laws** limited even trading contacts with the Chinese.

- In 1613 the **Mughal** emperor welcomed the English East India Company. The Portuguese were already there, and France and the Netherlands soon followed. The Mughals were badly paid for their openness. The French and British were able to seize the majority of the trade. Not limited to treaty ports, the British and French trading companies began to meddle in local affairs and won the right to acquire territory. In addition, the European rivalry between Britain and France began to play out in India. The British routed the French and took over a large area of the subcontinent. By 1800 **imperialism** had become the governing philosophy of the British East India Company, and it began actively to increase the company's holdings until 1857, when the company deposed the final Mughal emperor. The company was ultimately disbanded, and the subcontinent became part of the British Empire in 1876.

Slave Systems and the Slave Trade

Study Strategy

See also Chapter 6, Section 4, for information on slavery.

- **Slavery** has been known since ancient times in all parts of the world. Although **racism** had a part in justifying the enslavement of Africans by the English, slavery in other parts of the world did not necessarily have this component. Often slaves were prisoners captured in battle. For example, many defeated Russians, Slavs, Germans, and Poles were sent to Istanbul as slaves to serve the sultans. The **Mamluks** were Turkish and Mongol slave soldiers in the service of the Egyptian sultan; twice they overthrew their sultans and established ruling dynasties.

Connections Strategy

Serfdom as practiced in the Middle Ages in Europe and in Russia from 1649 until 1861 was similar to slavery. The lord/landholder had certain rights over the serf and the serf was bound to the land. If the land was sold to another lord, the serf had to stay and work for the new owner.

- The enslavement of prisoners of war was a practice also known in Africa. The external slave trade began around the 1100s when Africans began supplying captives from the interior to **Arab merchants** for sale in North Africa and the Middle East. The trade remained relatively small in East Africa until the arrival of the Portuguese, who were interested in buying slaves for a European market. The slave trade expanded greatly in the 1700s after the Portuguese left and the trading cities of the East Coast assumed control of the trade. For much of the nineteenth century, these **Swahili** cities provided Africans as slaves to the plantation islands off the East Coast of Africa and to the Arabian Peninsula.

- The most widespread and largest systems of slavery were those on (1) the plantations of the Caribbean, (2) the southern British colonies in North America (later the southern states of the United States), and (3) Brazil. The **plantation system** required cheap, abundant labor, and the population of sub-Saharan Africa seemed to fit this description.

African Slavery in British North America

- The origins of **slavery** in the Americas began with the Spanish on their sugar islands in the Caribbean. To replace Native Americans, the Spanish, and later the English, began to import Africans as slaves. In 1619, the first Africans to arrive in the English colonies in North America came off a Dutch ship at Jamestown and were treated as **indentured servants.** As it became more difficult to find the large number of workers needed for tobacco agriculture, the policy changed.

- In a court case in Jamestown in 1640, the indenture of an African was changed to servitude for life, *durante vita*. In 1663, Maryland passed its first slave law. The plan for government for the Carolinas recognized Africans as slaves and, therefore, as property. Slavery was legalized in Georgia when the colonists came to realize that they would make money only through plantation agriculture. New York and New Jersey began as a single Dutch colony, and Africans were recognized as indentured servants. After the English seized and divided the colony, slavery was legalized. However, the Northern colonies did not farm large-scale **labor-intensive crops,** such as tobacco, rice, and indigo, so there was little need for slaves.

- Estimates vary, but it is generally agreed that some 20 million Africans survived the **Middle Passage** of the **triangular trade route** between Europe, Africa, and the colonies. They came from the **West Coast of Africa,** and most were sold into the Caribbean or South America. After being captured by fellow Africans and force-marched to the sea in chains for sale to Europeans, Africans were kept in **slave factories** until ships were available. The Africans were then marched on board ship in chains and kept below decks where an average of 13 to 20 percent of the human cargo died during a voyage. On arrival in the colonies, the Africans were sold without regard to keeping families together.

- The English **institutionalized** slavery because (1) they needed cheap, abundant labor and (2) they viewed Africans with their foreign languages and ways as less than human. The English had found neither Native Americans—who died from disease or who, as runaways, melted back into the forests—nor European indentured servants—who worked only for a specified time or who, as runaways, could melt into the general population—a satisfactory workforce.

- One reason that colonists used Africans as slaves was that the supply seemed limitless. In Virginia in the 1660s, there were only 300 Africans, but by 1756 there were 120,000 in a population of 293,000. About 3,000 were free blacks. In the forty years between 1714 and 1754, the number of Africans in the colonies rose from 59,000 to almost 300,000. **Natural increase** accounted for some of this, but most slaves were newly arrived Africans. New England and the Middle Colonies had few slaves in proportion to the overall slave population in the colonies. The climate and terrain were unsuited to plantation-style agriculture.

- Slaves had no legal rights: (1) slave marriages were not recognized, (2) slaves could not own property (they *were* property), (3) they had little legal protection against a cruel owner, (4) they could be sold away from their families, and (5) it was illegal to teach a slave to read and write.

Consequences of the Slave Trade for Africa

- The slave trade could not have grown into such big business without the cooperation of Africans, but the consequences for Africa were immense. (1) Areas were **depopulated** as slavers captured the youngest and healthiest, leaving the aged and infirm to fend for themselves. (2) Because of the hit-and-run nature of **slave raids,** a cross-section of any group was taken—farmer, village chief, craftworker, wife, father—thus, robbing the group of its leaders, its workers, and its social organization. (3) Arts and technology suffered as Africans turned to trade for what they wanted. (4) The **Sudanic empires** lost importance as trade shifted to the coast from its trans-Saharan network, thus causing a decline in interior empires and the growth of **forest kingdoms.** (5) To feed the desire for wealth, power, and more guns to ensure more wealth and power and more guns, the slave trade perpetuated itself, thus escalating slave raiding and warfare. (6) To justify the slave trade, Europeans (and later Americans) came to see Africans as inferior, or not quite human, which continues to affect **race relations** to this day.

Idea Bank

Although this chapter deals with the period from 1450 to 1750, this information and time line can help you make connections back and forth in time in case you need ideas for a change-over-time essay.

- **Peonage** is another form of slavery, or enforced servitude. Under the system of peonage, a debtor provides service until his or her debt is paid off. Debt bondage was the basis of **tenant farming** and **sharecropping** in the southern United States after the Civil War, methods that kept former slaves tied to the land they rented from former slaveowners. Peonage was also prevalent in Latin America in the nineteen and twentieth centuries and continues in some areas today.

\multicolumn{2}{c}{TIMELINE OF THE ABOLITION OF AFRICAN SLAVERY}	
1807	Britain abolishes the slave trade.
1808	External slave trade is abolished by the United States.
1833	Britain abolishes slavery.
1863	Lincoln issues the Emancipation Proclamation and frees slaves in areas held by the Confederacy.
1865	All U.S. slaves are freed at the end of the Civil War.
1873	Sultan of Zanzibar ends the slave trade, which controlled much of the trade on the East Coast of Africa.
1886	Cuba abolishes slavery.
1888	Brazil abolishes slavery.
1948	UN's Universal Declaration of Human Rights condemns slavery.

KEY PEOPLE

- Babur, son of Tamerlane; Akbar; Shah Jahan
- Charles I, Charles II, James I, James II
- Charles V, Holy Roman Emperor
- conquistadore
- Henry of Navarre, Huguenots
- Hideyoshi, Tokugawa Shogunate
- Ivan the Great, first tsar
- Louis XIV
- Prince Henry the Navigator, Portugal
- Oliver Cromwell, Puritans, Roundheads
- ronin: unsponsored, unemployed samurai
- Sikhs, adherents of religion combining Hinduism and Buddhism, no caste system
- Suleiman I, peak of Ottoman Empire
- Sunni Ali, Askia Mohammed, rulers of Songhay

KEY PLACES

- Guinea states
- Indo-Gangetic Plain
- Lepanto, site of naval battle, destroyed Ottoman fleet

KEY TERMS/IDEAS

- Act of Toleration, but not for English Catholics
- *capitalism, entrepreneur*
- joint stock company, underwrote trading ventures, Dutch East India Company, British East India Company
- Treaty of Tordesillas, moral authority of the papacy, Spain, Portugal
- Parlement, French governmental body

SECTION 2. SOCIAL, CULTURAL, AND INTELLECTUAL DEVELOPMENTS

This section describes a variety of social, cultural, demographic, and environmental changes that occurred worldwide between 1450 and 1750. Many were related directly to the changes in global interactions that began to escalate during this period. Others had more limited causes and their effects were more limited, but even societies that considered themselves closed found themselves changing. As you read this section, identify which changes were the result of global interactions.

FAST FACTS

Roles of Women

- The **roles of women** in this period were as varied as the cultures. However, there are some generalizations that can be made. (1) The higher up in social class a woman was and the more complex the society in which she lived, the more freedom she had to indulge in education and the arts; servants did the household work. (2) The lower down the social scale a woman was, the more her time was taken up in feeding and clothing her family and, in agricultural societies, in working in the fields and tending the livestock. (3) Cities opened up opportunities for women to learn crafts and to engage in commerce. (4) However, the higher in class status a woman was, the less valued her contribution might be, and the more "protected," whereas (5) women of lower class were more highly regarded within their class because they directly contributed to the welfare of the family. These points can also be made from the viewpoint of a social organization that is either urban/commercial and rural/agricultural or hierarchical and decentralized.

Study Strategy

To review Confucianism, see Chapter 6, Section 4.

- In China the principles of **Confucianism** governed the relationship of women to their families. They were to obey their fathers and brothers and then their husbands. A woman's role was always one of subservience. Confucianism along with **Buddhism** also influenced the Japanese attitude toward women. In Japan women were to obey their fathers, then their husbands, and if widowed, their sons.

- The **harem** is an example of how culture defines roles. Originally Islamic women were Arabic and had certain rights and freedom of movement. Over time Islam adopted practices such as **veiling** from non-Arab converts, and wealthy Muslims began to separate women in their households from the adult males by placing them in **harems,** special sections of the house where all female members, young sons, and their servants lived.

Environmental and Demographic Changes

Connections Strategy

See Chapter 6, Section 5, and Chapter 7, Section 4, for a review of cultural exchange.

- Students of U.S. history are familiar with what is called the **Columbian Exchange,** the exchange of peoples, plants, animals, technology, and disease between the Western and Eastern Hemispheres. You have already seen how goods, technology, and learning spread between and among the Middle East, Europe, and Asia prior to the 1400s. With direct European contact with Africa and the inclusion of the Americas in the global network of trade and settlement in the 1400s, the interchange became global and reciprocal.

- The following table lists a sample of the foodstuffs and animals that became part of the global exchange network after Columbus discovered the Americas in 1492. Whereas it is unnecessary to memorize which crops and animals were disseminated where, it is important to know the concepts demonstrated by this table: The exchange of crops and animals (1) was global in extent and (2) affected each region that it touched.

- The effects of the new crops were not seen immediately. Some historians do not think that they were of any consequence much before 1650. However, **populations** began to increase well before this time. In China, the population is estimated to have grown from 80 million in 1400 to 160 million by 1600. This was the result of bringing more land into cultivation and introducing new strands of rice. The Japanese also developed improved farming methods and increased their output of foodstuffs. Once the crops from the Americas began to take hold, populations increased rapidly. For example, in 1700 in Europe the population is estimated to have been 100 to 120 million; in a hundred years it had grown to close to 190 million. France's population on the eve of French Revolution was 26 million, up from 18 million at the beginning of the century. In general, (1) the cessation of frequent conflicts and invasions, (2) the lack of widespread outbreaks of disease, and (3) better farming techniques and strands of crops helped to increase populations.

- Another demographic characteristic of this period is the growth of **urban populations.** Cities were (1) always magnets for ambitious people from the countryside who wanted a better, more exciting life and (2) a place for a new start for people driven off their land by **famine** (French farmers and farm laborers in the late 1700s), the **enclosure movement** (English farmers in the 1500s), and too little productive land for too many people (Chinese peasants for much of China's history in this period).

Examples of Diffusion of Crops and Animals

Crop/Animal	Origin	Destination	Significance
Corn (maize)	Americas	Africa, Europe, China	Increase in food supply, leading to population increase
Potato	Andes in South America	Europe	Increase in food supply, leading to population increase
Sweet potato	Americas	China	Increase in food supply, leading to population increase
Peanut	South America	Africa	Increase in food supply, leading to population increase
Wheat	Europe	Americas	Remained staple of European diets
Sugar cane	Africa	Americas	When refined, sugar fueled the sugar plantation culture and African enslavement
Domestic animals such as cattle, goats, and chickens	Europe	Americas	Source of protein for Native Americans in settled communities
Horse	Europe	Americas	Means of transportation; new way to hunt buffalo, which helped to deplete herds

Study Strategy

For more on the bubonic plague, see Chapter 7, Section 4.

- **Disease** was an unintended part of the global exchange. Just as flea-infested rats carrying bubonic plague traveled from Asia to Europe on cargo ships, ships moving between Europe, Africa, and the Americas carried yellow fever, malaria, smallpox, and measles to the Americas and syphilis to Europe. The impact of the transmission of disease to Europe was minimal; however, the impact of European and African diseases on Native American populations was significant. European diseases—as well as mistreatment—wiped out the Arawak and Carib populations on the first islands taken by the Spanish. In the 150 years between 1500 and 1650, the Native American population in the areas claimed by Spain dropped to less than 4 million from 50 million.

Reformation

- The **Reformation** began as a movement from within to reform practices of the **Roman Catholic Church** and ended with the establishment of several **Protestant** religions and the fighting of several wars waged ostensibly to preserve religion but used to enlarge royal power and holdings. Both **secular** and **religious** issues lay behind the Church's problems. The emerging central monarchies (1) resented the secular power of the papacy and (2) the amount of land tied up as Church property that could not be taxed. There were also (1) disputes over a variety of **doctrinal issues,** such as the nature of the sacraments, clerical celibacy, indulgences, and the amount of ritual that had developed in the Catholic Church and (2) indignation over the lax lives led by some clergy. Reformers urged a return to a simpler form of Christianity without priests, candles, incense, stained-glass windows, and elaborate dogma.

- The act usually considered the beginning of the Reformation was **Martin Luther's** nailing to the church door his **Ninety-Five Theses** attacking Roman Catholic doctrine. Excommunicated when he refused to recant, Luther continued to teach, and his writings became the basis of Lutheranism and other Protestant denominations. Luther taught that (1) faith alone was all that was necessary for salvation and (2) the Bible was the only guide people needed to learn God's word.

Connections Strategy

Note all the consequences that become events in the cause-and-effect chain for future events.

- Many of the consequences of the Reformation were **secular** and often **political.** (1) Luther's insistence on the Bible as the guide to salvation and his translation of it into German helped to spread **literacy.** (2) His support for the German princes and his encouragement of their disobedience of the pope fed the spirit of German **nationalism.** (3) On the other hand, the division of German princes between Lutheranism and Catholicism and the **Thirty Years' War** kept Germany from becoming a unified nation until the end of the nineteenth century. (4) A **religious war** freed the Netherlands, which had embraced Calvinism, from Spain, which was Roman Catholic. (5) In England, Henry VIII severed his nation's ties with the pope over a personal conflict, proclaimed himself head of the Church in England, and through the **Act of Supremacy** stripped the Roman Catholic Church of its lands and authority. (6) By loosening the hold of the Roman Catholic Church on people's thinking and in many places destroying its political power as well, the Reformation led to the end of the medieval way of life, in which the Church provided stability and certainty. (7) **Anticlericalism** was a result not only of the dismay over the corrupt lives of the clergy but also the teachings of Luther and

Calvin that priests were not necessary. (8) With its insistence on good works and material success as a confirmation of salvation, the Reformation contributed to the growth of the **middle class.** (9) In the nineteenth century, this middle class would be instrumental in the establishment of European democracies.

Counter-Reformation

- The Roman Catholic Church that emerged from the **Counter-Reformation** of the 1500s and 1600s was similar to what it had been before the process but also different in that it had taken on many of the characteristics of the modern church. The movement (1) reformed the papacy, (2) established disciplinary reforms within the church, (3) reformed existing religious orders and established new ones, and (4) by the **Council of Trent** clarified those Catholic doctrines that were the cause of controversy with Protestants, such as the supremacy of the pope, the veneration of the saints, and indulgences. The emphasis was on renewing and revitalizing the **spiritual life** of the Church. Popes elected after this period tended to see their roles more as spiritual leaders than wealthy temporal rulers wielding political power.

Scientific Revolution

- The **Scientific Revolution** was actually a slow process of creating change in the way people viewed life. Begun in the 1500s, the Scientific Revolution by the 1700s had built a following of scientists and philosophers whose ideas gave rise in Europe and the Americas to the **Age of Reason,** or the **Enlightenment.** The Scientific Revolution itself was built on a belief in the efficacy of **natural science** and the **scientific method of observation** to explain the "mysteries" of life. These mysteries ranged from the fact that the earth moved around the sun **(Copernicus, Galileo)** to how the planets orbited the sun **(Kepler)** to the laws of gravity **(Newton)** to the discovery of oxygen **(Priestley)** to an understanding of the nature of disease **(Morgagni).** This was all part of the moving away (1) from the medieval view of life on earth as a step to salvation and (2) the reliance on supernatural explanations of earthly phenomena.

The Enlightenment

- The **Enlightenment** was an outgrowth of this belief in science and influenced European thought during the 1700s. Those who considered themselves enlightened thinkers believed in (1) science and **natural law,** the laws that govern human nature; (2) the power of human reason, or **rationalism,** to discern those principles of natural law; (3) and that once determined, people should live by those laws, (4) thus alleviating society's economic, political, and social problems and (5) ensuring **human progress.**

- In theory, if not always in practice, the Enlightenment called for (1) an end to injustice, inequality, and superstition; (2) toleration for all religions; and (3) a breaking down of institutions, such as the Church, that were corrupt and not based on natural law and human reason.

Major Developments in the Arts

- While knowing the artistic styles of individual painters might be personally interesting, for purposes of the AP World History test knowing the general characteristics of **Renaissance** art might be more useful. (1) While the themes of the art of previous centuries had been primarily religious, the **subjects** of Renaissance art were often the rich and powerful, such as monarchs, popes, and merchants; Greek and Roman deities; scenes of contemporary events; ordinary people doing ordinary things. (2) The **human figure,** whether a saint or a contemporary merchant, was shown more realistically because artists began to study anatomy to learn how the body worked. (3) Artists learned to use **perspective** to give their works a three-dimensional quality; previous art was flat, or one-dimensional. (4) The use of **tempera** gave way to **oil paints.**

- Toward the middle of the chronological boundary covered in this chapter, European art went through two artistic developments, **baroque** and then **rococo.** Both owed much to classicism, but Chinese influences were also evident in art and furniture design. This was a consequence of Europe's increasing trade with China.

- The following table provides one example society from each world region addressed in this chapter in case you need to do crosscultural comparisons of the arts.

REPRESENTATIVE DEVELOPMENTS IN THE ARTS BETWEEN 1450 AND 1750

Empire/State	Artistic Achievement
Ming Dynasty	• Construction of the Forbidden City in capital of Beijing • Fine porcelain, sought after as trade good
Tokugawa Shogunate	• **Kabuki,** new style of musical drama • **Haiku,** 17-syllable poems • **Bunraku,** plays performed by large-scale puppets
Mughal Empire	• Merger of Persian and Indian (Hindu) artistic styles and themes to form Indo-Muslim style • **Miniature painting** • Architecture: Pearl Mosque, Taj Mahal
Russian	• Merger of Russian styles (onion dome) and Italian motifs and stonework to produce new Russian architectural style and form • Cathedral of St. Basil • Merger of artistic styles of Italy and Byzantine Empire to produce peak period **icon** painting
Benin City-State	**Lost-wax method** of casting bronze of the Yoruba peoples; **Benin** famous for its bronze artwork

KEY PEOPLE

Review Strategy

See if you can relate these people to their correct context in "Fast Facts."

- **Baroque: Rubens, Van Dyck, Rembrandt, Le Brun, painters; Inigo Jones, Wren (architect)**

- **Elizabeth I, Thirty-Nine Articles, Church of England (Anglicanism) as state religion**

- **John Calvin, Calvinism; influence on Switzerland, Germany, France, the Netherlands, and Scotland**

- **English Enlightenment: Locke, *Second Treatise of Civil Government;* Hobbes, materialism; Hume, empiricism**

- **footbinding**

- **German Enlightenment: Kant, Goethe, Schiller**

- **Huguenots, French Protestants**

- **Italian Renaissance: Michelangelo, Titian, Leonardo da Vinci, painters; Palladio, architect**

- **Jesuits, Society of Jesus, as missionaries**

- **Northern Renaissance: Durer, Hans Holbein the Younger, El Greco, painters**

- philosophes: Voltaire; Rousseau, *Social Contract;* Diderot; Descartes

- Puritans

- Rococo: Watteau, Hogarth, Reynolds, painters; Louis XV style

Key Terms/Ideas

Review Strategy

See if you can relate these terms and ideas to their correct context in "Fast Facts."

- architecture of the Renaissance: classical in form, Greek columns, Roman arch and dome

- deism

- patronage of the arts, the papacy, the nobility

- printing press, importance for the dissemination of information in the vernacular, Bible in the vernacular, spread of literacy

Chapter 9

FROM 1750 TO 1914

From 1750 to 1914 marks another period in world history. During this 164-year chronology, the West became the major causal agent of change. It both underwent vast changes and caused vast changes in all other areas of the world. Western Europe had begun the process in the 1400s through its voyages of exploration, colonization efforts, and appropriation of world trading networks as well as establishment of new trade routes. From 1750 to 1914, western Europe consolidated its hold on foreign colonies and global trade and began a process of industrialization that, over time, changed the way the world made goods and did business. Political changes on the European continent that culminated in the first world war—the Enlightenment, attempts at radical reform, the unification of Germany and Italy, and shifting balances of power among European nations—also affected events in other parts of the world. This is not to say that important changes independent of Europe were not happening in other world regions, but the industrialization of western Europe began a global process that continues today.

As you study this period in history, look for continuities with the past—the continuation of absolutism in the France and the continuing sense of cultural superiority of the Chinese—and breaks with the past—the French Revolution and the end of Japanese isolation and rapid modernization of Japan after 1867. As you read, add examples to your Idea Bank to help you in writing your essays.

Connection Strategy

The sense of cultural superiority by the Chinese continues in the present.

DIVERSE INTERPRETATIONS

- Two different and competing theories, depending on one's viewpoint, are cited to explain the history of world regions in the modern period.

- The **modernization,** or **Westernization,** theory holds that as nations become more economically prosperous, various social changes will occur, such as improved health care, more educational opportunities, more rights for women, and so on. A desire for democratic government will evolve as people learn more about what the world holds, and they give up old ways and old attitudes. Scholars who hold this view cite the process that western Europe underwent as proof and believe that, in time, developing nations will evolve into developed nations.

- The **dependency theory,** which is cited by other scholars, claims that developing nations are economically dependent because developed nations have in the past and continue in the present to grow wealthy by draining the resources from developing nations. The latter nations export agricultural products, natural resources, and the production of assembly-line workers and sweatshop labor for the benefit of companies in other nations. For example, oil that has been refined for use as gasoline is more expensive than raw crude oil just pumped from the ground. The seller of the raw crude will get less money than the company that refines and sells gasoline. This theory is based on the idea that dependency is inherent in the system of **capitalism.**

- **Marxist theorists** dispute both theories and counter that only the adoption of **socialism** will enable developing nations to become viable economic entities.

SECTION 1. INDUSTRIALIZATION AND ITS CONSEQUENCES

Study Strategy

See Section 3 of this chapter for more on the way industrialization affected global trade.

The **Industrial Revolution** began in Great Britain in the mid 1700s and spread from there to the United States, other European nations, Japan, some Latin American countries, and eventually to much of Asia and Africa in the twentieth century. Its effects, however, were felt globally within a short time. While vast numbers of Asians and Africans were not forced into the life of a factory worker, they did provide the labor that farmed the **plantations** and mined the natural resources that fueled industrialization and world trade. The patterns of world trade changed as European nations seized trading networks from local and regional control and connected them into a truly global network.

FAST FACTS
Industrial Revolution

- Several factors came together to encourage the development of industrialization: (1) the **Agricultural Revolution,** (2) an increase in population, and (3) improvements in technology. The increase in agricultural production resulted from improved farming techniques. Because there was more food available and less chance of famine, life expectancy rose and with it the size of the population. Between 1700 and 1800, the population of Europe increased by slightly more than 50 percent to 190 million. This so-called **population explosion** resulted less from an increase in the **birth rate** than to a decline in the **death rate** and has continued into the present. Beginning in the 1800s, (1) improved medical care, (2) nutrition, (3) hygiene, and (4) sanitation have led to rising rates of **life expectancy** worldwide, although the gains in life expectancy in **developing nations** are still small.

- The third factor, improved technology, included (1) new sources of energy, such as **steam power;** (2) new materials, such as steel; and (3) new methods, such as the **factory system.** The widespread use of steam power resulted from (1) the invention of the **steam engine** and (2) the availability of sources of coal to fuel the new steam-powered machinery. Later, natural gas and then petroleum became important industrial fuels.

- The fact that **Great Britain** had large domestic deposits of coal is one reason that it was the early leader of the Industrial Revolution. The fact that **Japan** lacked its own sources of these fuels was one reason it embarked on its territorial expansion.

Study Strategy

See Section 2 of this chapter for more on reform movements.

- The Industrial Revolution resulted in a number of consequences: (1) a **Transportation Revolution,** (2) **urbanization,** (3) development of the **factory system,** (4) rise of the **middle class,** and (5) **reform movements.** The so-called Transportation Revolution was sparked by the invention of the **steam locomotive.**

- The Industrial Revolution came to different areas of the world at different times. France and Germany developed complex industrial economies during the nineteenth century. Russia made less progress and remained predominantly an agricultural country. By the early 1800s, the textile factory system of the British had been transported to the United States. Improvements in technology and **industrial production methods** moved quickly into various U.S. industries and spurred the development of an extensive railway system. By the second half of the nineteenth century under the **Meiji Restoration**, Japan quickly industrialized. Latin American nations and Asian and African colonies were seen more as sources of natural resources and markets than as potential industrial nations. Latin American nations as independent political units were also hampered by the lack of local capital for the investment in industrialization. Any industrialization that occurred was bankrolled by foreign investors.

- The emphasis in Protestant religions on earthly success as a sign of personal salvation indirectly resulted in the acquisition of capital and thus the development of industrialization. This belief in the value of hard work is the culture trait known as the **Protestant work ethic.**

COMPARING INDUSTRIALIZATION IN GREAT BRITAIN AND JAPAN

	Great Britain	Japan
Source of Capital	• Private entrepreneurs, capitalists • Limited foreign investment	• Government investment in initial stages of development • Zaibatsu, a few wealthy banking and industrial families, developed large business interests • Limited foreign investment
Energy Resources	• Large domestic deposits of coal for steam power • Large domestic deposits of iron for building machinery	Had to import energy sources
Availability of Technology	Much of the technology that spurred the Industrial Revolution developed originally in Great Britain • Textile mills • First steam engine • First steel-making process	Had to import machinery
Pool of Workers	• Almost doubling of population, from 5 to 9 million in the 1700s • In clothing industry, piecework by poorly paid women in sweatshops	• Also rapid population growth • In clothing industry, piecework by poorly paid women in sweatshops
Transportation System	• Internal railway system • Shipping companies for export	• Internal railway system • Shipping companies for export

Societal Changes	• Reform movements
	  • Class tensions
	  • Labor unions
	  • Socialism
	  • Women's suffrage
	  • Universal education
	• Middle class
	• Leisure time
		• Some increased opportunity for education for women
		• Continued reliance on traditional family life, including subordinate position of women
		• Class tensions

• Industrialization went through basically the same process wherever and whenever it occurred—in early nineteenth-century Great Britain or late twentieth-century Nigeria. (1) Factories were built in areas in or near towns and cities with access to sources of power, transportation, and pools of workers. (2) A shift of people from countryside to city occurred as a result of poor harvests, too little land and too many people to feed, and the allure of life away from a farm; this movement resulted in **urbanization.** (3) A **middle class** of factory managers, shopowners, and professionals such as lawyers and accountants developed. (4) The brutal working conditions and unsafe and unhealthy living conditions that factory workers endured resulted in calls for reforms, some political and some socioeconomic.

- While there are commonalities in how industrialization occurred in various nations, there are also differences. For this reason, it is useful to compare and contrast the development of industrialization in a western European nation such as Great Britain and Japan.

Gender Issues

Connection Strategy

The following are generalizations that apply to those women affected by industrialization. Those women who remained in rural areas in these nations continued in the same patterns as before.

Study Strategy

See Section 2 of this chapter, pp. 263–270, for more on social reforms for women.

- The position of women in industrial societies did and did not change. Poor women who had taken care of the home and children and worked in the fields when needed shifted from doing a great deal of domestic work to working in factories or in **sweatshops** and doing piecework at home and having little time or space for domestic work. Upper-class women had more wealth and more servants to manage but less influence and less power outside the home than they had had in previous eras.

- A new group of **middle-class housewives** developed, who lived on the outskirts of the new cities in large homes with a servant or two to do the work. These women sent their husbands off to work in the cities to manage the factories, run the new department stores, or protect their corporate legal clients. Like upper-class women, they were isolated from the work world and relegated to making afternoon social calls and drinking tea. This was the **Victorian Age** in which women were idealized, manners (etiquette) counted, and nothing distasteful—like how money was made—should ever be seen by women. The contradiction between the values supposedly appropriate and applicable for middle- and upper-class women and the realities of the lives of poor working-class women moved a number of reformers to action.

The Emancipation of Russian Serfs

Study Strategy

See Chapter 8, Section 1, p. 247, for the abolition of the slave trade.

- Two other areas that attracted reformers' interest in the nineteenth century was (1) the abolition of the African slave trade and slavery and (2) the emancipation of the serfs in Russia.

- While a variety of factors had worked to end the practice of **serfdom** in western Europe much earlier, serfdom continued in Russia until 1861. It had several negative effects on the economic development of the nation. (1) Dissatisfaction with their lives encouraged acts of violence and rebellion among serfs. (2) Serfs were not free to leave the land, so Russia lacked a large pool of labor for factory work. (3) Russia also lacked a large internal market for any goods it might produce because the mass of its population, serfs, were mired in poverty. (4) Most importantly, however, serfs bound to someone else's land had no reason to work harder, grow more, or improve the land.

- **The Emancipation Act of 1861** was meant to change some of the evils of the system. Serfs were now free and no longer bound to land owned by large landholders. (1) As a result, former serfs could take work off the land, so there was now a labor pool available for factory work. (2) The change from serf to indebted freeman did not improve agricultural output. (3) While the land now belonged to the former serfs, now called peasants, they had to pay off the price of the land they received. The valuations of the land were high, as were taxes.

KEY PEOPLE

Review Strategy

See if you can relate these people to their correct context in "Fast Facts."

- **Karl Marx, Fredrich Engels,** *Communist Manifesto,* **Marxism**
- **James Watt, inventor of the steam engine**

KEY PLACES

Review Strategy

See if you can relate these places to their correct context in "Fast Facts." Can you locate them on historical maps?

- **Sierra Leone as safe haven for former slaves, British colony**
- **Liberia, colonization scheme for freed slaves from U.S.**

KEY TERMS/IDEAS

Review Strategy

See if you can relate these terms and ideas to their correct context in "Fast Facts."

- **arts: romanticism, realism, impressionism as reaction to industrialism, post-impressionism**
- **enclosure movement: removal of land from farming, Great Britain, loss of means of livelihood by peasants**
- **impressionism in the arts**
- **labor unions**
- **philosophy: materialism as dominant school of thought, influence of the Industrial Revolution, idealism**
- **progressives in the United States, settlement houses, muckrakers**
- **realism in the arts**
- **socioeconomic theories: laissez-faire capitalism, socialism, communism**
- **telecommunications: telegraph, telephone, radio**
- **transformative nature of industrialization on societies**

SECTION 2. POLITICAL REVOLUTIONS AND INDEPENDENCE MOVEMENTS

While centralized monarchies were the norm in Europe, including Russia, the power of the monarch varied from the constitutional limits of Great Britain to the autocracy of France. The years between 1750 and 1914 saw a number of revolutions and independence movements with varying degrees of success. The precipitating causes may have been different, but the long-term causes were often the same.

FAST FACTS

Comparing Revolutions

The following table outlines basic facts about five revolutions between 1789 and 1949. There are several common strands in modern revolutions: (1) the influence of intellectual movements and ideas, for example, the democratic principles of the Enlightenment and the Marxist principles that underlie communism; (2) the importance of peasants and urban workers as actors in the revolutions; and (3) the shift to authoritarian rule in movements that began as democratic uprisings.

Latin American Independence Movements

- Mexico's revolution of 1810–1820 was unlike the other independence movements in the Spanish colonies in Central and South America in the early 1800s because it was a revolution of **mestizos** and Native Americans. The other rebellions were led by wealthy, educated **creoles.** As a result, the newly independent nations replaced the governing power of the **peninsulares** with a small powerful **elite** of creole families. Little changed for the majority of the people—mestizos, mulattoes, and Native Americans.

- Independence came to Spanish South America through the efforts of **Simon Bolivar** and **José de San Martin,** both **creoles** and both familiar with the writings of the **Enlightenment.** With Spain engaged in wars with Napoleon, they and like-minded men acted to free their colonies from Spanish rule. Between 1808 and 1824, all the Spanish colonies became independent nations. Bitter rivalries for power led to civil wars and more turmoil and suffering for the mass of people. Little in the way of social, political, or economic reform was accomplished in the former Spanish colonies. One legacy of this period in Latin America is the **caudillo,** the strong man, or military ruler, as head of government.

A COMPARISON OF REVOLUTIONS OVER TIME

World Area	Impetus	Stages	Outcome
United States	• **Mercantile** policies of Great Britain • Dependent status of colonies symbolized by "no taxation without representation" • Enlightenment ideas	• Noncompliance with British laws • Reprisals by the British • Protests: boycotts, violence, letters and declarations to the British crown • Cycle of escalating protests and reprisals • **Declaration of Independence, 1776** • War • Alliances with Britain's enemies • Defeat of the British forces • Peace treaty, 1783	• Establishment of the United States of America in 1776 • Recognition by other nations and finally the British • Loss of territory and revenues by the British
France	• Long-term effects of rule by **absolute monarchy** • Policies of Louis XVI • National debt and financial collapse • Privileges accorded the nobility; abuses • Privileges accorded the Roman Catholic Church; abuses • Rise of the **bourgeoisie;** rivalry for power with nobles and Church • Conditions of peasants; series of poor harvests • Conditions of urban workers, **sans culottes** • Enlightenment ideas; *philosophes*	• Four Stages • Aristocrats challenge king • Bourgeoisie challenge voting process in Estates-General • Popular revolution, the people in the cities, Paris, especially; support the bourgeoisie • Peasants in the countryside; support the revolution in Paris • **French Republic: National Convention** • **Directory** • Unsolved problems: • Continuing war with Great Britain, Austria • Corrupt politicians • Bread riots • Anger over policies related to the Church • Growing **royalist** support	• **National Assembly** • Formal abolition of feudalism • **Declaration of the Rights of Man and the Citizen** • Revocation of privileges of the Roman Catholic Church; reorganization of the Church under the state • Set up limited monarchy • National Convention • Abolished the monarchy and the aristocracy • Extended **suffrage** to more but not all male citizens • **Committee of Public Safety** • **Reign of Terror (Jacobin Club)** • **Directory** • 5-man council, absolute power • Napoleon asked to assume power

264

A COMPARISON OF REVOLUTIONS OVER TIME

World Area	Impetus	Stages	Outcome
Haiti (Saint-Domingue)	• Appeal of Enlightenment ideals to **creoles** and **mulattoes** • French Revolution as inspiration to slaves	• **Slave insurrection** in 1791 • Britain and Spain send troops; slaves and French join to oust them • At end of civil war, slaves freed and in power; still a French colony 1802, troops under Napoleon sent to end rule of former slaves • Defeat of the French by rebels and disease	• Independence declared in 1804 • Civil war among rival factions • Independent republic established in 1820
Mexico	1810–1820 • Revolution in Haiti • Distraction of Spain by its war with France 1910–1917 • Long dictatorship of **Porfirio Diaz** (1876–1910) • Unequal distribution of wealth: a few wealthy landowners and mass of desperately poor peasants, factory workers, miners • **Liberal reformers**	• **El Grito de Dolores!** Call to arms by priest; led **mestizos** and Native Americans in rebellion in 1810 • Fighting continued under new leader; killed in 1815; some scattered fighting • In 1821 **conservative creole** joins with rebels and declares Mexico independent empire • In 1823 emperor overthrown by liberals • In 1824 republic created • Demand for free elections; Diaz resigns • Succeeded by **Francisco Madero** as president; murdered after two years • **Civil war: Francisco "Pancho" Villa, Emiliano Zapata** • 1917 election: Venustiano Carranza as president	• First rebellions demanded reforms such as abolition of slavery • Lack of support from creoles for insurrection; collapsed • Under republic, after years of turmoil, little change for ordinary mestizos and Native Americans • French occupation • Reforms instituted under Benito Juarez (1861–1864 and 1867–1872) • Constitution of 1917, still in effect • Broke up large landholdings • **Nationalized** ownership of natural resources and Church property • Restricted religion • Provided for **minimum wage** • Extended **suffrage** to all males

A COMPARISON OF REVOLUTIONS OVER TIME

World Area	Impetus	Stages	Outcome

China	• Increasing power of foreign nations
	• Defeat in Sino-Japanese war in 1895
	• Spread of reform ideas among **Western-educated Chinese**
	• Discontent of poor rural peasants
	• Grant of power to provincial governments by Qing in an effort to stem uprisings
		• Abortive rebellions in late 1800s
		• **Chinese Revolution of 1911**
		  • Provincial secessions
		  • Declaration of republic
		• Empire under **Yuan shih-K'ai**
		• Years of civil war and chaos
		• Establishment of republic in 1927 under **Nationalist**, or **Kuomintang Party**
			• Abdication of **Qing (Manchu) emperor** in 1912
			• **Sun Yat-sen (Sun Yixian)** briefly president; steps aside for Yuan Shih-k'ai, premier under the Qing
			• Usurping power, Yuan declares self emperor; dies in 1916
			• **Warlords** in power across China
			• Unification of much of China begun under Sun; aided by Soviets
			• **Chiang Kai-shek (Jiang Jie Shi)** successor to Sun; leads Nationalist or Kuomintang, and republic
			• Fight for control of China with Communists under **Mao Zedong**

	• Difference in ideology between Western-educated Nationalists and Russian-trained leaders • Influence of **Marxism** on latter	• Civil war between Nationalist and Communist forces for control of China: 1927–1937 and 1946–1949	• Cessation of fighting between Communists and Nationalists • Defeat of Nationalists who flee mainland to Taiwan in 1949 • Establishment of **People's Republic of China** on mainland; Communist state

Latin American Independence Movements

- Mexico's revolution of 1810–1820 was unlike the other independence movements in the Spanish colonies in Central and South America in the early 1800s because it was a revolution of **mestizos** and Native Americans. The other rebellions were led by wealthy, educated **creoles.** As a result, the newly independent nations replaced the governing power of the **peninsulares** with a small powerful **elite** of creole families. Little changed for the majority of the people—mestizos, mulattoes, and Native Americans.

- Independence came to Spanish South America through the efforts of **Simon Bolivar** and **José de San Martin,** both **creoles** and both familiar with the writings of the **Enlightenment.** With Spain engaged in wars with Napoleon, they and like-minded men acted to free their colonies from Spanish rule. Between 1808 and 1824, all the Spanish colonies became independent nations. Bitter rivalries for power led to civil wars and more turmoil and suffering for the mass of people. Little in the way of social, political, or economic reform was accomplished in the former Spanish colonies. One legacy of this period in Latin America is the **caudillo,** the strong man, or military ruler, as head of government.

Nationalism in the Nineteenth Century

- After the fall of the Roman Empire in western Europe, governing power was **decentralized** among a number of **feudal lords.** The first liege lord to attempt to unify **vassals** on a large scale was **Charlemagne** in 800. After his death, his kingdom was divided, and no one attempted to unify the Franks again until **Hugh Capet** in 987. His Capetian dynasty established a central monarchy and laid the basis for the later French **absolute monarchy.** After 1066, **William the Conqueror** systematically reduced the power of the English lords, but his successors, while able to centralize the monarchy, were less successful than the French ruling house in establishing the concept of **divine monarchy.**

- By the end of the Middle Ages, a sense of **national identity,** or **national consciousness,** was developing among groups of people united under a single ruler, be it king, duke, or prince. An unintended consequence of the **Napoleonic wars** was to intensify this sense of **nationalism** among people of various European countries.

- Unfortunately for later developments, the men who divided Europe at the **Congress of Vienna** in 1815 after Napoleon's defeat had little interest in supporting burgeoning national feelings of lesser nations. They were more interested in establishing and maintaining a **balance of power** among the dominant nations—**Great Britain, Austria, Prussia,** and **Russia.** The Congress, (1) in addition to establishing the balance of power, (2) restored monarchs to the thrones of France, Netherlands, and several German and Italian states and (3) redrew national boundaries with no regard to ethnic and cultural differences among peoples. To the victor belonged the spoils, although France was treated fairly easily by the victors.

- Italian nationalists began as early as 1820 to fight the Austrian Hapsburg rulers of northern Italy and the French Bourbon rulers of various southern Italian states. The nationalists had some success in 1848, but it was short-lived. After a series of alliances and secret deals, **Victor Emmanuel II** of Sardinia became king of a united **Italy** in 1861.

- During the uprisings across Europe in 1848, the **Frankfurt Assembly,** a parlement of German states, met to write a constitution for a unified Germany, but when **Frederick Wilhelm** of Prussia declined to lead the proposed nation, the effort came to nothing. **Otto von Bismarck,** prime minister of Prussia, through a series of clever maneuvers, including war against France, united German princes with Prussia to create a single united **Germany** under **Kaiser Wilhelm I** in 1871.

Revolutions of 1848

- While nationalist feelings were stirring some Europeans to action—for example, the Germans and Prussians—the need for economic and political reforms was motivating others. A series of events culminated in the **Revolutions of 1848** across Europe. While spontaneous, the causes of the uprisings were similar: (1) the repressive policies of conservative monarchies, (2) economic problems caused by bad harvests and unemployment, and (3) working and living conditions under growing industrialization. While nationalists were unsuccessful in Austria and Hungary and efforts to write liberal constitutions came to little, the Revolutions of 1848 are notable because (1) the concept of **absolute monarchy** outside of Russia died with the uprisings and (2) manorialism came to an end.

- The French sparked the conflicts with an uprising against **King Louis Philippe's** policies, which favored the bourgeoisie over the poor—rural farmers and urban workers. He was forced to abdicate, and a provisional government was installed. A huge system of relief was set up, but when the middle class realized the amount of money needed to support it, they returned a majority of conservative candidates to the National Assembly. The relief effort was ended, and Parisians rioted. By December 1848, the National Assembly had proclaimed the **Second French Republic**, written a democratic constitution, and called for a presidential election. Voting conservatively again, the voters (males only) elected **Louis Napoleon,** nephew of Napoleon Bonaparte. Within four years, he had himself made emperor and the Second French Republic gave way to the **Second French Empire.** France now had another **autocratic ruler** who would remain in power until his disastrous foray into power politics and France's defeat in the Franco-Prussian War of 1870. After Louis Napoleon went into exile, the **Third French Republic** was born and a new constitution was written, establishing a **parliamentary system** of government.

Women's Suffrage Movement

- Women in the United States and in Great Britain had been agitating for the right to vote throughout the nineteenth century. In the United States, **women's suffrage** had taken a backseat to the abolition of slavery. When that was accomplished with the passage of the Thirteenth Amendment after the Civil War, American suffragists began a long and aggressive campaign that did not end until passage and ratification of the **Nineteenth Amendment**—in time for women to vote in the 1920 elections. By this time, about half of the states had granted women the right to vote in some or all elections, beginning with Wyoming in 1869.

- Women in Great Britain adopted aggressive tactics as well that included protests and demonstrations. When women jailed for their activities went on hunger strikes, they were force-fed. By 1918, women over 30 were allowed to vote and women between the ages of 21 and 30 were not able to vote until 1928.

- While a number of European nations granted women the right to vote between 1906 and 1919, women in France did not gain the right until 1944. Women's suffrage was one result of the new order after the Russian Revolution of 1917. Nations in Asia, Africa, and the Middle East tended to grant women the right to vote as each nation became independent. However, in some nations such as Saudi Arabia women may not vote.

KEY PEOPLE

Review Strategy

See if you can relate these people to their correct context in "Fast Facts."

- John Adams, Benjamin Franklin, Thomas Jefferson, Thomas Paine, George Washington
- George III, William Pitt
- Miguel Hidalgo, priest of Mexican mestizos and Native Americans; succeeded in first Mexican Revolution by Father José Morelos; Augustin de Iturbide
- Klemens Metternich, Austrian minister, Vienna System, restoration of monarchs to the throne after Napoleon, conservative policy
- Emmeline Pankhurst, Christabel Pankhurst, Sylvia Pankhurst, Women's Social and Political Union
- Elizabeth Cady Stanton, Susan B. Anthony
- Pierre Toussaint L'Ouverture, Jean-Jacques Dessalines

KEY TERMS/IDEAS

Review Strategy

See if you can relate these terms and ideas to their correct context in "Fast Facts."

- cahiers, Tennis Court Oath, storming of the Bastille, Paris commune
- Chartist movement, England, movement of artisans and laborers to extend suffrage, provide for a secret ballot, and annual elections to Parliament
- Declaration of the Rights of Women, Seneca Falls Women's Rights Convention, United States, 1848
- Dual Monarchy of Austria-Hungary, ethnic unrest, tensions among competing nationalist ideals
- Enlightenment ideas, influences on independence movements
- Estates-General: First, Second, Third Estates
- Three Principles of the People: nationalism, democracy, livelihood; Sun Yat-sen

SECTION 3. RISE OF WESTERN DOMINANCE

The period between 1750 and 1914 continues the rise to world power of western Europe that was begun in the previous era. By the end of the nineteenth century, the United States joined Europeans in empire building.

NEW PATTERNS OF TRADE

Connection Strategy

In the 1400s, the Ming Dynasty had put an end to long-distance, oceangoing trading voyages by the Chinese in order to concentrate on internal affairs. China is considered the only nation that would have had the resources and technology to challenge Western nations for this maritime trade.

- Before the voyage to India of Vasco da Gama, Arabs, Egyptians, and Turks had a **monopoly** on Eurasian trade. The Portuguese were soon followed into this lucrative network by the Spanish, Dutch, English, and French. By 1542, the Portuguese had reached Japan and established trading rights there. They took over the East African trading centers as refueling stops and seized **Goa,** an island off the Indian subcontinent, to use as their base. The Portuguese left internal trade routes to the locals and concentrated on long-distance trade.

- In time, the Dutch, British, and French were able to usurp much of Portugal's trade. While the former was a **royal monopoly** and subject to government regulation, the Dutch, British, and French enterprises were privately owned companies. They were able to move more quickly and were motivated by the lure of **profit** to be as efficient and as productive as possible. By the early nineteenth century, the Dutch—like the Portuguese—had lost out to larger and more powerful rivals in Asia. Great Britain had come to dominate the Indian subcontinent, and Africa was ripe for the taking in the mind of Europeans. By the end of the century, the United States and Japan would join the race for global advantages.

IMPERIALISM AND COLONIALISM

- **Imperialism** is the policy by which a more powerful nation extends its influence over a less powerful nation. Nineteenth-century imperialism was spurred by (1) the Industrial Revolution, (2) the desire to maintain a balance of power among competing European nations, and (3) the desire for military power and prestige. While some of the consequences of colonialism may be viewed by Westerners as progress, such as increases in life expectancy and literacy, these benefits came about through (1) the destruction or diminishment of traditional patterns of life and (2) the imposition of new values, customs, and possibly religious systems in their place.

- In 1885, German chancellor **Otto von Bismarck** called together a meeting of major European nations and the United States to divide up sub-Saharan Africa among them. The United States took no land, but Germany, Great Britain, France, Belgium, Portugal, Italy, and Spain did. By 1914, **Ethiopia** remained the only independent nation on the subcontinent. No regard was given to ethnic divisions among peoples who were forced within colonial boundaries. Africans resisted their new rulers but could not overcome European firepower.

- The European powers used different systems for governing their African colonies. The British governed **indirectly** through African rulers, changing as few customs and traditions as possible on the theory that the fewer the changes, the more smoothly things would run. Some British also thought that their charges in time would be able to govern themselves. Only a governor and council of advisers were appointed from Great Britain. The British established schools to educate local young men for civil service jobs. The French, Belgians, Germans, and Portuguese used **direct rule** and replaced local leaders with men sent out from their own nations. These European nations also introduced their own laws, court systems, and governmental bodies. They did not believe that the Africans would be capable of governing themselves.

- By the late 1800s, the United States stretched from the Atlantic to the Pacific. In 1890, the frontier was officially closed, and the nation began to look beyond its shores for ways to bolster its economy and to become a player on the world stage. The United States found several ways to flex its international muscles: (1) the partition of Samoa; (2) the annexation of Hawaii; (3) the annexation of Puerto Rico and the Philippines, spoils of the Spanish American War; and (4) the right to administer a protectorate over Cuba. First under Theodore Roosevelt and then under later Presidents, the United States used the "big stick policy"(1) to aid Panamanian rebels to gain the rights to a canal zone and (2) to intervene later in the twentieth century in an independent Cuba, Dominican Republic, Nicaragua, Haiti, and Mexico. While the latter instances of U.S. involvement were not colonialism, it was a form of imperialism, because the goal was to preserve U.S. interests.

RACISM AND SOCIAL DARWINISM

- **Racism** is the idea that some races are superior and others are inferior. This attitude justified the trans-Atlantic slave trade and the institution of slavery in the former British colonies and new United States. During the late nineteenth century, the **theory of evolution—natural selection**—of plants and animals that **Charles Darwin** developed was applied to societies to justify imperialism. Known as **Social Darwinism,** this theory held that like plants and animals, some people—and, therefore, some races—were superior to others, and it was the duty of these more fit to govern the less fit.

REACTION TO FOREIGN DOMINATION

- The following table outlines some of the major interactions between Westerners and Asian and Middle Eastern peoples as Europe and the U.S. implemented their imperialist policies. (1) In the case of the Ottoman Empire, China, and India, internal weaknesses within each region contributed to the unequal relationship that developed with the West. (2) The economic stimulus that the Industrial Revolution created for Western nations spurred their desire for new markets in which to sell their increasing production and new sources of raw materials to feed their factories to produce more goods. (3) In most cases, the West's superior firepower made it possible to subdue the local populations. Note also that not all imperialist activity was Western in origin.

LOCAL REACTION TO FOREIGN DOMINATION

World Region	Imperialist Action	Local Reaction	Outcome
Ottoman Empire	In a series of wars, Russia moves against Ottomans and supports **Pan-Slavic nationalism.**	• Turks fight back but are not a match for Russians. • In an effort to maintain **balance of power,** Britain and France aid Turks.	• Ottoman Empire as **"sick man of Europe"** • When Turks defeated by the Russians in 1878, Turks lose large part of **Balkans.** • Britain and Austria-Hungary unhappy over Russian gains, so they redraw map and take large areas for themselves.
China	• Foreign merchants come to trade. • The opium trade is forbidden, but British import opium from India to China. • Japan in 1894 moves against China. • Western influences continue to grow. • Discontent with Qing Dynasty grows. • Western-education intellectuals seek reforms, but conservatives refuse.	• China allows foreigners to trade and live in limited number of **treaty ports.** • Opium Wars, 1839–1842, 1856–1860 • China is badly defeated in the **Sino-Japanese War.** • In an attempt to diffuse the reformers, Dowager Empress supports the Boxer Uprising, which attacks foreigners and Chinese Christian converts.	• China loses wars and is forced to open more ports to foreigners and to grant **extraterritoriality,** the first of several **unequal treaties.** • Europeans exploit the situation and divide China into **spheres of influence.** • U.S., lacking any territory in China and to protect its own trading interests, insists on Open Door Policy. • European nations, U.S., and Japan defeat the Boxers. • Reforms are implemented, but the provinces begin to secede. • In 1911, a republic is declared.

LOCAL REACTION TO FOREIGN DOMINATION

World Region	Imperialist Action	Local Reaction	Outcome
India	• Portuguese, Dutch, English, and French vie for control of Indian trade during the **Delhi Sultanate** and then the **Mughal Empire.** • European rivalry spills over into India and the British defeat the French in 1757. • **British East India Company** builds an empire in India; introduces reforms, education, civil service. Varying degrees of compliance with policy of **nonintervention** in Indian affairs.	• British East India Company's attempts at acquiring territory is met by armed resistance by various states, Marathas and Sikhs, for example. • Long-standing issues that Indians had with the East India Company, such as the British attitude toward Indians and British interference with traditional Hindu practices, boiled over in the **Indian Mutiny** of 1857.	Control of India is removed from the East India Company in 1858 and placed under British government by the **Act for Better Government for India.**
Japan	U.S. forces Japan to open its ports to foreign trade in 1854.	• In reaction to the **Tokugawa Shogunate's** inability to resist foreign power and to deal with its own internal problems, it is overthrown. • The **Meiji Restoration** occurs. • After 1868 under the Meiji, Japan begins a process of **modernization and industrialization.**	• Feudalism ends. • Japan becomes a world power and begins its own **imperialist campaign** in Asia, at least in part to secure natural resources and markets to satisfy its production capacities.

Idea Bank

As you study, add examples of each form of reaction to your Idea Bank.

- The data on the table also point out that in general there were three forms of reaction to imperialism: (1) reform of internal practices that weakened the nation, (2) resistance, and (3) rebellion against imperialism.

KEY PEOPLE

Study Strategy

See if you can relate these people to their correct context in the "Fast Facts" section.

- Muhammad Ali (Mehmet Ali), seized Egypt from Mamlukes, increasing British dominance although part of the Ottoman Empire
- African resistance fighters: Chaka and the Zulu, the Mahdi of Sudan, Ashanti in West Africa, Mandingo in West Africa, Maji Maji in East Africa

KEY PLACES

Study Strategy

See if you can relate these places to their correct context in "Fast Facts." Can you locate them on modern maps?

- Crimea
- Panama Canal
- Suez Canal, French-built, British managed

KEY TERMS/IDEAS

Study Strategy

See if you can relate these terms and ideas to their correct context in the "Fast Facts" section.

- Crimean War
- dollar diplomacy, gunboat diplomacy
- economic imperialism
- policy of assimilation
- "scramble for Africa"
- Spanish American War: Puerto Rico, Cuba, Philippines

Chapter 10

FROM 1914 TO THE PRESENT

One of the themes of this period is the globalization of diplomacy and conflict. Up to this time, a war might have begun as a fight between two European nations and possibly their European allies and even spread to their colonies, but the wars were relatively small. World War I drew in all regions—if not as principal actors like the United States and Germany then as sources of supplies or soldiers like Latin American nations and Europe's African colonies.

By the mid-twentieth century, the United States had taken on a role as **police officer** and **peace negotiator** for the world. It played the Soviet Union to a standoff in Berlin with the **Berlin Airlift** in the 1940s and sent troops to **Grenada** in the 1980s and **Somalia** in the 1990s, among other places. It acted as mediator between **Israel and the Palestinians** in the 1970s, 1980s, and 1990s and between the republicans and unionists in **Northern Ireland** in the 1990s. In the **Persian Gulf War** in 1991 and in the attack on the **Taliban** in Afghanistan in 2001, the United States used diplomacy to gather a wide coalition of supporters and co-combatants before launching a military response.

Political relations between and among nations is only one area in which this period is different from earlier eras. But how also are foreign relations the same? As you study, look for changes over time that signal why this period is different from other chronological boundaries in world history. What continuities remain from earlier times? Look at contacts among and between nations—trade, conflict, **popular culture,** migrations—and such other topics as technology, the environment, and communications.

SECTION 1. WAR AND PEACE

War has characterized a large amount of the period from 1914 to the present—World Wars I and II and a number of localized conflicts, such as **Korea, the two Pakistans, Vietnam, Israel and the Arab states, the Persian Gulf War, Sudan, Bosnia,** and **Kosovo.** The local conflicts often were surrogate wars in which the superpowers did not confront each other but supported combatants on opposing sides. In 1989, the Berlin Wall collapsed and the **Cold War** was over, but a new kind of war had begun, the war of **terrorism** against citizens of nations that the terrorists wish to destroy. The largest such attack was caused by adherents of a strict Islamic fundamentalist sect against the World Trade Centers and the Pentagon in the United States in 2001.

WORLD WAR I

- The causes of World War I are rooted in nineteenth-century Europe: (1) the bitter rivalry between France and Germany as a result of the humiliating peace terms forced on France after the Franco-Prussian War; (2) rising **nationalism** among Slavs, known as **Pan-Slavism;** (3) the Balkan Wars and their aftermath; (4) economic rivalry between Great Britain, the originator of the Industrial Revolution, and Germany, a rapidly growing industrial competitor; (5) colonial rivalries in Africa; and (6) **the arms race.**

- Prior to World War I, the desire by Slavs to have their own nation was spreading through eastern Europe, fanned by Russia's ambitions as the largest Slavic nation. Both the **Austro-Hungarian** and the **Ottoman Empires** were concerned that Pan-Slavism would destabilize their nations. In 1912 and 1913, Ottoman fears turned out to be well founded. In the First **Balkan War,** the Turks lost almost all their European territory to a coalition formed by Serbia, Montenegro, Greece, and Bulgaria. In the Second Balkan War, **Serbia** gained more territory, and its goal to create a Slavic nation was threatening Austria-Hungary's power. The direct cause of World War I was the assassination by a Serbian nationalist of the Archduke Franz Ferdinand of Austria-Hungary while visiting Bosnia.

Test-Taking Strategy

Remember that you won't be asked about specific battles but about large general pieces of information such as the causes and effects of the wars.

- Although the war was centered in Europe, it drew in other areas. (1) Japan entered the war on the side of the Allies and took territory from Germany in China and the Pacific. (2) The United States entered the war on the side of the Allies. (3) The Ottoman Empire entered the war on the side of the Central Powers and fought the Allies in the **Dardenelles** and in the Arab Middle East, losing almost all of what was left of its territory. (4) Britain, France, and South Africa took German possessions in Africa.

- The peace treaty that ended World War I was not signed by the United States because one of its provisions was (1) the establishment of the **League of Nations,** which the U.S. Senate refused to endorse. Other provisions of the treaty included (2) $30 billion in reparations to be paid by Germany, (3) division of German territory by the victors, and (4) creation of the new nations of Latvia, Lithuania, Estonia, Poland, Czechoslovakia, Austria, Hungary, Yugoslavia.

- The League of Nations turned out to have little value because it lacked power, especially without the membership of the United States. Its charter called for (1) collective security for member nations, (2) disarmament, and (3) arbitration of international disputes.

- The decision to impose a huge debt on Germany and the separation of ethnic groups across several nation-states became causes of World War II. In addition, Russia was antagonized because Latvia, Lithuania, Estonia, and Poland had been created from its territory. Japan was antagonized because it was not allowed to keep the territory in the Pacific that it had seized from Germany. Italy was antagonized because it wanted more territory than the Allies were willing to give it.

- At the end of World War I, colonists in the Middle East, Asia, and Africa hoped that their participation in World War I would put an end to European colonialism. Instead, the diplomats turned the former Germany territories into **mandates** under the League of Nations, in effect continuing their status as colonies. Turkey did win its own independence with the collapse of the Ottoman Empire in 1923.

WORLD WAR II

- Economic problems that contributed to war included (1) huge reparations to be paid by Germany; (2) spiraling **inflation** in Germany; (3) decrease in prices for farm products, especially from the United States; (4) collapse of the U.S. Stock Market; and (5) the consequent deepening worldwide depression. Japan also faced the problem of lack of energy resources to power its industrial development.

- Political problems included (1) fallout from the economic problems, especially the worldwide depression, and (2) anger and frustration over the peace treaty that ended World War I. **Hitler** in Germany and **Mussolini** in Italy responded to these concerns and promised (1) an end to economic problems and (2) recapture of world power. Hitler also promised to purify the nation and remove all Jews, gypsies, physically defective people, and the like and reserve Germany for the pure Aryan race. Both Hitler and Mussolini established **totalitarian states** to curtail any dissent.

- World War II was fought on two fronts, **Europe/North Africa** and the **Pacific.** There was concern that Great Britain might fall if the Germans defeated the **Soviet Union** and took the Suez Canal. The Allies, therefore, adopted a strategy to defeat Germany and its ally Italy before turning to the Japanese in the Pacific. Short-term goals to accomplish this strategy were (1) control of the sea lanes to keep war matériel moving to Europe, (2) effective use of the Allies superior air power, and (3) supplying Soviet forces to fight the Nazi assault on the Eastern front. This strategy put a burden (1) on the Chinese to repel the Japanese who had already taken control of parts of China and (2) also on U.S. and Filipino troops to hold off the Japanese in the Philippine islands. **Chinese Communists** and **Chinese Nationalists** put aside their civil war in 1939 to fight the Japanese invaders.

- The conduct of the war itself, European governance after the war, and the future **United Nations** were the topics of a series of conferences during World War II. The divisions of the **Cold War** could already be seen in the decisions made by the **Big Three.**

WARTIME ALLIED CONFERENCES

- When the "secret agreements" were made known after Roosevelt's death, many critics faulted Roosevelt and Churchill for abandoning Poland, East Germany, the rest of Eastern Europe, and **Nationalist China** to communism. In truth, Soviet forces already occupied **Eastern Europe.** Short of another war, there was little that the Western powers could do to force Stalin to live up to his promises in Europe. In February 1945, the United States and Great Britain were still fighting the war in the Pacific, and British and U.S. troops had not yet entered Germany.

- The end of the war brought a number of changes. Europe was exhausted and without the resources to rebuild. The United States and the Soviet Union found themselves as the only two **superpowers.** As soon as the common enemies were vanquished, the rifts in the wartime alliances began to show.

WARTIME ALLIED CONFERENCES

Conference	Purposes
Moscow Conference of Foreign Ministers, October 1943 (Great Britain, USSR, United States)	• Agreed to an invasion of France in 1944 • Discussed the future of Poland but reached no agreement • Set up a committee to draft policy for postwar Germany • Agreed to set up an international peace-keeping organization
Teheran, November 1943 (Churchill, Stalin, Roosevelt)	• Agreed on timing of D-Day to coincide with Russian offensive • Renewed promise from Stalin that USSR would join war in Asia after the defeat of Germany • Agreed in vague terms to giving USSR some concessions in Asia for joining the war against Japan • Discussed structure of international peace-keeping organization
Bretton Woods, July 1944 (Forty-four nations represented)	Set up **International Monetary Fund**
Dumbarton Oaks, August–October 1944 (Representatives of China, Great Britain, USSR, United States)	Drafted plans for United Nations, including a **Security Council** as the seat of permanent peace-keeping responsibilities

Yalta, February 1945 (Churchill, Stalin, Roosevelt)	• Agreed to divide Germany into **four military zones of occupation** (France would administer the fourth zone)
	• Agreed to **free elections** in Poland "as soon as possible" but also agreed to accept the Soviet-dominated **Lublin Committee** as the interim government
	• Agreed to "broadly representative" interim governments throughout Europe (Communist-backed governments in the areas the Soviets controlled)
	• Worked out voting procedures in the proposed United Nations for the sixteen Soviet territories
	• Agreed to call a conference in San Francisco on April 25, 1945, to write a charter for the new international organization
	
	"Secret Agreements"
	In exchange for entering the war against Japan and signing a treaty of friendship and alliance with China, Stalin asked for and received:
	   • Recognition of the independence of the Mongolian People's Republic under Soviet protection
	   • Possession of the Kurile Islands, part of Sakhalin Island, an occupation zone in Korea, and rights in Manchuria

Potsdam, July–August 1945 (Churchill replaced by the new Prime Minister, Clement Atlee; Stalin; Truman)	• Agreed to policies for the occupation and administration of Germany, including disarmament, "denazification," democratization, and payment of reparations • Issued **Potsdam Declaration,** demanding Japan's unconditional surrender

THE COLD WAR

Review Strategy

See Section 2 of this chapter for the end of the Cold War.

- President Harry Truman adopted a policy of **containment** in dealing with the Soviet Union. According to this idea, the Soviet Union and its **satellites,** if left alone, would change and possibly collapse from internal economic and political pressures. The **free world** only had to keep the Soviet Union from expanding.

- The policy of containment was the basis of the **Truman Doctrine.** When Great Britain announced it was no longer able to provide economic and military aid to **Greece** and **Turkey** to fight **Communist takeovers,** Truman asked Congress for $400 million in aid. Mindful of the fine line between support and interference, Truman did not ask to commit troops. Without this aid, Greece and Turkey would most probably have fallen to the Communists, and the Soviet Union could then have dominated the eastern Mediterranean, thus upsetting the balance of power in Europe.

- Another indication of the reduced circumstances of Western Europe after World War II was the need for aid for its economic recovery. The U.S.'s **Marshall Plan** was designed to help European nations rebuild after the war. The plan met heated resistance in Congress. Opponents claimed it (1) would end any possibility of working with the Soviets, (2) would reestablish the United States as an imperialist power, (3) would bankrupt the nations, (4) could be a waste of money or could set up European nations as competitors for U.S. markets, and (5) should be aimed at Asia, not Europe. Senator Arthur Vandenberg, a Republican, defended Truman's strategy and argued that it was in the nation's self-interest to ensure that Europe did not fall to communism, and the plan was approved.

ARMS RACE

- Shortly after the end of World War II, the Soviet Union exploded its first atomic bomb. The two superpowers found themselves locked in an **arms race** as they built up **stockpiles of nuclear arms** and threatened each other. **Deterrence** was the basic concept that underlay the arms race. According to this theory, each side would be deterred from striking first because the other side had a matching arsenal of weapons that would be launched in retaliation against the aggressor.

- Pursuing a policy known as **détente,** President Richard Nixon eased tensions with the Soviet Union. As early as 1969, the two nations had signed a **nuclear nonproliferation treaty.** The Soviet Union was interested in relaxing tensions with the United States to strengthen its own position against China and to buy U.S. wheat to ease its own food shortages. The Soviet Union and the United States signed the first round of the **Strategic Arms Limitation** treaties **(SALT I),** limiting the spread of antiballistic missiles, and agreed to cooperate in health research, space exploration, trade, and pollution control. Although President Jimmy Carter and the Soviet Union signed **SALT II,** the U.S. Senate did not ratify it. In 1996, nations began signing a permanent test-ban treaty that would not go into effect until all nuclear powers signed it.

INTERNATIONAL ORGANIZATIONS

- The **United Nations** was established in 1945 as the successor to the League of Nations to work for (1) peace, (2) **collective security,** and (3) cooperation among its member nations, now numbering 185. Its main body, the **General Assembly,** can only pass recommendations. In order to approve actions, the **Security Council** must vote, and the five **permanent members**—China, France, Russia, the United Kingdom, and the United States—of the fifteen-seat Security Council must vote "yes" on any substantive matter, such as the use of UN-sponsored **peacekeeping** troops in a nation. Peacekeeping is an important function of the UN, as is providing relief to poor and war-torn nations. During the Cold War, the need to have agreement among the five permanent members has blocked various efforts at collective security. Perhaps the most important document to come from the UN is the **Declaration of Universal Human Rights,** outlining what should be considered the basic human rights of all peoples.

- In addition to the UN, nations have organized into regional defense and economic pacts to further their collective interests. Among them are the **European Union, North Atlantic Treaty Organization (NATO), Organization of African Unity (OAU), Association of South East Asian Nations (ASEAN),** and **Central American Common Market (CACM).** One of the largest is the **Nonaligned Movement** of 110 nations established in 1961. This group of mostly **developing nations** seeks to cooperate on political, economic, and cultural issues. How successful these organizations are depends (1) on their missions, (2) on the resources member nations can provide, and (3) on their clout, whether military or economic.

KEY PLACES

Study Strategy

See if you can relate these places to their correct context in "Fast Facts." Can you locate them on modern maps?

- **Balkan Peninsula**
- **Serbia**

KEY TERMS/IDEAS

Study Strategy

See if you can relate these terms and ideas to their correct context in the "Fast Facts" section.

- **Appeasement, Munich Conference**
- **Axis Powers**
- **ethnic cleansing, genocide, Bosnia**
- **fascism**
- **genocide, Armenia**
- **Holocaust, genocide, Nuremburg war crimes trials**
- **Iron Curtain**
- **limited war, Korean War, U.N. police action**
- **massive retaliation**
- **"powder keg of Europe"**
- **Russian Revolution**
- **Spanish Civil War, General Francisco Franco**
- **Star Wars, Strategic Defense Initiative**
- **Third Reich**
- **Triple Alliance, Central Powers**
- **Triple Entente, the Allies**
- **World Bank, International Monetary Fund**
- **World War I as "total war"**

SECTION 2. FORCES OF CHANGE

Flip on a television in Chicago, Rome, or Islamabad and you can watch CNN. Check the newspaper in Dublin, Amsterdam, or Hong Kong and you find an American movie to attend. Why visit Disney World in Orlando when you can see one in Paris or Tokyo? On the other hand, walk down a street in many U.S. cities and towns and you can choose from a Thai or an Ethiopian restaurant to eat in, hear languages from Russian to Farsi, and pass by a Buddhist temple, a Hispanic evangelical church, and a mosque.

Globalization of U.S. culture has vastly changed the world, but the world has changed the United States as well. The twentieth century is one of heightened contacts on a global level. Migrations of people from continent to continent (not just from nation to nation), the beaming of television programs via satellite and now instant communication and access to information via the Internet, and the popularization of the consumer society have all had their effects on national cultures.

DECOLONIZATION

- **Decolonization,** the process of freeing colonial possession, began in earnest after World War II. The main reasons for decolonization were (1) African independence movements, (2) world opinion, and (3) the cost of maintaining colonies. It was difficult for European nations to mount a defense of colonialism when the same nations had just fought a war to make the world safe for democracy.

- A few generalizations can be made about the decolonization process. (1) In African colonies in which blacks were clearly in the majority, nationhood was accomplished fairly easily. (2) In colonies in which large numbers of whites lived, the process was often protracted and sometimes bloody, as whites attempted to hold on to their positions. **Southern Rhodesia,** which ultimately became Zimbabwe, and the **Republic of South Africa** are two examples of the latter. (3) France did not release its former colonies as willingly as Great Britain. This should not be a surprise considering the attitude toward its colonies that each nation showed in setting up its colonial administrative structure.

COMPARING THE DECOLONIZATION PROCESS IN REPRESENTATIVE NATIONS

Colony/Nation	European Nation	Process to Independence
Morocco	France, Spain/ **Protectorate**	• Divided and under protectorate status in 1912 • Rebel fighting throughout 1920s and 1930s • Area of heavy fighting in World War II • Open warfare on French by independent fighters from 1947 on • French withdraw in 1955 • Independence in 1956 • Spanish area returned in 1969
Persian Gulf States: United Arab Emirates, Bahrain, Qatar, Kuwait, Oman	Great Britain/ Protectorates	British withdrew in 1961 because of the cost of defense; states had been important for strategic and commercial reasons
Formerly Gold Coast/ Ghana	Great Britain	• Strikes, protests by nationalists • British policy of gradual independence; constitution but British still in control of foreign policy, defense, the economy, law • Demands by nationalists for complete freedom • British bow to pressure • Complete independence in 1957
Kenya	Great Britain	• Mau Mau, secret organization, bloody campaign against British rule • Military response to Mau Maus • British bow to pressure • Independence in 1963

Connection Strategy

Compare and contrast these movements with the revolution in China.

• Comparing this table with the nationalist movements in Egypt and India provides some interesting comparisons and contrasts. The kingdom of **Egypt** was a British protectorate from 1914 to 1936, and Great Britain continued to be influential in the nation because of its investment in the **Suez Canal.** After World War II, the Egyptians inspired by the same nationalist forces that were roiling European colonies ousted the king and declared itself independent. The new nation signed an agreement with Britain to remove its troops from the Suez Canal and then **nationalized** it.

COMPARING THE DECOLONIZATION PROCESS IN REPRESENTATIVE NATIONS—*cont'd*

Colony/Nation	European Nation	Process to Independence
Belgian Congo/ Democratic Republic of the Congo	Belgium	• Removed as personal fiefdom of King Leopold II in 1908 because of brutality • Reforms instituted, including education • Rebellions in the late 1950s • Belgians bow to world opinion and violence • Independence in 1960
Myanmar/Burma	Great Britain	• As a province of British India rebelled against British in 1931–1932 • Made a crown colony in 1938 • Sided with British in World War II • Independence in 1948
Vietnam/Part of French Indochina	France	• Occupied by the Japanese in World War II • Declaration of independence in 1945 • Reoccupation by the French • French-Indochinese War • Partitioned by Geneva Conference into Communist north and non-Communist south • Overthrow of president in the south in 1963, Vietcong insurgency; Vietnam War • After U.S. pullout in 1975, Communist-led united Vietnam declared in 1976

Review Strategy

See Chapter 9 for the British takeover of India.

• After the removal of the East India Company, Britain established a colonial administration over **India.** Indians, however, agitated for independence. This agitation took the form of strikes and demonstrations. Finally, after World War II, exhausted by war and with its empire unraveling, Great Britain agreed to Indian independence in 1947. However, the Muslim minority worried about its future in a Hindu-dominated India. Fighting broke out between Hindus and Muslims. Britain agreed to a **partition** of India into Hindu India and Muslim Pakistan, but Pakistan was split into East and West with India in between. In 1971 after a civil war with **West Pakistan** motivated in part by ethnic differences, **East Pakistan** became the sovereign nation of **Bangladesh.**

Legacies of Colonialism

Review Strategy

Remember that the following are generalizations, which means there are exceptions.

- In Africa, the new nations were faced with (1) **civil wars** because of the clustering within national boundaries of rival **ethnic groups,** (2) military takeovers because of the lack of democratic experiences among the citizenry, (3) a **population explosion,** (4) low **per capita income,** (5) the lack of local capital for investment in **infrastructure** and industry, (6) urbanization, and (7) government corruption. Responses included (1) the imposition of **socialism (ujamaa** in Tanzania), (2) the call for African authenticity, (3) the adoption of one-party political systems, and (4) the assumption of huge debtloads.

- The Middle Eastern nations were faced with similar problems: (1) ethnic divisions, (2) military coups, (3) government corruption, (4) population explosion, (5) poverty with its all-attendant problems such as low life expectancy, and (6) lack of capital. The Middle East also suffered from dwindling supplies of fresh water. In an effort to solve these problems, some Middle Eastern nations (1) turned to **socialism** and (2) took on large debts from international lenders.

- Although colonialism ended in Latin America more than a century before independence came to Africa and much of Asia and Africa, the region suffered from many of the same problems. Perhaps the fundamental problem was the **unequal distribution of wealth.** Since colonial days, land, mines, and business enterprises had belonged to a few wealthy families or, since the nineteenth century, to foreign investors.

Breakup of Soviet Union

- It had been clear for many years that the **command economy** of the Soviet Union was not working. By the 1980s, the nation was in grave difficulty. (1) The economy was stagnating because of the problems inherent in **central planning,** (2) consumer lines were longer for fewer goods, (3) alcoholism had become a national concern, and (4) its foreign policies—the arms race, the war in Afghanistan, and the aid to developing nations to counter Chinese and U.S. offensives— were draining its resources. In 1985 under **Mikhail Gorbachev,** the Soviet Union (1) signaled an end to the Cold War; (2) introduced **glasnost,** or openness in government; and (3) introduced **perestroika,** restructuring of the economic and political process. His reforms led to the intensification of discontent in the Soviet Union and in its **satellites.** In 1991, the Soviet Union was dissolved. Its republics had begun declaring their independence, and the nations of Eastern Europe turned out their Communist leaders.

NEW NATIONS

- Like other nations that won their independence in other parts of the world in the twentieth century, some of the new nations of Eastern Europe were the result of Western European statesmen at some point in the past redrawing the map of Europe. Some of the nations that emerged from the shadow of communism had been created after World War I. No matter how carefully these diplomats had attempted to preserve ethnic unity, it had been impossible because of the number and locations of the various ethnic groups. The force of the Soviet Union had kept ethnic tensions in the nations underground. Once these nations no longer had the Soviet Union to enforce union, the ethnic tensions flared up. Fighting, secession, and **ethnic cleansing** marred the future of **Bosnia, Kosovo, Yugoslavia,** and **Chechnya,** among others.

- The new nations of the former Soviet Union, including the Republic of Russia and the newly free nations of Eastern Europe, faced similar problems: (1) the privatizing of national industries, (2) the end of central planning, and (3) the adoption of free-market economies. These, in turn, created the additional problems of (1) high unemployment and (2) inflation, which (3) in some places energized the Communist opposition to agitate for a return to communism.

CHANGING ROLE OF WOMEN

- How women fared in twentieth-century revolutions depended (1) on the type of revolution and (2) on the culture in which the revolution occurred. In **Iran** where the revolution was **conservative** in nature, women lost ground. Under the Shah who was deposed, women had made progress in Western-style rights and freedoms. The **Iranian Revolution of 1979** imposed **Islamic fundamentalist values** on the people and introduced a **theocracy.**

ENVIRONMENTAL ISSUES

- Among the threats to the environment are (1) **deforestation,** (2) **global warming,** and (3) **acid rain.** Increasingly, deforestation has become an issue between **developed** and **developing nations.** The latter claim they should be able to exploit their land because they need the resources to spur their economies, while developed nations want to preserve such areas as the Amazon rain forest, which environmentalists see as belonging to all people. However, acid raid and global warming are often the byproduct of nonenvironmentally friendly practices of developed nations.

REVOLUTION AS A CATALYST FOR WOMEN'S ROLES

Revolution	Education/Job Opportunities	Law	Social Status
Russian, 1917	• Education free and open to all • No restrictions on training in medicine, engineering, and the sciences • Able to work in any industry	Granted equality	• Wage earner, income needed to help support family • Legal identities tied to husbands, difficult to get divorces.
Chinese, 1949	• Lower rate of literacy among women • Few college-educated women • Duty to work but employed in the more menial jobs	Granted equality	• Ideal of extended family weakened but women still in inferior position • Stereotypes about what women can and can't do • Few women in government and politics • Male child still preferred to female
Cuban, 1959	• Education free and open to all • Duty to work	Granted equality	Wage earner, income needed to help support family
Iranian, 1979	Greatly limited	Greatly limited	Freedom of action greatly limited

KEY PEOPLE

Study Strategy

See if you can relate these people to their correct context in the "Fast Facts" section.

- **Mahatma Gandhi, soul force, nonviolence**
- **Muhammad Ali Jinnah, Muslim League, India, Pakistan**
- **Jomo Kenyatta, Kenya**
- **Kwame Nkrumah, Ghana**
- **Julius Nyerere, Tanzania**

KEY PLACES

Study Strategy

See if you can relate these places to their correct context in "Fast Facts." Can you locate them on modern maps?

- **Persian Gulf States**

KEY TERMS/IDEAS

Study Strategy

See if you can relate these terms and ideas to their correct context in the "Fast Facts" section.

- collapse of the Berlin as symbol of change

- desalinization

- feminism

- human rights as global issue

- multinational corporations

- National Congress Party, India

- nongovernmental organization (NGO)

- Pacific Rim

- Terrorism: Northern Ireland, Palestinians and Israel, Islamic fundamentalist jihad

PRACTICE TEST

AP WORLD HISTORY

On the front page of your test booklet, you will find some information about the test. Because you have studied this book, none of it should be new to you, and much of it is similar to other standardized tests you have taken.

The front page will tell you that the following exam will take 3 hours and 5 minutes—55 minutes for the multiple-choice section and 2 hours and 10 minutes for the three essays. Ten minutes of the time for Section II is a mandatory reading period for the DBQ. There are two booklets for this exam, one for the multiple-choice section and one for the essays.

The page in your test booklet will also say that SECTION I:

- is 55 minutes.

- has 70 questions.

- counts for 50 percent of your total grade.

Then you will find a sentence in capital letters about not opening your exam booklet until the monitor tells you to open it.

Other instructions will tell you to be careful when you fill in the ovals on the answer sheet. Fill in each oval completely. If you erase an answer, erase it completely. If you skip a question, be sure to skip the answer oval for it. You will not receive any credit for work done in the test booklet, but you may use it for making notes.

You will also find a paragraph about the guessing penalty—deduction of one-quarter point for every wrong answer—but also words of advice about guessing if you know something about the question and can eliminate several of the answers.

The final paragraph will remind you to work efficiently and to pace yourself. You are told that not everyone will be able to answer all the questions and that it is preferable to skip questions that are difficult and come back to them if you have time.

SECTION I

Directions: Each question or incomplete statement is followed by five suggested responses. Choose the best answer and fill in the correct oval on the answer sheet.

1. A major difference between the teachings of Buddhism and Hinduism is

   (A) belief in nirvana.
   (B) the cycle of rebirth.
   (C) the principle of nonviolence.
   (D) belief in karma.
   (E) belief in dharma.

2. Bantu-speakers settled in all of the following areas of Africa EXCEPT

   (A) West Africa.
   (B) East Africa.
   (C) Central Africa.
   (D) Southern Africa.
   (E) South-central Africa.

3. An element of Chinese culture that the Japanese did not adopt was

   (A) the Chinese system of writing.
   (B) the concept of filial piety.
   (C) respect for the merchant class.
   (D) the civil service examination system.
   (E) the Chinese emphasis on learning.

4. The Delhi Sultanate and the Aztecs had which of the following methods of governing in common?

   (A) Use of slaves and prisoners of war as human sacrifice
   (B) Tribute system
   (C) Use of priests as advisors
   (D) Use of viceroys to administer far-flung parts of the empire
   (E) Calpulli as the basic unit of governance

5. Which of the following was a major problem that led to the decline of both the Roman Empire and the Ottoman Empire?

   (A) Both empires experienced invasions by the Mongols.
   (B) Rivals competed with one another for power.
   (C) Revolutionaries attempted to affect reforms, but their ideas were opposed.
   (D) A downturn in agricultural prices displaced small farmers, thus leading to the emergence of a poor and disaffected urban population.
   (E) Neither empire had a clear policy on the succession of the ruler.

6. Which of the following most clearly differentiates the period from 1450 to 1750 from earlier periods?

   (A) Decline of manorialism in western Europe
   (B) The rise of the Ottoman Empire
   (C) The inclusion of the Americas in the global trade network
   (D) The opening of Japan to the West
   (E) The replacement of Romanesque architecture with the Gothic style in western Europe

7. Although different in their sources of power, the governments of Great Britain and France had which of the following characteristics in common?

   (A) Both nations were constitutional monarchies.

   (B) The power to levy taxes was controlled by the monarch in both nations.

   (C) Neither nation had wide class differences.

   (D) By the mid-1700s, the prime minister had become the real power in British and French politics, not the monarchy.

   (E) Both nations had a small elite of landowning aristocrats who were considered the "natural" ruling class with power and influence in the government.

8. Which of the following developments in the Americas accounted most directly for the growth of the slave trade?

   (A) The dominance of cotton agriculture in what is known as the Deep South in the United States

   (B) The establishment of the plantation system of sugar production in the Caribbean and Brazil

   (C) The discovery of gold in Brazil

   (D) The establishment of the Triangular Trade Route

   (E) The introduction of coffee agriculture into Mexico

9. A major idea that the framers of the U.S. Constitution absorbed from the Enlightenment was

   (A) that all men are created equal.

   (B) liberty, equality, and fraternity.

   (C) the concept of a federal republic.

   (D) the social contract theory.

   (E) the due process.

10. What was the direct cause of the rebellions in Latin America in the first part of the nineteenth century?

   (A) Slave revolt in Haiti

   (B) The spread of Enlightenment ideas

   (C) The American Revolution

   (D) Napoleon's invasion of Spain

   (E) The French Revolution

11. All of the following are causes of the Industrial Revolution EXCEPT

   (A) population growth.

   (B) urbanization.

   (C) enclosure movement.

   (D) the development of new sources of energy.

   (E) the agricultural revolution.

12. Which of the following best describes the most significant aspect of relations between China and European nations during the nineteenth century?

   (A) China's relations with the outside world were characterized by its claim to cultural superiority.

   (B) Western nations applied pressure to force China to make concessions.

   (C) China, under pressure, granted Western nations a series of unequal treaties that gave them most-favored-nation trading status.

   (D) Europeans living in China were given the right of extraterritoriality.

   (E) Great Britain lost the Opium War to China.

13. "The main conclusion here arrived at, and now held by many naturalists who are well competent to form a sound judgment, is that man is descended from some less highly organised form."

Which of the following wrote these words?

(A) Montesquieu
(B) Charles Darwin
(C) Thomas Malthus
(D) Andrew Carnegie
(E) John Locke

14. Newly independent nations in Africa have been confronted by all of the following problems EXCEPT

(A) rule by the military.
(B) one-party rule that evolved into authoritarian government.
(C) ethnic rivalries that have culminated in civil war.
(D) dependent economies.
(E) lack of cash crops for export.

Question 15 relates to the table shown below.

Daily Life in Selected Countries

	China	India	Russian Republic	United States
Life Expectancy (years)	67 (male) 69 (female)	57 (male) 59 (female)	62 (male) 72 (female)	73 (male) 80 (female)
Infant Mortality (Rate per 1,000 births)	34	89	23	10
Percentage of Labor in Agriculture	61%	67%	20%	2%
Percentage of 20-24 Year Olds in Higher Education	1%	9%	21%	58%
Literacy Rate	Over 75%	36%	99%	99%

15. Based on the statistics on this table, which two nations show the greatest amount of difference?

(A) India and the United States
(B) Russia and China
(C) United States and China
(D) Russia and India
(E) There is little or no difference among nations.

16. Which of the following actions had a long-term effect on relations between western and eastern Europe in the Middle Ages?

    (A) The invasion of Spain by the Moors
    (B) The acceptance of the Orthodox Church as the official religion of Kievan Russia
    (C) The evolution of feudalism in western Europe
    (D) The crowning of Charlemagne by the pope
    (E) The rise of the Seljuk Turks

17. All of the following were direct results of the Crusades EXCEPT

    (A) the growth of a money economy in Europe.
    (B) the growth of European trading centers.
    (C) the decline of feudalism.
    (D) an increase in the power of the papacy.
    (E) exposure to intellectual and cultural traditions of the Middle East.

18. Which of the following is the most accurate description of the similarities between the Sudanic empires of Africa and the empires of the Aztecs and Inca?

    (A) The empires developed in similar physical environments.
    (B) The empires relied on military force to enlarge their territories.
    (C) The peoples of these empires practiced monotheistic religions.
    (D) The major economic activity of these empires was trade.
    (E) None of these empires had a system of writing.

19. All of the following are accurate descriptions of the difference between Hinduism and Islam EXCEPT

    (A) Hinduism is polytheistic and Islam is monotheistic.
    (B) the Hindu caste system conflicts with Islam's belief in the equality of all people.
    (C) Islam's simple prayer ceremonies are the opposite of Hinduism's elaborate religious ceremonies filled with music and dance.
    (D) Hinduism is thousands of years old, whereas Islam is relatively new, having been founded in the seventh century C.E.
    (E) Hinduism rejects the use of the human form in religious and secular art, whereas the human form is an important subject in Islamic art.

20. All of the following were unintended results of the Mongol invasions EXCEPT

    (A) the rise of Moscow as the most important city-state in what eventually would become tsarist Russia.
    (B) the spread of bubonic plague from China to Europe and the Middle East.
    (C) the rise of the Ottoman Turks and the eclipse of the Seljuk Turks.
    (D) the collapse of the Byzantine Empire.
    (E) the adoption of Islam by the Mongols and their assimilation into Turkish culture.

21. "It is the imminent peril threatening you and all the faithful, which has brought us hither. From the confines of Jerusalem and the city of Constantinople a horrible tale has gone forth . . ."

The above was probably spoken about which of the following?

(A) The creation of the modern state of Israel
(B) The establishment of the Abbasid dynasty
(C) The invasion of Europe by the Huns
(D) The capture of the Holy Land by the Seljuk Turks
(E) The invasion of the Middle East by the Yuan branch of the Mongols

22. Which of the following that occurred in western Europe in the period from 1450 to 1750 did not result in long-term changes?

(A) Renaissance
(B) The growth of capitalism
(C) Scientific Revolution
(D) Agricultural Revolution
(E) The growth of strong centralized monarchies

23. Which of the following is the best description of the effect of the Age of Exploration on Europeans?

(A) As a result of the increased amount of gold and silver in circulation, people were able to buy more.
(B) As a result of the decline in the fortunes of the feudal nobility and the rise in the fortunes of the merchant class, monarchies were able to limit the influence of the feudal nobility.
(C) Trading centers shifted from English, French, and Dutch cities to the Italian city-states of the Mediterranean and Adriatic.
(D) Diseases from the Americas killed large numbers of Europeans.
(E) Mercantilism was abandoned as the leading economic principle of European nations.

24. The European balance of power in the 1700s was made up of a set of shifting alliances among all of the following nations EXCEPT

(A) Russia
(B) France
(C) Prussia
(D) Italy
(E) England

25. European politicians made which of the following mistakes both in redrawing the map of Europe after the Napoleonic wars and in drawing the boundaries of their colonies in Africa?

(A) The leaders ignored the amount of resources that each colony would need in order to support itself.

(B) They ignored the lack of language uniformity among the various peoples within the new nations and colonies.

(C) Both sets of boundaries ignored the ethnic and cultural differences of the peoples they put within common national borders.

(D) The new boundaries ensured that France would be surrounded by strong rival nations.

(E) The former African sovereign states had no part in the decisions about their new borders.

26. Which of the following men was the first to state that history was "the history of class struggles"?

(A) Mao Zedong

(B) Machiavelli

(C) Cardinal Richelieu

(D) Marx

(E) Lenin

27. All of the following are characteristic of Japan under the Meiji Restoration EXCEPT

(A) the rise of the zaibatsu.

(B) the revocation of the special status afforded the samurai.

(C) modernization of the bureaucracy.

(D) shift of population from the agricultural countryside to urban industrial centers.

(E) equal rights for women.

28. U.S. foreign policy at the end of the nineteenth century was motivated by all of the following EXCEPT

(A) a sense of patriotism.

(B) the profit motive.

(C) Social Darwinism.

(D) Gospel of Wealth.

(E) desire for most-favored-nation status with China.

29. The only nation to respond to Sun Yat-sen's request for help against the Chinese warlords was

(A) Great Britain.

(B) the United States.

(C) Russia.

(D) Japan.

(E) France.

30. Which of the following is the best justification for Truman's decision to use the atomic bomb to end World War II?

(A) Experts projected that it would take one million Allied soldiers to invade the Japanese home islands.

(B) Kamikaze fighters were inflicting heavy damage on Allied ships and personnel.

(C) The fire bombing of the Japanese home islands seemed to have little effect.

(D) The civilian Japanese government had accepted the idea of surrender, but the military had rejected it.

(E) Despite mounting losses, the Japanese leaders were continuing to tell their people to expect a great victory.

31. The major reason why pastoral nomadism did not develop in the Americas was

(A) the lack of large domesticated animals such as cattle.

(B) the inability of Native Americans to domesticate the buffalo.

(C) the lack of savanna for grazing.

(D) the lack of horses for herders to use in order to control herds.

(E) the uneven amount of moisture that falls across the two continents.

32. Which of the following is an accurate description of an economic difference that existed between the Roman Empire and Han China?

(A) Manufacturing was an important activity in the Roman Empire because it provided trade goods, whereas the Han Chinese had little manufacturing.

(B) Roman society during the Roman Empire was matrilineal, whereas Chinese society during the Han dynasty was patrilineal.

(C) Han China relied less on a slave labor system than did the Roman Empire.

(D) The economy of the Roman Empire was based on agriculture, whereas China during the Han dynasty had an economy based on trade.

(E) Women in Han China had greater freedom of action than did women in the Roman Empire.

33. Which of the following is an accurate description of a cultural characteristic that the Celts, Slavs, and Germans of northern Europe had in common around 200 C.E.?

(A) These peoples were primarily hunters and gatherers.

(B) The overall political organization of the Celts, Slavs, and Germans evolved into regional kingdoms.

(C) These cultures lacked all knowledge of metallurgy.

(D) The Celts, Slavs, and Germans were matriarchal.

(E) Their social organization was highly stratified.

34. Bedouins were instrumental in spreading which of the following religions?

(A) Buddhism throughout China

(B) Christianity in Africa

(C) Islam on the Arabian Peninsula

(D) Presbyterianism in Scotland

(E) Shintoism throughout Japan

35. Which of the following is not an accurate description of why Islam appealed to so many peoples?

(A) Muhammad, as the last of the great prophets, accepted earlier Judaic and Christian revelation and incorporated them into Islam.

(B) Islam's Five Pillars provided simple and clear guidance to believers.

(C) Islam was monotheistic and thus shared a common element with Judaism and Christianity at a time when most people practiced polytheism.

(D) Islam preached the equality of all peoples, thus appealing to the poor and oppressed.

(E) Because Islam lacked any legal code, it was possible to adapt Islam to any form of governmental organization.

36. Which of the following were trading partners of the Abbasid Empire?

    (A) India and Japan
    (B) Kingdom of Kongo and China
    (C) The Mediterranean region and Benin
    (D) West Africa and Japan
    (E) The Mediterranean region and China

37. Which of the following best describes the East African trading centers prior to the arrival of the Portuguese?

    (A) The trade network to and from the East African coast was fairly local and limited to a small portion of the interior and to nearby coastal islands.
    (B) The slave trade was an important element of the economies of the East African trading centers.
    (C) Ife was the most important of these East Coast cities.
    (D) The cities were a mix of black African and Islamic peoples and culture traits.
    (E) The predominant religion was a traditional African-based animism with an overlay of Islamic teachings known as Swahili.

38. Which of the following nations acquired territory in Asia in the 1700s through the initiative of agents working for joint-stock companies?

    (A) Great Britain and the Netherlands
    (B) Spain and the Netherlands
    (C) Great Britain and France
    (D) Prussia and Austria-Hungary
    (E) The Netherlands and France

39. The area of the African continent that was most significantly affected by the slave trade was

    (A) North Africa.
    (B) East Africa.
    (C) West Africa.
    (D) South Africa.
    (E) South-central Africa.

40. What was the major difference between Marxist theory and Lenin's view of it?

    (A) Marx saw no limitation to the use of violence to impose his economic theories, whereas Lenin took a more cautious view, believing that political tools should be used first.
    (B) Lenin believed that the proletarian revolution could occur without the middle-class phase, whereas Marx saw a more orderly progression through several phases.
    (C) Marx understood that the proletarian revolution could occur without industrialization, whereas Lenin did not.
    (D) Neither man understood that the Russian peasantry was a group that could be cultivated to support a revolutionary movement.
    (E) Marx believed in the need for small groups of committed revolutionaries, known as cells, who could carry out revolutionary activities, whereas Lenin discounted the usefulness of such groups.

41. Which of the following is the most accurate description of the fundamental difference that lay behind what Woodrow Wilson expected from the treaty ending World War I and what the Allies wanted?

    (A) The Allies wanted reparations from Germany, and Wilson opposed them.
    (B) Establishment of the League of Nations was of less importance to Wilson than it was to the British and French representatives to Versailles.
    (C) Wilson wanted autonomy and independence for various eastern European nations affected by the war, whereas the Allies had secretly agreed during the war to divide up these territories when they won the war.
    (D) Wilson wanted a peace that would not lead to another war, whereas the Allies wanted revenge.
    (E) Wilson was hampered by the need to negotiate a treaty that would pass the Senate, whereas the Allies had no political concerns.

42. "Liberalism denied the State in the name of the individual; Fascism reasserts the rights of the State as expressing the real essence of the individual. And if liberty is to be the attribute of living men and not of abstract dummies invented by individualistic liberalism, Fascism stands for liberty, and for the only liberty worth having, the liberty of the State and of the individual within the State."

    The words above were written by which of the following?

    (A) Boris Yeltsin
    (B) Fredrich Engels
    (C) Adolph Hitler
    (D) John Locke
    (E) Benito Mussolini

43. All of the following statements are true about the status of women in developing nations EXCEPT

    (A) the rights and freedom of action of women in nations that have become fundamentalist Islamic states have declined.
    (B) women in developing nations have lower life expectancy rates than women in industrialized nations.
    (C) in general, while higher education may be open to all women, it is only women of the upper class in developing nations who are able to attend.
    (D) most women in developing nations spend their time in child care and providing for their families.
    (E) women readily take advantage of newly gained legal and civil rights in these nations.

44. Which of the following is the most accurate description of the world economy in the late twentieth century?

    (A) The decolonization of the African continent made little difference in who was in charge.
    (B) The West—now Europe and the United States—continues to dominate world trade, as it has done since the globalization of the economy in the 1500s.
    (C) Latin American nations moved from the status of dependent economies to equal partners in the world trading arena.
    (D) Japan has taken on a major role in the world economy.
    (E) GATT has poured billions of dollars into the economies of various nations to shore up their national governments.

Question 45 relates to the graphs shown below.

Religious Membership in the Subcontinent of India

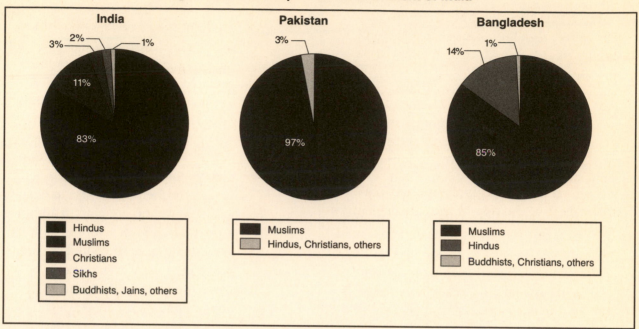

45. Which of the following is not demonstrated by the information on the following
graphs?

(A) India has the greatest amount of
religious diversity.

(B) Pakistan has the highest percentage
of a single religion.

(C) Bangladesh has the highest percentage of Christians.

(D) Together, the three graphs show the
results of the virtual eradication of
Buddhism from the subcontinent by
Muslims.

(E) The reason for the division of India in
1947 explains the high percentage of
Muslims in Pakistan and Bangladesh.

46. All of the following are general characteristics of pastoral nomadic societies EXCEPT

(A) kinship was patrilineal.

(B) there was little social stratification.

(C) wives lived with their husbands' families.

(D) there was little intertribal warfare.

(E) a dependent relationship existed between those who had more resources and those who were less well off.

47. According to Confucius the most important aspect of the role of the scholar-gentry was

(A) to maintain harmony among the social classes by administering the state and advising the ruler wisely.

(B) to administer the civil-service examination system.

(C) to staff the bureaucracy that ran China.

(D) to educate the sons of the upper-class who would become the new scholar-gentry.

(E) to ensure that China remained isolated from non-Confucian teachings by censoring all communications from outside China.

48. Which of the following was a major difference between the way the Roman Empire was administered and the way the later Byzantine Empire was governed?

(A) The Roman Empire was an autocracy and the Byzantine Empire was an oligarchy.

(B) The Roman Empire lacked the bureaucratic system of administration that the Byzantine Empire developed.

(C) Byzantine emperors were greatly influenced by the Orthodox Church, whereas the Roman emperors paid little attention to their pantheon of deities.

(D) The government of the Byzantine Empire was characterized by intrigues, hence the meaning of the word *byzantine* as devious.

(E) The Roman Empire had a large contingent of foreign mercenaries in its army, whereas the Byzantine Empire relied on Mamluks from Egypt.

49. Which of the following challenged Hinduism?

(A) Daoism

(B) Confucianism

(C) Shintoism

(D) Polytheism

(E) Buddhism

50. All of the following are true about sub-Saharan African societies prior to the arrival of Europeans EXCEPT

(A) Islam was an important force in the Sudanic kingdoms.

(B) Bantu provided a base for the majority of languages south of the Sahara.

(C) the idea of kings as rulers rather than kinship groups with a chief and council of elders never became popular among the rain forest or savanna peoples.

(D) most Africans practiced traditional animism.

(E) generally agricultural economies included some trade, if only on a local or regional level.

51. All of the following modern nations lacked centralized monarchies at the end of the Middle Ages EXCEPT

(A) Germany.

(B) the Netherlands.

(C) Belgium.

(D) Italy.

(E) Spain.

52. A major difference between the Amerindians of North America and the Aztec of Mesoamerica prior to the arrival of Europeans was

(A) the lack of hunting and gathering among the North Americans.

(B) the importance of kinship as the unit of organization among the North Americans.

(C) the lack of a class system among the Aztec.

(D) the absence of large-scale building among the North American culture regions.

(E) the use of horses by North American Plains Native Americans.

53. Which of the following was instrumental in making Europeans the leaders of global trade in the 1400s?

(A) European ships were faster and more seaworthy than the vessels of other world regions.

(B) The Japanese closed their ports to all foreigners.

(C) The Crusades created an appetite for Asian goods, which the Italian city-states exploited.

(D) The Ming ended all Chinese trading ventures to India, the Middle East, and Africa, opening the way for others.

(E) Europeans had invented such technological advances as the astrolabe and compass and thus could navigate farther distances than sailors from other regions.

54. All of the following resulted from the Protestant Reformation EXCEPT

(A) a rise in literacy.

(B) a series of religious wars.

(C) the general acceptance of personal freedom of religion.

(D) a new work ethic that considered doing well on earth to be a sign of one's salvation.

(E) the establishment of married clergy in Protestant religions.

55. By 1600, the expansion of which of the following had ended invasions from Central Asia?

(A) Russia and the Ottoman Empire
(B) Mughal Empire and Russia
(C) Ming China and the Ottoman Empire
(D) The Khanates of the Mongols
(E) Ming China and Russia

56. Which of the following was a major difference between industrialization in Japan and in Great Britain?

(A) Japanese workers were paid comparatively well, unlike British workers.
(B) Japan and Great Britain had extensive railway systems to transport goods.
(C) The Japanese were more technologically advanced than the British and exported machinery to the West.
(D) The Japanese government played a far larger role in the development of industrialization and the infrastructure to support it than did the British government.
(E) Great Britain had to import coal to fuel its industries, whereas Japan had large reserves.

Question 57 relates to the cartoon shown below.

The Crime of the Ages—Who Did It?

57. Which of the following is the most accurate statement of the cartoonist's meaning?

(A) World War I is the crime of the ages.

(B) All nations involved in World War I at its outbreak are to blame for it.

(C) Russia and Austria are blamed unfairly.

(D) The nations of Europe are blaming one another.

(E) War is a terrible crime.

58. "Then the world will enter upon a new stage of its history—the final competition of races, for which the Anglo-Saxon is being schooled. Long before the thousand millions are here, the mighty centrifugal tendency, inherent in this stock and strengthened in the United States, will assert itself. . . . [and] spread itself over the earth."

The author of these words was an advocate of which of the following principles?

(A) "Big stick" policy
(B) Imperialism
(C) Absolutism
(D) Gunboat diplomacy
(E) Dollar diplomacy

59. All of the following are examples of the new role that the United States played as a superpower after World War II EXCEPT

(A) issued the Eisenhower Doctrine.
(B) issued and funded the Marshall Plan.
(C) voted to admit the People's Republic of China to the United Nations.
(D) advocated the policy of deterrence.
(E) denounced the Suez invasion.

60. Which of the following is the most accurate description of twentieth-century revolutions?

(A) Revolutions in the twentieth century generally resulted from movements to restore power to the traditional ruling elite.
(B) Twentieth-century revolutions were generally based on some ideal, such as nationalism or communism.
(C) By the end of the century, the movement known as Islamic fundamentalism had become the predominant force for change in Southwest Asia and South Asia.
(D) The Mexican Revolution is an example of a revolutionary action taken by peasants against the wealthy, especially large landowners.
(E) The Cuban revolution was atypical of twentieth-century revolutions in that it sought to replace one autocratic ruler with another.

61. A major difference between the Inca and the Aztec was

- (A) the development of monumental architecture by the Aztec.
- (B) the Inca's use of a tribute system with dependent states.
- (C) the development of limited pastoralism by the Inca.
- (D) the use of military force by the Aztec to enlarge their empire.
- (E) that the Aztec was the base culture of Mesoamerica, whereas the Inca was a later adaptation of earlier Andean cultures.

62. Which of the following were important trading cities along the East Coast of Africa?

- (A) Kilwa, Gao, and Timbuktu
- (B) Gao, Great Zimbabwe, and Mogadishu
- (C) Benin, Gao, and Great Zimbabwe
- (D) Timbuktu, Gao, and Nok
- (E) Kilwa, Mogadishu, and Sofala

63. Which European nation did not experience revolution in 1848?

- (A) Austria
- (B) France
- (C) Russia
- (D) Hungary
- (E) Prussia

64. "It is the object of that system to enrich a great nation rather by trade and manufactures than by the improvement and cultivation of land, rather by the industry of the towns than by that of the country."

In this quotation from the *Wealth of Nations,* Adam Smith is referring to which system?

- (A) Factory system
- (B) Industrialization
- (C) Mercantilism
- (D) Monetary system
- (E) Capitalism

65. Which of the following is the most accurate description of the effect of the Industrial Revolution on European society?

- (A) All classes were better off than they had been before industrialization.
- (B) The wealthy were the only class to profit from the Industrial Revolution.
- (C) The middle class grew in size, while the number of poor and upper-class Europeans remained constant.
- (D) Class and wealth distinctions in Europe remained as they had been in the eighteenth century before the Industrial Revolution.
- (E) The poor became poorer, while the middle and the upper classes prospered.

66. In assuming its role as superpower, which of the following was not an issue that the United States faced in safeguarding its own security?

(A) Determining how to balance its security and national interests against powerful unfriendly nations

(B) Helping to protect the sovereignty of nations in Europe, Latin America, and Asia without provoking hostile reactions from them or the Soviet Union

(C) Establishing ties to the newly independent nations of Asia and Africa

(D) Balancing the cost of domestic programs with defense needs

(E) Determining how to use protective tariffs to ensure the greatest gain for the U.S. economy

67. Which of the following is an example of an international policy on which both the United States and the Soviet Union agreed?

(A) Economic sanctions against Cuba

(B) Exclusion of Taiwan from the United Nations

(C) Support for the Solidarity government of Poland

(D) Partition of Palestine

(E) Overthrow of the government of Salvador Allende in Chile

Question 68 relates to the map shown below.

Oil and Gas Resources

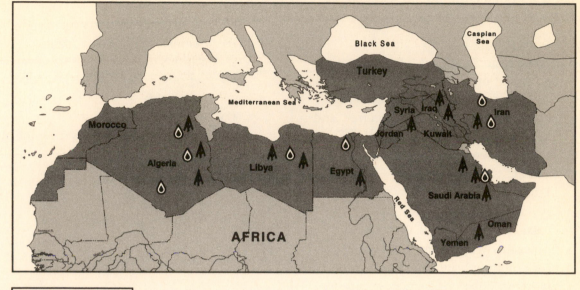
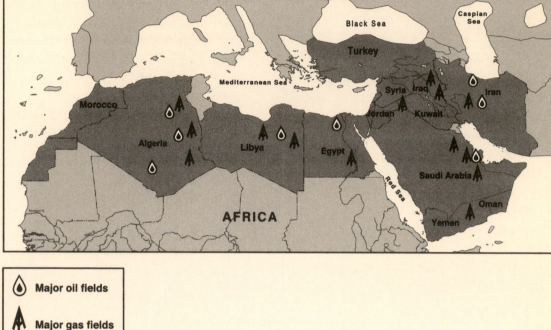

Major oil fields

Major gas fields

68. Which of the following is supported by the information displayed on the map?

(A) Arab nations gained great influence in the world because of their oil and natural gas resources.

(B) The oil boom of the 1970s enabled oil-rich Arab nations to promote Islamic missionary work.

(C) Thousands of foreigners went to work on new construction projects and in new industries in the oil-rich nations of the Middle East.

(D) The majority of Arab nations do not have vast resources of oil and natural gas.

(E) The oil-rich nations formed a cartel known as OPEC.

69. Which of the following problems that Latin American nations face today has its roots in colonial times?

    (A) Population explosion
    (B) Uneven distribution of wealth
    (C) Urbanization
    (D) Lack of natural resources
    (E) Hostile natural environment

70. Which of the following is a problem that pits developing nations against developed nations?

    (A) Desalinization
    (B) Desertification
    (C) Deforestation
    (D) Use of nuclear-powered energy plants
    (E) Urbanization

SECTION II

PART A

(Suggested planning and writing time—50 minutes)

Directions: The following question asks you to write a coherent essay that incorporates your interpretation of documents 1-5. (Some editing of the documents has been done for this test.)

This question will assess your skill in working with and understanding historical documents. Consider both the sources of the documents and the authors' point of view. Do not summarize the documents individually, but integrate your analysis. Cite relevant evidence from your outside knowledge of world history.

1. The Industrial Revolution began in England in the eighteenth century and spread throughout the world. As nations responded to the challenge of the Industrial Revolution and the imperialism of the West that it spawned, they were faced with significant consequences. Analyze the following documents to determine the nature of these consequences and their effects on various peoples.

   What other documents would you include, and why?

DOCUMENT 1

SOURCE: As Great Britain industrialized, entire families, including children as young as 5 and 6 years old, had to work to survive. This selection comes from a female factory worker's testimony before a British parliamentary committee holding hearings in 1831 and 1832 on the nature of industrial problems.

At what time in the morning, in the brisk time [cold weather], did those girls go to the mills?

In the brisk time, for about six weeks, they have gone at 3 o'clock in the morning, and ended at 10, or nearly half-past, at night.

What intervals were allowed for rest or refreshment during those nineteen hours of labour?

Breakfast, a quarter of an hour, and dinner half an hour, and drinking of ale a quarter of an hour.

Was any of that time taken up cleaning the machinery?

They generally had to do what they call dry down; sometimes this took the whole of the time at breakfast or drinking, and they were to get their dinner or breakfast as they could; if not it was brought home.

Had you not great difficulty in awakening your children to this excessive labour?

Yes, in the early time we had them to . . . shake them; when we got them on the floor to dress them, before we could get them off to their work; but not so in the common hours.

What was the length of time they could be in bed during those long hours?

It was near 11 o'clock before we could get them into bed after getting a little victuals [food], and then at morning my mistress used to stop [worry] all night, for fear that we could not get them ready for the time. . . .

So that they had not above four hours' sleep at this time?

No, they had not.

Were the children excessively fatigued by this labour?

Many times; we have cried often when we have given them the little victualling [food]we had to give them; we had to shake them, and they have fallen to sleep with the victuals [food] in their mouths many a time.

Did this excessive term of labour occasion much cruelty also?

Yes, being so very much fatigued the strap was very frequently used.

What was the wages in the short hours?

Three shillings [about 36 cents] a week each.

When they wrought [worked] those very long hours, what did they get?

Three shillings and sevenpence halfpenny.

DOCUMENT 2

SOURCE: Upton Sinclair's *The Jungle*, a novel describing labor conditions in the meat-packing industry in the United States, was published in 1906.

Of course Jurgis had made his home a miniature fertilizer mill a minute after entering. The stuff was half an inch deep in his skin—his whole system was full of it, and it would have taken a week not merely of scrubbing, but of vigorous exercise, to get it out of him. As it was, he could be compared with nothing known to men, save the newest discovery of the savants, a substance which emits energy for an unlimited time, without being itself in the least diminished in power. He smelt so that he made all the food at the table taste and set the whole family to vomiting; for himself it was three days before he could keep anything on his stomach- he might wash his hands and use a knife and fork, but were not his mouth and throat filled with poison?

And still Jurgis stuck it out! In spite of splitting headaches he would stagger down to the plant and take up his stand once more and begin to shovel in the blinding clouds of dust. And so at the end of the week he was a fertilizer man for life-he was able to eat again, and though his head never stopped aching, it ceased to be so bad that he could not work.

DOCUMENT 3

SOURCE: This letter to a government official details treatment under chiabaro, a forced labor system used to provide labor for gold mines in southern Africa.

Bulawayo
South Rhodesia, (Gumtree garden)
P.O. Uvuma, 19th July, 1919

Dear Bwana Casson,

We are very sorry, because here we are killed, and for this reason we are telling you that we are suffering much we are killed like fowls, they say you have commanded that the people of Zomba and Blantyre must be killed without reason. We are severely beaten and chained without reason, so we are asking you that you might tell us if it is true. This Boma is Gumtree they say "your master has ordered this" if these are true tell us that we may know very well that these rules come from Zomba to the Head Office. This is what is happening here, the European of Bulawayo are not saying anything, they are just confessing that it is true these rules have come from your own home in Nyasaland. There are no other word the real words are only these. Our master has killed Che Diaman without doing wrong because he had no pass for walking with, so he was captured by the Police of Gumtree Boma and was beaten about 40 lashes and the same day he died, also Che Habit was beaten 14 lashes and he was in bed about a week and died, the reason we are killed is on account of Passes.

I remain,
Malikwa M. K. Manoro

DOCUMENT 4

SOURCE: This excerpt by Max Havelaar describes the coffee auctions of the Dutch Trading Company and labor conditions in Java.

But strangers came from the West, who made themselves lords of his [a Javanese chief's] land. They wished to benefit from the fertility of the soil, and commanded its occupant to devote part of his labor and time to growing other products which would yield greater profit in the markets of EUROPE. To make the common man do this, a very simple policy sufficed. He obeys his Chiefs; so it was only necessary to win over those Chiefs by promising them part of the proceeds. . . . And the scheme succeeded completely.

On seeing the immense quantity of Javanese products auctioned in the Netherlands, one must be convinced of the effectiveness of this policy, even though one cannot consider it noble. For, if anyone would ask whether the man who grows the products receives a reward proportionate to the yields, the answer must be in the negative. The Government compels *him* to grow on his land what pleases *it;* and *it* fixes the price it pays him. . . .

It is true, then, that the poor Javanese is lashed outward by the whip of a dual authority; it is true that famine is often the outcome of these measures. But . . . merrily flutter the flags of Batavia, Semarang, Surabaya, Pararuan, Besuki, Problingo, Pachitan, Chilachap, on board the shops which are being laden with the harvest that make Holland rich!

Famine? In rich, fertile, blessed Java-*famine?* Yes, reader. Only a few years ago, whole districts died of starvation. Mothers offered their children for sale to obtain food. . . .

I see I have been bitter. But what would you think of someone who could write such things *without* bitterness?

Document 5

Source: In the following excerpt from his encyclical, *Rerum Novarum,* written in 1891, Pope Leo XIII expresses the Catholic Church's interest in the condition of labor.

. . . We thought it expedient now to speak on the condition of the working classes. It is a subject on which we have already touched more than once, incidentally. . . . The discussion is not easy, nor is it void of danger. It is no easy matter to define the relative rights and mutual duties of the rich and of the poor, of capital and of labor. And the danger lies in this, that crafty agitators are intent on making use of these differences of opinion to pervert men's judgments and to stir up the people to revolt.

In any case we clearly see, and on this there is general agreement, that some opportune remedy must be found quickly for the misery and wretchedness pressing so unjustly on the majority of the working class: for the ancient working-men's guilds were abolished in the last century, and no other protective organization took their place. . . . Hence, by degrees it has come to pass that working men have been surrendered, isolated and helpless, to the hard-heartedness of employers and the greed of unchecked competition. The mischief has been increased by rapacious usury, which, although more than once condemned by the Church, is nevertheless, under a different guise, but with like injustice, still practiced by covetous and grasping men. To this must be added that the hiring of labor and the conduct of trade are concentrated in the hands of comparatively few; so that a small number of very rich men have been able to lay upon the teeming masses of the laboring poor a yoke little better than that of slavery itself.

SECTION II
PART B AND PART C

(Suggested planning and writing time for each part—40 minutes)

Directions: You are to answer the following question. In writing your essay, use specific examples to support your answer.

2. Discuss the changes in modes of transportation from around 700 C.E. to the present. Explain how the changes have impacted people, societies, and cultures.

Directions: You are to answer the following question. In writing your essay, use specific examples to support your answer.

3. Compare and contrast the role of women from 1900 to the present in three of the following countries. Include historical facts, specific historical figures, and any other factors you believe significant in shaping the role of women in the countries listed.

- China
- Japan
- India
- Arab Middle East

SUGGESTIONS FOR THE DOCUMENT-BASED QUESTION

PART A

Be sure that you analyzed each document. Notice that you are asked to determine the consequences of both Industrial Revolution and imperialism and their effects on various groups. You might have noticed that the documents were in chronological order, but you did not need to write about them in that order. The rubric for the DBQ states that documents should be grouped in one, two, or three different ways for a basic score and in additional ways for extended points. Chronology is one method, but you might also have chosen categories such as location, Europeans and non-Europeans as speakers, and problems of industrialization versus problems of securing raw materials.

Regardless of the forms of organization you chose, you should have incorporated references to all the documents in your essay in a way that best supports your thesis. You should also have noted any documents that you think would present other events or other points of view that you may consider more important or that present a more balanced view than those included in the question. You might have chosen the following points about Documents 1 through 5 to discuss in your essay.

Document 1

- Transcript of a government committee hearing on labor
- Witness identified as female factory worker
- Eyewitness, not objective but testimony seems lacking in emotion
- Questions seem to be leading the witness
- 1831–1832, early in industrialization process

- Social relationships within the family changed by Industrial Revolution
- Altered nature of workforce
- Much exploitation
  - Sixteen-hour or longer workdays
  - Children as part of factory system
    - As little as 4 hours sleep
    - Little or no food
    - Corporal punishment

- Forced to work because wages needed to maintain subsistence living for family
- Paid a pittance

Relevant Historical Facts

- Increase in population

- Urbanization

- Growing middle class

- Small but wealthy upper class whose wealth was increasing

- Unequal distribution of wealth among social classes

- Squalid living conditions for laborers

- Yet all classes were better off in Europe as a result of industrialization

Document 2

Test-Taking Strategy

Be sure to write about the point of view of the author of the document.

- Upton Sinclair, novelist and social reformer

- Similar to intent of a group of reformers known as muckrakers

- Observer, secondhand account

- Fictionalized true experiences in powerful prose

- Horrible working conditions in the meat-packing industry

- Unable to clean off chemicals and pollutants

- Odors caused entire family to become ill, severe headaches

- Polluted air

- Filthy factory environment

Relevant Historical Facts

- Environment of the stockyards was so shocking to readers that the public rallied to support pure food legislation then pending in Congress

- Passage of the Meat Inspection Law and the Pure Food and Drug Act

Document 3

- Worker under the forced labor system in Rhodesia, a British colony
- Evidently appealing for help from a government official
- No objectivity
- Question of whether an emotional appeal can be totally believed
- What additional information might explain acts noted

- Description of mine workers in the region that is now Zimbabwe
- Forced labor system
- Long contracts, live in guarded compounds
- Movements controlled
  - Passes to leave
  - Without one, punished
- Conditions, squalid and dangerous
- Punishment brutal: whipped, chained, killed
- Wives and families not allowed

Relevant Historical Facts
- Mining profitable only because costs kept low
- Vast fortunes for whites
- Despair and anger led to violent uprisings

Document 4

- Dutch observer of colonial practices in Java
- Maybe visitor out from Netherlands but knows a great deal about how the system works
- Maybe official of the Dutch East India Trading Company
- Sympathetic to the Javanese
- Question of objectivity, last sentence

- Westerners take advantage of local conditions
  - Create what is in effect a captive labor force
  - Forced locals to grow products that sell in Europe
  - Scheme-win over chief by offering portion of profit
  - Tremendous profits in Europe for the Dutch

- Indentured indigenous workers
  - Must grow required crops
  - Purchased by Dutch at government-determined price
- Result–abysmal conditions
  - Dutch prosper, Javanese workers die
  - Famine because food crops not grown, cash crops instead
  - Children sold for money to get food

Relevant Historical Facts
- Some plantations like prisons
- Villages forced to set aside land to grow cash crops for government
- Price of local farmers' harvest determined by the buyer, the government
  - No profit
  - Neglect own fields to work for Dutch
- Dutch government
  - Gained about one third of total income from these exports
  - If harvest poor, farmers forced to make up difference
  - Pay taxes
  - Provide free labor

Document 5

- Pope Leo XIII
- Famous encyclical on behalf of workers
- Advocate of justice, Christian teachings
- A call by the Roman Catholic Church to improve working conditions of workers

- Concern about conflict between workers and employers
  - Recognizes capital's and labor's differences
  - Agitators cause trouble, stir up revolt
  - Way to block appeal of agitators, improve conditions of labor
- Current conditions
  - Grave injustice to workers
  - Virtually slaves

- Terrible living and working conditions
- Guilds that once protected workers were abolished
- No other organizations for protection
- Workers surrendered to conditions, isolated, helpless
- Employers: hard-hearted, greedy
  - Avaricious usury
  - Unchecked competition
- Church's position
  - Draw rich and poor together, remind each of duties
  - Obligations of justice
  - Crime to defraud workers of a rightful wage
  - Advocate establishment of workers' associations

Relevant Historical Facts
- Christian socialist movement and the Roman Catholic Church
- Stressed evils of industrialism
- Exercise Christian charity, ruthless competition and exploitation

Other Points
- To some industrialization, for some synonymous with progress
  - Increased production
  - Greater potential for imports
  - Greater profits for individuals and governments
  - Inspired competition among nations
  - Exploration of new lands
  - Efficient management of time and labor
- Industrial Revolution, criticized by others
  - The mistreatment of labor standard in the factories and mines of the first stages of industrialization
  - Created problems
  - What to do with unemployed from rural areas who moved to cities to find jobs
  - Dull monotony of routine work
  - Dangerous working conditions
  - Subsistence living conditions

- Reforms needed
    - Restrictions: child labor, working hours
    - Fair wages
    - Government inspections
- Worker's cooperatives
- Unions
- Women's suffrage
- Catalyst for social change
    - Communist Manifesto
    - Utopians
    - Less radical socialists and reformers
    - Greater class animosity
- Establishment by European nations of political control over major portions of Africa and Asia
    - Desire for natural resources, raw materials, and markets
    - Huge colonial structures
- Mass migrations
    - British Dominions
    - United States
    - Latin America: Argentina, Brazil
    - Asiatic Russia
    - Europeanization of Siberia, British Dominions (except south Africa), the Americas

You might have asked for documents suggesting other important aspects of the time period:

- Testimony of factory owners, government officials, mine owners, plantation owners
- Establishment of public education in the United States and Europe
- The growth of the middle class
- The growth of national infrastructures in Europe and the United States
- The work of mission societies
- Japanese industrialization

SUGGESTIONS FOR THE CHANGE-OVER-TIME ESSAY

You might have chosen the following points to include in your essay on changes in modes of transportation from the 700s C.E. to the present.

Test-Taking Strategy

Create a thesis that shows that you understand the concept in the question. Then support your main idea with examples, facts, and details.

Early Transportation
- Domestication of animals for transportation, beasts of burden
  - Horses
  - Mules
  - Oxen
  - Goats
  - Llamas
  - Alpacas
  - Dogs
  - Animals carry more weight than humans can

Wheeled Vehicles
- Wheeled vehicles in Sumeria in 3000 B.C.E.
- Horse-drawn chariots in Egypt in 2000 B.C.E.
- Larger loads and longer distances

First Water Vessels
- Rafts, boats, canoes
- Ability to travel to distant places
- Transporting cargo by water

Sailing Ships
- Small wooden sailboats
- Best original shipbuilders: India, China
- 1500s improvements in shipbuilding, navigational instruments, maps
  - big hulls, more seaworthy craft, better sails and large sail configurations
  - astrolabe, compass
- Bigger ships meant
  - Longer voyages
  - More cargo
  - More profit
- Better instruments meant
- More accurate navigation
- Longer voyages

Test-Taking Strategy

Remember to use any information that you have read or learned outside the classroom to help you in writing your essay.

Steamships

- Late 1700s, steamships replace sailing ships

- Late 1800s, steam-powered freighters with iron hulls

- Steamships not dependent on winds

- Steamships much larger than sailing ships

- Iron hulls less vulnerable to damage than wooden hulls

    - Longer distances

    - More cargo

    - More profit

Railroads

- 1830, first steam locomotive

- 1870s railroads cross

    - Europe

    - Canada

    - United States

    - India

- Fast overland transportation

    - Long distances in relative comfort

    - Carry heavy freight long distances

    - Transcontinental network of tracks

Automobiles

- 1890s, first gas-powered internal combustion engine for automobiles (Germany)

- 1900s, Ford develops automobiles, assembly line for mass production

- Then trucks (USA)

- Individual, personal transportation available

- Trucks: freight to individual, specific destinations

Air Travel

- 1920s, airplanes carry passengers, freight

- 1944, jet airplanes carry passengers, freight

- Travel to anywhere in the world quickly

- International trading and business network: transport certain goods anywhere quickly

SUGGESTIONS FOR THE COMPARATIVE ESSAY

Test-Taking Strategy

As you work through your list of brainstormed items to include in your outline, look for just the evidence that substantiates your thesis.

You might have chosen the following points to include in your essay on the role of women in Japan, China, India, and the Middle East. Consider them as you complete your self-evaluation of your essay.

Early Japan
- Women, subordinate to men
- Women, power in the household only
- Family, basic unit of society
- In absence of men, women manage estates, handle businesses
- Women's principal role, homemaker

Modern Japan
- After World War II, U.S. occupation
- Educational opportunities for women improve
- 1947 Constitution gives women
  - Right to vote
  - Right to sue for divorce
- 1985 Equal Employment Opportunity Law
  - Bans job discrimination based on gender
- Women enter higher education, medicine
- Still barriers to women in entering business and politics
- Still very much a "man's world"

Early China
- Women, subordinate to men
- Women, power in the household only
- Must obey male relatives throughout life
  - Fathers
  - Then husbands
  - Then sons
- Chinese respect for age raises women's status in later life
- During times of famine
  - Female babies killed
  - Sold as slaves

Modern China
- After Communist revolution of 1949
- Women more active in government and workforce
- 1950 Marriage Law
  - Bans arranged marriages
  - Gives right to sue for divorce
- 1980s, one-child-per-family policy
  - Sons preferred
  - Female infanticide increases
  - International adoption for girl babies

Early India
- Women, subordinate to men
- Women, little power even in the household
- Hindu wives
  - Submission
  - Obedience
  - Burning of widows on husbands' funeral pyre
- Islam introduces
  - Purdah, practice of secluding women in the household
  - Child marriages
  - Polygamy

Modern India
- After independence
  - Ban on polygamy and child marriage
  - Granted right to sue for divorce and right to vote
- Greater opportunities for education and jobs
  - More women in politics
- Hindu traditions still strong
  - Male superiority
  - Subordination of women
  - Caste system

Early Arab Middle East
- Women, subordinate to men

- Women, few and in some places no rights

Modern Arab Middle East
- Women, still subordinate to men in many countries

- Exception Iran, 1930s to the Iranian revolution in 1979

    - Legal reforms

    - Educational opportunities opened

    - Backlash in 1970s, Shi'ite Muslims' return to more traditional roles

- Exception Turkey, 1920s

    - Banned polygamy, veils

    - Women in public office

    - Rural areas, more traditional ways

- Education

    - Free public elementary education for boys and girls in most countries

    - Most high school education, boys

    - University: coed or in Saudi Arabia, single-sex classes

- Women, still at risk for maiming and death

    - For disobedience, adultery, violating purdah

ANSWERS AND EXPLANATIONS

QUICK-SCORE ANSWERS

1. A	11. B	21. D	31. A	41. D	51. E	61. C
2. A	12. B	22. E	32. C	42. E	52. B	62. E
3. D	13. B	23. B	33. B	43. E	53. D	63. C
4. B	14. E	24. D	34. C	44. B	54. C	64. C
5. E	15. A	25. C	35. E	45. C	55. A	65. A
6. C	16. D	26. D	36. E	46. D	56. D	66. E
7. E	17. C	27. E	37. D	47. A	57. B	67. D
8. B	18. B	28. D	38. A	48. B	58. B	68. D
9. C	19. E	29. C	39. C	49. E	59. C	69. B
10. D	20. D	30. D	40. B	50. C	60. B	70. C

PRACTICE TEST 1

Test-Taking Strategy

For not/except questions, ask yourself if the answer is correct in context. If it is, cross it off and go on to the next answer choice.

1. **The correct answer is (A).** Buddhists believe in nirvana, the release of humans from the cycle of rebirth and union with the universe, whereas Hindus believe that the essential self, or soul, known as atman, achieves moska, union with brahman. The latter is the spiritual force of which everything is a part. Another difference is the Hindu practice of caste, which the Buddhists do not have. Both Hindus and Buddhists believe in the cycle of rebirth, choice (B); the principle of nonviolence, choice (C); karma, one's actions that affect one's fate in the next life, choice (D); and dharma, one's religious and moral duties, choice (E).

2. **The correct answer is (A).** Bantu-speakers may originally have lived in eastern Nigeria south of the Benue River Valley or in the southeast Congo Basin, neither of which is in West Africa, choice (A). They moved east, choice (B), northeast and south, choice (D), and into Central, choice (C), and South-central Africa, choice (E), but they did not settle in West Africa, so choice (A) is correct.

3. **The correct answer is (D).** While the Japanese adopted and adapted a number of elements of Chinese culture, they did not embrace the civil service examination system. Positions within the government continued to be filled based on heredity and social class. Nobles and sons of nobles held power from generation to generation. The Japanese did adopt the Chinese system of ideographic writing, choice (A), and they also developed their

own system, known as kana, to complement the Chinese characters. The Japanese also adopted the concept of filial piety, based on Confucian teachings, choice (B). Choice (C), respect for merchants, is the opposite of the Chinese attitude toward the merchant class, so it is wrong regardless of whether the Japanese valued merchants, which they came to do. Choice (E), adoption of the Chinese emphasis on learning, is true about the Japanese.

Test-Taking Strategy

To be correct, an answer choice must be true for all parts of a question, in this case, the Delhi Sultanate *and the* Aztec.

4. **The correct answer is (B).** Both the Delhi Sultanate and the Aztec exacted tribute from subject states. Choice (A), the use of slaves as human sacrifice, is true only for the Aztecs, so it is the wrong answer. Even if you did not know for sure that choice (C) is incorrect, you could eliminate it because the Delhi Sultanate was an Islamic dynasty and Islam does not have priests. Choice (D), the use of viceroys, is true only for the Delhi Sultanate, so it is incorrect. Choice (E), the calpulli, is true only for the Aztec.

5. **The correct answer is (E).** Because neither the Roman Empire nor the Ottoman Empire had a clear policy about the succession of its emperor, rivals competed both openly and covertly for power, thus weakening the empire. Choice (B), rivals competed for power, may seem like a good answer and it is true, but choice (E) gives the reason why rivals were able to compete—the lack of a succession policy—and so is a better answer. Always look for the answer that is the most inclusive and gives the most complete information. Choice (A), invasions by the Mongols, is incorrect because the Romans had disappeared long before the Mongols moved westward. The Roman Empire had fallen victim to the Huns. Choice (C), revolutionaries who attempted reforms, is incorrect because this answer refers only to the Young Turks who took over the government and introduced reforms near the end of the Ottoman Empire. It does not include the Roman Empire, so choice (C) is incorrect. On the other hand, choice (D), a discontented urban population, refers to the Roman Empire.

6. **The correct answer is (C).** While choice (A), the decline of manorialism in western Europe, and choice (E), the eclipse of the Romanesque by the Gothic style, are true, the inclusion of the Americas in the global trade network, choice (C), had far greater impact on the world at that time and in subsequent periods. Choice (B), the rise of the Ottoman Empire, is incorrect. Ottomans were on the move in the 1200s. Japan did not open to the West, choice (D), until the mid-1800s, so it is also incorrect.

7. **The correct answer is (E).** Power and influence in both Great Britain and France was wielded by small elites of landowning aristocrats. Even though England had male suffrage and elected members to the House of Commons, those who stood for elections were for the most part wealthy landowners, as were those men who advised the monarch. Choice (A) is incorrect because only Great Britain was a constitutional monarchy. The king of France had absolute power. Choice (B), power to levy taxes, was controlled by Parliament in Great Britain, while the French king exercised the right of divine monarchy, but the spending and taxing polices of the French monarchs was a major factor in the events that precipitated the French Revolution. Choice (C) is incorrect; both nations had wide class differences. However, this answer is incorrect for another reason. The question asks about common characteristics of the governments. Choice (C) lists a socioeconomic characteristic—class distinctions. Choice (D) is incorrect because the prime minister was an English post only. Note, however, that this answer choice is correct about the relative importance of the prime minister in British government.

8. **The correct answer is (B).** The establishment of the plantation system required abundant, cheap labor on a large scale. Africans who appeared to be in endless supply were the only group that seemed to match this need. Cotton agriculture in the southern part of the United States, known as the Deep South, choice (A), did not take hold until the early nineteenth century, after the trans-Atlantic slave trade had peaked. Gold was discovered in Brazil, choice (C), in 1695 but had little effect on the African slave trade. Note, however, that anywhere from 3.5 to 5 million Africans were transported to Brazil, mostly to work on plantations. Choice (D), the establishment of the Triangular Trade Route, is a distracter. The trade route was a result of the market for slaves, not the cause of it. Choice (E), introduction of coffee agriculture into Mexico, is incorrect. However, the introduction of coffee plantations into Brazil increased the need for enslaved workers.

9. **The correct answer is (C).** If you read this question carefully, you saw that it asks about the men who originally wrote the U.S. Constitution. You are looking then for an idea that appears both in the Constitution and in Enlightenment thinking. While that might mean that choice (B), liberty, equality, and fraternity—the slogan of the French Revolution—could be the correct answer, it probably isn't. Choice (A), that all men are created equal, is from the Declaration of Independence, so cross it off. Choice (E), due process, comes from the Magna Carta, a document in the evolution of English government, so eliminate it also. That leaves

choice (C), a federal republic, and choice (D), social contract theory. This is when looking at the big picture helps. The federal republic flows from the idea of the social contract between those who govern and those who are governed. Choice (C) then is the more inclusive and better answer.

Test-Taking Strategy

The key word is direct.

10. **The correct answer is (D).** When Napoleon invaded Spain, Spain had little time or resources to keep its American colonies in line. Revolutionaries took advantage of Spain's distraction to launch their independence movements. Choice (A), the slave revolt in Haiti, occurred in 1804 and undoubtedly fanned the flames for independence, but it was not the direct cause of the slightly later campaigns. The same is also true of choice (B), Enlightenment ideas; choice (C), the American Revolution; and choice (E), the French Revolution. They all helped create an environment conducive to wanting independence from Spain.

11. **The correct answer is (B).** This is another question that asks you to distinguish causes from effects. Choice (B), urbanization, is an effect of the Industrial Revolution more than a cause. Cities attracted people displaced by the enclosure movement in England, choice (C), poor harvests in other areas, and the agricultural revolution, choice (E). The new factories and mills provided work, and urban infrastructure, housing, retail businesses, schools, houses of worship, and so on increased greatly to serve the ever-growing mass of workers and their families. Choice (A), population growth, helped to make the Industrial Revolution possible by providing both an increasing labor force and also an increasing market for the products of the Industrial Revolution. The use of steam power, choice (D), is another factor that made the development of heavy industry possible.

Test-Taking Strategy

When you review the answer choices, see if one of them isn't a "big picture" choice, and one or two others aren't supporting details.

12. **The correct answer is (B).** The key phrase in this question is *most significant.* This clues you to look for the most important, most inclusive answer. Choice (A), China's claim to cultural superiority, is true and did shape how the Chinese dealt with other cultures. Choice (B), Western pressure to force concessions, is also true, as are choices (C), a series of unequal treaties, and choice (D), the grant of extraterritoriality. Choice (E) is the opposite of what occurred. China lost the Opium War, but that still leaves four choices. Look at choices (B), (C), and (D). Choice (C), the unequal treaties, and choice (D), the grant of extraterritoriality, are results of choice (B), the pressure applied by Western powers, so choice (B) is the best, more general, more inclusive answer. If you still think that choice (A) may be the best answer, consider that China's attitude could not help it counter the offensives of the Western powers who used force—economic and military.

13. **The correct answer is (B).** The key words in this quotation, *naturalists, man,* and *descended,* should point you to choice (B), Charles Darwin, the author of the *Origin of Species.* Choice (A), Montesquieu, was a member of the Enlightenment who developed the idea of dividing government power among the executive, legislative, and judicial branches. Thomas Malthus, choice (C), wrote in *Essay on Population* that the population increased in a geometric progression while food production increased in an arithmetic progression. Population would always outstrip agricultural capacity unless checked by war, disease, or famine. Choice (D), Andrew Carnegie, an American millionaire business tycoon, developed the "gospel of wealth" that called on those with wealth to live up to their responsibility to help those less fortunate. A Scottish immigrant to the United States as a teenager, Carnegie amassed a fortune and gave much of it away to various causes in the United States. John Locke, choice (E), was the author of the social contract theory.

14. **The correct answer is (E).** Choice (E), lack of cash crops, is the opposite of the situation. The newly independent nations of Africa continued to export cash crops and other commodities, such as precious metals and diamonds. As colonies, they had been dependent economies, and as nations, they retained the same dependent economic activities, choice (D). Choice (A), rule by the military in Africa, is similar to what has occurred in Latin American nations where juntas have overthrown various governments since the early days of independence. An example in Africa is General Idi Amin of Uganda; a Latin American example is the successive military governments that ruled Brazil from 1964 to 1989. Perhaps the best-known example of one-party rule in an African nation that evolved into authoritarian government, choice (B), is Tanzania under Julius Nyerere. Rivalries among a number of groups have erupted into civil war, choice (C), for example, between Ibo and other groups in Nigeria and between the Hutu and Tutsi in Rwanda.

15. **The correct answer is (A).** The largest differences over the greatest number of categories is between India and the United States. In answering questions about visuals, be sure you know what you are being asked to look for and then what the data say. Sometimes you will be required to interpret the data. In this case, however, you are being asked a simple comprehension question, so you need to read and analyze exactly what the visual says.

Test-Taking Strategy

If a question asks you about two or more items, be sure the answer you select answers all parts of the question.

Test-Taking Skill

The key word is direct.

16. The correct answer is (D). The crowning of Charlemagne as emperor of the Holy Roman Empire by Pope Leo III antagonized the emperor of the Byzantine Empire, who considered himself the rightful and only heir of the original Roman Empire. The question asks about an event that affected relations between eastern and western Europe, so choice (A), invasion of Spain by the Moors, makes no sense in the context of the question; it relates to a portion of western Europe only. For the same reason, choice (B), the acceptance of Orthodox Christianity by Kievan Russia, does not fit; it relates only to a part of eastern Europe. The same is true of choice (C), the evolution of feudalism in western Europe, and choice (E), the rise of the Seljuk Turks, which affected the Byzantine Empire through conquests and western Europe by capture of the Holy Land, which precipitated the Crusades.

17. The correct answer is (C). The Crusades contributed to the growing power of western monarchies, which resulted in a corresponding decline in the power of lesser feudal lords. But this decline was not a direct result of the Crusades; it was an indirect result of the increasing power of the kings, so choice (C) is incorrect and, therefore, the correct response for this *except* question. Choice (A), the growth of the money economy in Europe, occurred because nobles who needed money to underwrite their expeditions to the Holy Land permitted their serfs to substitute money for payments in kind for their rents, so eliminate choice (A). (An indirect result of the growth of the money economy was the weakening of manorialism and its attendant system of serfdom in the West.) Choice (B), the growth of European trading centers, is also true and, therefore, an incorrect answer choice. The power of the papacy rose during this period, choice (D), because of the attention given to the Crusades, which were called by the pope, so cross it off. Crusaders themselves as well as the goods their ships brought back opened Europe to the knowledge of a wider world beyond their borders, so choice (E) is also true but the wrong answer to this *except* question.

18. The correct answer is (B). Sudanic empires and the empires of the Aztec and the Inca used military power to enlarge their territories. Choice (A) is incorrect because the Sudanic empires developed in savannah, whereas the Aztecs ruled from the fertile Valley of Mexico and the Inca established their empire in the Andes Mountains. The ruling classes and urban dwellers of the Sudanic empires were typically Muslims, whereas the rural peoples tended to practice animism, which is polytheistic. The Aztec and Inca also worshipped many deities, so choice (C) is incorrect. While trade was important to the Sudanic empires, the majority of people were engaged in some form of agriculture. This was also true for the Aztec and Inca, making choice (D) incorrect for all three groups. Choice (E) is incorrect for the Sudanic empires, which used Arabic, and the Aztec, who had developed a system of writing. The Inca did not have a system of writing.

Test-Taking Strategy

For not/except *questions, ask yourself if the answer is correct in the context of the question. If it is, cross it off and go on to the next answer choice.*

19. **The correct answer is (E).** Choice (E) is the opposite of what is true. Hindus created statues and other artistic representations of the human form. Strict adherents of Islam reject the use of the human form in art and use geometric and floral patterns exclusively. (All Islamic art does not necessarily follow this prohibition; the miniature paintings of the Mughals, for example, depict humans.) Choice (A), that Hinduism is polytheistic and Islam is monotheistic, is true, so choice (A) is the wrong answer to this *except* question. (Judaism, Christianity, and Islam are founded on the same base and are the world's three largest monotheistic religions.) Choice (B), the conflict between Islam's belief in the equality of people and the caste system of Hinduism; choice (C), the difference in the ceremonies and rituals of Islam and Hinduism; and choice (D), the difference in the age of the two religions, are all correctly stated and, therefore, incorrect responses for this reverse question.

Test-Taking Skill

The key word is unintended.

20. **The correct answer is (D).** The Mongol invasions did not cause the collapse of the Byzantine Empire. That was the work of the Ottoman Turks. Choice (A), the rise in importance of Moscow, occurred as a result of its becoming the collector of tribute for the Mongols. This was not intended by the Mongols, so choice (A) is true and, therefore, the wrong answer for this *except* question. Choice (B), the spread of bubonic plague, occurred through the transportation either of animals infested with disease-carrying fleas or goods infested with rats carrying the diseased fleas. It was not deliberate, so cross off choice (B). The Seljuk Turks hired the Ottoman Turks to protect their holdings in Asia Minor from the Mongols. The Seljuk Turks were unable to withstand the force of the Mongols overall, and their empire collapsed. In the meantime, the Ottomans used their base in Asia Minor to begin their own rise to imperial power. This makes choice (C) correct but the wrong answer. Choice (E) is also correct but the wrong answer. The Mongols who stayed in the areas of their conquest on the central and western steppes adopted Islam and were assimilated into the dominant Turkish culture. This cultural assimilation of the conqueror by the conquered has often been true in world history.

21. **The correct answer is (D).** This quotation is taken from the sermon of Pope Urban II, exhorting Christians to free the Holy Land from the Turks. Did you notice the clue words *faithful, Jerusalem, Constantinople,* and *horrible tale?* Choice (A), the creation of the modern state of Israel, is incorrect because Constantinople is now called Istanbul and has been since shortly after the creation of the modern state of Turkey in 1923. Choice (B), the establishment of the Abbasid Dynasty, might make you think twice, but it was confined to primarily what is today Iraq and, therefore, would not pose a threat to Jerusalem or Constantinople, so cross it off as illogical. The invasion of Europe by the Huns, choice (C), would not affect Jerusalem or Constantinople, so eliminate it. The Yuans were Mongols, choice (E), but they set up a dynasty that ruled China from 1260 to 1368, so they were not a threat to Jerusalem.

22. **The correct answer is (E).** The effects of the development of strong, centralized monarchies such as France did not last as long as the change in worldview that resulted from the Renaissance, choice (A); the change from a manorial to capitalist economy, choice (B); the escalating developments in science and technology that have occurred since the Scientific Revolution, choice (C); or the increase in food production as a result of the Agricultural Revolution, choice (D). The change in worldview that the Renaissance sparked resulted in such far-reaching changes as a turning from religious to natural explanations of phenomena, a greater interest in life on earth rather than in life after death, and a general turning outward that ultimately resulted in European explorations and a global community. Similar long-term transitions and developments can be traced from each of the other answer choices but not from the rise of strong monarchies, most of which have long since ended.

23. **The correct answer is (B).** One of the effects of the Age of Exploration was the rise of capitalism and the increasing wealth and importance of the merchant class. With their rise came a concomitant decline in the influence of the feudal lords, which monarchs, interested in increasing their own power, exploited. Choice (A) is incorrect because the increase in the amount of gold and silver in circulation caused inflation and made it more difficult for people to buy goods. This is the basis of the price revolution. Choice (C) is incorrect because English, French, and Dutch cities eclipsed the Italian city-states as the most important international trading centers. Choice (D) is a distracter. Something about it is correct, but it was diseases that Europeans spread that killed large numbers of Native Americans, so

eliminate this answer. Choice (E) is the opposite of what occurred. Mercantilism, in which the home country sought to amass large amounts of gold and carefully regulate its balance of trade, became the guiding economic principle of the era and led to some of the issues between Great Britain and its American colonies.

24. **The correct answer is (D).** During the 1700s, there was no Italian state. The Italian peninsula was made up of a number of city-states, duchies, and small kingdoms, which were no unified until 1861. The other nations, Russia, choice (A); France, choice (B); Prussia, choice (C); and England, choice (E) chose allies and enemies as their interests dictated.

25. **The correct answer is (C).** The inattention to ethnic differences shown by both those European statesmen who redrew the map of Europe at the Congress of Vienna and those who carved up sub-Saharan Africa in the 1880s would result in such ethnic initiated conflicts as World War I and civil wars in African and eastern European nations. Choices (A), (D), and (E) all have the same problem with their statements, so you could eliminate them immediately without even knowing whether the statements are correct. None of them address both parts of the question: Europe and Africa. Choice (A) deals only with African colonies; it is also illogical since the European nations would have wanted to make sure that their colonies were profitable. Choice (D) is true but deals only with France, not with African colonies, so it is only half true and, therefore, incorrect. The same is true for choice (E), which deals only with Africa. It is true about Africa but does not deal with France and so cannot be the correct answer. Choice (B) is another problem. It is true, but it is a subset of choice (C). Language is a part of cultural identity. Choice (C) is a better answer because it is a more inclusive response.

26. **The correct answer is (D).** History as "the history of class struggles" was a basic principle of Karl Marx's theories. If you recognized the idea of class struggle as being part of Communist ideology, you might have also considered choice (A), Mao Zedong, and choice (E), Lenin. However, the question asks for "the first," and since Marx predates both these other men, he is the best choice. The phrase *class struggle,* a key phrase in the question, would not have been part of the rhetoric of the much earlier Machiavelli, choice (B), or Cardinal Richelieu, choice (C), so eliminate them.

27. **The correct answer is (E).** While there was some interest in increasing the rights and status of women under the Meiji, nothing ever came of the efforts, so choice (E) is incorrectly stated but the correct response to this *except* question. Choice (A), the rise of the zaibatsu, or industrial and banking conglomerates concentrated in the hands of single families, occurred under the Meiji. The zaibatsu wielded great power until 1948 when their activities were limited by law. The samurai, a hereditary caste, were the soldier warriors of Japan until the Meiji made all men subject to military service, choice (B). In an effort to learn from the West and modernize the nation, the Meiji established separate government departments and modernized its bureaucratic practices, choice (C). Industrialization occurred rapidly and with it the movement of people to the cities from rural areas, choice (D). Eliminating as true choices (A), (B), (C), and (D) leaves choice (E) as incorrect but the right response to the *except* question.

28. **The correct answer is (D).** This is another *not/except* question, so you are looking for the answer that does not fit. The Gospel of Wealth as articulated by Andrew Carnegie advocated that the wealthy had a responsibility to help the poor and less fortunate. It does not fit with the concept of imperialism as illustrated by U.S. foreign policy at the end of the nineteenth century, so it is the correct answer to the question. Perhaps the greatest motive for U.S. imperialism at the end of the nineteenth century was a sense of patriotism, choice (A). The profit motive, choice (B), was less of an incentive when businessmen looked at the problems of running faraway businesses, such as the cost involved in administration and defense and difficulty of controlling rebellious local peoples, but was still an operative motive. Choice (C), Social Darwinism, gave an intellectual veneer to less noble motives. It applied Charles Darwin's principle of natural selection in the animal and plant worlds to human society and determined that some races and nations were more "fit" than others and, therefore, destined to rule over the inferior peoples. Choice (E), the desire for most-favored-nation trading status with China, was a factor in the U.S.'s insistence on the Open Door Policy in China.

29. **The correct answer is (C).** Only Russia—after its own successful Communist revolution—answered Sun Yat-sen's request for aid in 1921. None of the non-Communist nations agreed to help. Both Great Britain, choice (A), and France, choice (E)—on opposite sides of the war—were reeling from their losses in World War I. The United States, choice (B), had entered a period of isolation after World War I, and Japan, choice (D), was about to launch its own assault on China.

30. **The correct answer is (D).** While answer choices (A), (B), (D), and (E) were factors, choice (D), the split in the Japanese government between the civilians who agreed to surrender—but not the unconditional surrender the Allies wanted—and the military who rejected surrender showed that the Japanese intended to continue fighting. Choice (C) is incorrect. The fire bombings were doing heavy damage, but the government continued to fight on. Choice (E), exhortations of Japanese leaders to fight on to final victory, is a subset that supports choice (D) as the correct answer. Of the two answer choices, choice (D) is the more inclusive.

31. **The correct answer is (A).** There were no animals similar to cattle or horses in the Americas. The closest was the llama of the Andes. Even if Native Americans had been able to domesticate the buffalo, this would not have enabled pastoral nomadism to develop on a large scale since the buffalo lived on only a small part of the two continents, so eliminate choice (B) as illogical. Large parts of both continents had savanna, so choice (C) is also illogical. Not all nomads used horses—for example, the camel and reindeer herders—so choice (D) is incorrect. Moisture is related to choice (C) and so is illogical also.

32. **The correct answer is (C).** One of the practices of the Roman Empire that led to its decline was its reliance on slave labor, which displaced small farmers. The Han Empire did not use slave labor extensively. Choice (A) is incorrect because manufacturing in the sense of handcrafted goods was not an important economic activity in either empire at this time. Choice (B) is incorrect because neither part of the answer deals with economic activity; the statement is about a social practice. (Both societies were patrilineal.) Choice (D) is incorrect because agriculture was the basis of the economies of both the Roman and Han Empires. Choice (E) again is a statement about social practices and not economic practices, so eliminate it. It is also the opposite of the position of women in the two empires; women in the Roman Empire had more freedom of action than women in the Han Empire.

Test-Taking Strategy

In answering this question, you need to make sure that the answer is true for all three groups. A partially correct answer is a partially incorrect answer—and a quarter-point deduction.

33. **The correct answer is (B).** The Celtic, Slavic, and Germanic peoples evolved into small regional kingdoms around the 200s C.E. Choice (A) is incorrect because these peoples were both hunters and agriculturalists; they did not rely on hunting and gathering for their subsistence. Choice (C) is incorrect because they worked in iron, although not in other forms of metal such as bronze or copper. These peoples were patriarchal in organization, so choice (D) is incorrect. Like most agricultural and nomadic societies, the Celts, Slavs, and Germans had little in the way of social and class distinctions, so choice (E) is incorrect.

34. **The correct answer is (C).** The Bedouins were the original nomadic inhabitants of the Arabian Peninsula and the people to whom Muhammad preached his new religion, so as they converted to Islam, it spread throughout the peninsula. Choice (A) is incorrect; Buddhism was carried to China along the trade route and by the work of Buddhist monks. Catholic missionaries carried Christianity to Africa, choice (B). Presbyterianism spread to Scotland from Switzerland through the work of John Knox, choice (D). Shintoism was the indigenous religion of Japan, whose popularization coincided with the development of the belief that the imperial family was descended from the sun goddess, choice (E).

35. **The correct answer is (E).** Islam developed the shar'ia, which is the Islamic legal code, so choice (E) was not the reason why Islam appealed to so many people. Choice (A), that Muhammad accepted earlier Judaic and Christian revelations, and choice (C), the commonality of monotheism among all three religions, were both reasons why Islam seemed familiar to people and thus appealed to them. Choice (B), the simple nature of the belief system, and choice (D), belief in the equality of all people, also appealed to people, the latter especially to the poor and oppressed.

Study Strategy

It's a good idea to review these questions and answers—and the review chapters in this book—with a world atlas, historical atlas, or your world history textbook handy so you can check relative locations.

36. **The correct answer is (E).** The Abbasid Empire was centered in what is today modern Iraq, and its natural trading partners were the Mediterranean region to the west and China to the east. Choice (A) is illogical because the Abbasid Empire had no outlet to water on the east to trade with Japan or a manageable overland route southeast to India. Choice (B) is partially true because China was a major trading partner, but the Kingdom of Kongo did not exist during the Abbasid Dynasty; it was not founded until the 1300s. Choice (C) also is partially true because the Mediterranean was a trading partner, but Benin in West Africa was not only far beyond any possible trade route but also was not founded until around the 1200s. Choice (D), West Africa and Japan, were beyond the possible manageable routes of the Abbasid.

37. **The correct answer is (D).** The East African coastal trading centers had become a mix of black Africans and Islamic traders by the 800s, although Muslim Arabs had been trading in the area from the 600s. In time, a distinctive culture and language known as Swahili had developed. The language was based on Bantu with Arabic and Persian words. Among the Islamic traditions that were adopted were Islam itself, the building of mosques, and the use of other Islamic design motifs. This information points out

the fallacy in choice (E); Swahili was not a religion. Choice (A) is incorrect because the trading network of the East Coast cities spread as far as China, Indonesia, and Malaysia. The slave trade was not a large part of the economy until after the arrival of the Portuguese, so cross off choice (B). Ife, choice (C), was a city-state in the interior of West Africa, not one of the East Coast trading centers.

38. **The correct answer is (A).** Both the East India Company (British) and the Dutch East India Company enlarged the area under the control of their respective companies and thus their nations in the 1700s. The Dutch government dissolved the Dutch East India Company in 1799. The British took control of India from the East India Company in 1858, and the company was finally dissolved in 1873. Spain makes choice (B) incorrect because the government had always controlled the economic activity in its colonies. Choice (C) and choice (E) are both incorrect because France did not have similar successful charter or joint-stock companies. Choice (D) is incorrect because neither Prussia nor Austria-Hungary had successful colonial entrepreneurs in the eighteenth century. They had turned their attention to European rivalries.

39. **The correct answer is (C).** The estimates of historians vary, but somewhere between 10 and 40 million Africans, almost all from West Africa between what is today Mauritania and Angola, were taken in chains to the Americas. For the most part, North Africa, choice (A), provided slaves for markets locally. East Africa, choice (B), provided slaves for the markets of the East African coastal trading cities. Slavery also existed in other parts of Africa.

Test-Taking Strategy

Be sure you know what the question is asking. Highlight the key words, in this case difference.

40. **The correct answer is (B).** Marx believed that the development of industrialization and with it the evolution of a middle class was needed in order for a proletarian revolution, whereas Lenin believed that such a rising could occur in an essentially agricultural economy without a middle class, such as Russia had at the time. In showing that choice (B) is correct, this information also shows that choice (C) is incorrect and the opposite of the two men's beliefs. Choice (A) is also the opposite of what the two men believed. Lenin believed that violence could and should be used, whereas Marx believed in the need to exercise political action. Choice (D) is incorrect for two reasons. First, the information is incorrect, because Lenin did understand that the peasants, formerly serfs, could be cultivated to support revolution. Second, the question asks about a major difference, and this answer indicates a supposed similarity. Choice (E) is incorrect, because it states Lenin's position about the usefulness of cells as Marx's position and vice versa.

41. **The correct answer is (D).** Choice (D) is the best description of the fundamental difference that lay behind what Wilson wanted—a peace that would not lead to another war—and what the Allies wanted—revenge, to bring Germany to its knees and make it extremely difficult for the country to recover. Choice (A), the desire for heavy reparations on the part of the Allies, which Wilson opposed, is a specific example of their differences, but choice (D) is a better statement of the reason behind the opposing positions of Wilson and the Allies. Choice (C), that the Allies had divided up among themselves sovereignty over eastern European nations while the war was still being fought, is also true, but again it is an example that supports choice (D) as the most inclusive answer. Choice (B) is not true. Establishment of the League of Nations was of extreme importance to Wilson. Choice (E) is also not true. While Wilson did have to negotiate a treaty that would pass the Senate, his insistence on the League of Nations and his own lack of consideration of political realities doomed the treaty; the Allies had their own political considerations and that was one reason why they pushed for harsh terms for Germany.

42. **The correct answer is (E).** The word *fascism* should tell you immediately that the author of these words was Benito Mussolini, choice (E), the Fascist dictator of Italy before and during World War II. Choice (A), Boris Yeltsin, was the first president of the Russian Republic after independence. Choice (B), Fredrich Engels, socialist and philosopher, with Karl Marx published the *Communist Manifesto.* Choice (C), Adolph Hitler, more likely would have written about Nazism than Fascism. John Locke, choice (D), was the author of the social contract theory who greatly influenced the development of the U.S. Constitution.

43. **The correct answer is (E).** If you don't know the answer immediately, common sense can help you answer this *except* question. Even when women are granted legal and civil rights, their lack of education and lack of financial resources make it difficult for women in developing nations to take advantage of them. Choice (A), that the rights of women in nations that have turned to a fundamentalist version of Islam have declined, is true, so cross it off. Depending on the strictness of the fundamentalism, women are not allowed to go about in public unveiled and may not drive, and female children are not allowed to attend to school. Choice (B) is also true and stands to reason since proper sanitation, health care, and good nutrition are less available. Because this is a reverse answer question, eliminate choice (B) as true but the wrong answer. Choice (C) is also a

reasonable answer and thus one that should be eliminated. In nations with developing economies, there would be few women who could afford to attend secondary schools, let alone postsecondary institutions. Choice (D), that most women in developing nations spend their time in child care and providing for their families, is true and also supports choice (C). Only choice (E) is untrue and, therefore, the correct answer to this question.

Test-Taking Strategy

Be sure you know what the question is asking. The key words in this question are most accurate, world economy, *and* late twentieth century.

44. **The correct answer is (B).** While the Pacific Tigers are important in the world economy, the United States and Western Europe still dominate the global economy. Choice (A) is incorrect because it deals with political activity—"who is in charge"—rather than the economy. The statement also deals only with Africa. Choice (C) is incorrect; for the most part the nations of Latin America are developing nations and still dependent economies. Choice (D) is true; Japan has taken on a major role in the world economy, but choice (B) is a more general statement—encompasses more the world economy—than does choice (D). Choice (E) is incorrect. GATT, stands for General Agreement on Tariffs and Trade, is an attempt to regulate world trade; it does not give or lend aid. It was succeeded by the World Trade Organization (WTO). The International Monetary Fund (IMF), affiliated with the UN, and the World Bank lend money.

45. **The correct answer is (C).** This is a *not* question, so you are looking for the statement that is not supported by the data on the graph. The highest percentage of Christians is in India, not Bangladesh, which has only 1 percent of people who are neither Hindu nor Muslim. The data supports all the other answers, choice (A), India with a population divided among at least five religions is the most religiously diverse; choice (B), Pakistan has the highest percentage of one religion, Islam, at 97 percent of the population; choice (D), there are almost no Buddhists on the subcontinent; and choice (E), division of India in 1947 to give Muslims their own nation, which was later divided into Pakistan and Bangladesh, is reflected in the data about Muslims in these countries.

Test-Taking Strategy

For not/except *questions, ask yourself if the answer is true in the context of the question. If it is, cross it off and go on to the next answer. Repeating the question each time helps you keep in mind that you are looking for the incorrect response.*

46. **The correct answer is (D).** A common characteristic of pastoral nomadism was intertribal warfare. The warrior culture was a large part of the societies of such peoples as the Huns and the Mongols. Choice (A), patrilineal kinship, is true for pastoral nomads, so eliminate this answer. Choice (B), little social stratification, is also true, so cross it off. Common sense would tell you that this is true even if you did not know the answer immediately. People who had to rely on a nonsedentary existence based on grazing herds for subsistence would lack occupational specialization and have little need for a ruling hierarchy

other than group chief and perhaps elders. Choice (C) is also true, so rule it out. It makes sense generally that residence in a patrilineal society would be patrilocal. Choice (E) is also true in that relatively well-off individuals would have some responsibility to look after those who were less well off. That leaves choice (D) as the only untrue statement but the correct answer.

47. **The correct answer is (A).** The role of the scholar-gentry was to maintain harmony among the social classes by administering the state and advising the ruler wisely. The scholar-gentry, in turn, was prepared for this role by years of education. Choice (D), to educate the sons of the upper class who would become the new scholar-gentry, is not true. The civil-service examination system made it possible for a boy even from the most humble circumstances to become a member of the scholar-gentry. (This was a major difference with the Japanese system, where government posts were hereditary.) Choice (E), too, is simply not true. The scholar-gentry did not censor all communication from outside China to keep it isolated. However, choice (B), to administer the civil-service examination system, and choice (C), to staff the bureaucracy, are true about the role of the scholar-gentry in China, but neither is the best answer. If you were confused by the answers, look again at the question. It asks for the most important aspect of the role of scholar-gentry. Administering the civil system and staffing the government's bureaucracy were means to the end—maintaining harmony. Therefore, choice (A) is the most inclusive answer and choices (B) and (C) are specific examples, or supporting details.

48. **The correct answer is (B).** The Byzantine Empire's government is an exemplar of bureaucratic government, whereas the Roman Empire lacked this highly structured system of government administration. Choice (A) is incorrect because both the Byzantine and Roman Empires were autocracies, absolute rule by one person. An oligarchy is ruled by a small elite group. Choice (C) is partially true. The Roman emperors paid little heed to their deities. However, the Byzantine emperors exerted considerable authority over the patriarchs of the Orthodox Church. Choice (D) is true about the intrigues in the Byzantine Empire but lacks any information that compares it with the Roman Empire, so you could eliminate this answer whether you knew anything about intrigues in the Byzantine Empire or not. Choice (E) is correct about the foreign mercenaries in the Roman army, but the Mamluks fought for the Ayyubid sultan in Egypt, overthrew him, stopped the Mongols in the Middle East, routed the Crusaders from Syria, and controlled Egypt until 1517.

49. **The correct answer is (E).** Buddhism developed in Hindu India, but it was not able to sustain a presence. Hindu priests known as brahmans were able to weaken Buddhism's appeal by introducing changes in Hinduism to make it more attractive to the people. The establishment of the Hindu Gupta dynasty (320 C.E.–c. 500 C.E.) also strengthened Hinduism's standing. Another blow to Buddhism was the invasion and occupation of India by the Huns who found the peaceful nature of Buddhism alien. The invasion of Mongols who embraced Islam and established the Mughal dynasty all but ended the adoption of Buddhism; few practice Buddhism today on the subcontinent. Choice (A), Daoism, is an ancient Chinese philosophy that was not transported to India, so it is incorrect. Choice (B), Confucianism, an ancient Chinese ethical system, also did not travel to India, so eliminate it. Shintoism, choice (C), is a mature religion indigenous to Japan. State Shinto, which worshipped the emperor as a deity, was banned after World War II. Choice (D), polytheism, is illogical since Hinduism is polytheistic, that is, a religion with many male and female deities.

50. **The correct answer is (C).** Various rain forest and savanna peoples replaced chiefs with kings as the basic unit of governance, among them the Sudanic empires, the city-states of the Yoruba, and the Kingdom of Kongo. This makes choice (C) incorrect, but the correct answer for this *except* question. Choice (A), that Islam was important in the Sudanic kingdoms, is true, as is choice (D), that most Africans south of the Sahara practiced traditional animistic religions. Islam did not penetrate the countryside in the Sudanic empires but was the religion of city-dwellers. Nonetheless, Islam was important in creating a network of trading ties with North Africa and the Middle East and an intellectual ferment in the universities and schools in West Africa. Choice (B), that Bantu was the base language for the majority of languages south of the Sahara, is true, so eliminate it. Choice (E) is also true; generally agricultural societies would have at least some rudimentary trading activity.

51. **The correct answer is (E).** Spain alone of those listed had a centralized monarchy at the end of the Middle Ages. Choice (A), Germany, did not become a unified state until 1871 when the other German princes joined with Prussia in the German Second Empire. The Netherlands, choice (B), was still part of Spain at the end of the Middle Ages. The Netherlands declared its independence in 1581, but Spain did not recognize its sovereignty until 1684. Choice (C), Belgium, was part of Netherlands until the 1830s. Italy, choice (D), did not become a single nation until 1861.

52. **The correct answer is (B).** North American Amerindians organized their governing structure around kinship. A chief and a council of elders often aided by a priest, or shaman, all of whom were related, typically made decisions for the clan or tribe. The overall Aztec unit of government was the empire. An emperor, a council of nobles, and priests oversaw the management of a vast amount of territory. Choice (A) is incorrect because the North Americans relied heavily on hunting and gathering, whereas the Aztecs had an agricultural economy. Choice (C) is the opposite of the situation; the Aztec had a class system, whereas there was little social stratification among North Americans. Choice (D) is incorrect because the Moundbuilders, in what is today the U.S. Midwest and Southeast, built ceremonial mounds on a large-scale, and the Anasazi of the Southwest created cliff dwellings. The Plains Native Americans did not have horses until the Europeans came, and by the time horses were in widespread use on the Plains, the Aztec Empire had been destroyed.

Test-Taking Strategy

Just because an answer is true does not make it the correct answer to the question. Be alert to this type of distracter.

53. **The correct answer is (D).** When the Ming abruptly ended Chinese trading ventures to India, the Middle East, and Africa, the way was opened for other nations to step in. There was no other single Asian nation or African nation at the time that had the resources or technological advances of the Chinese to pursue trade on a large scale. Europeans who had begun to explore outward from Europe took advantage of this vacuum to establish their own trading networks and tap into existing networks in Africa, South Asia, Asia, and Southeast Asia. Choice (A), the seaworthiness of European ships, was not the reason why Europeans took the lead, so eliminate this answer. Choice (B), the closing of Japanese ports to foreigners, is illogical. Europeans already had developed wide-ranging trading contacts by the time the Japanese closed their ports between 1633 and 1639. It was to exclude Europeans that the Japanese government took this step. While the Crusades spurred an interest in goods from Asia, which the Italian city-states exploited, choice (C), this is not the answer to the question, so cross it off. Choice (E) is incorrect. The ancient Greeks invented the astrolabe, but the Chinese invented the compass during the Han Empire.

54. **The correct answer is (C).** Individuals were expected to follow the religion of their ruler. Among the northern German states, this meant becoming a Protestant; in England, an Anglican; and in France, remaining a Roman Catholic. There was no concept of personal religious freedom, so choice (C) is wrong but the correct answer to this *except* question. The remaining answer choices are all correct and, therefore, the wrong answers to the *except* question. Choice (A), the rise in literacy, was an indirect result of Luther's teaching that the Bible was the sole guide for Christians. In order to know what the Bible said, people needed to learn to read. Up until the Protestant Reformation, the Bible was published only in Latin, the language of the Roman Catholic Church. Because ordinary people now needed to read it for spiritual guidance, it was translated into vernacular and education became more important. Choice (B), a series of religious wars, was in part a result of rulers forcing those they ruled to follow whatever religion the ruler chose and in part power struggles among competing princes in Germany and national monarchies on a continental basis. A major outcome of the Protestant Revolution was the development of the Protestant work ethic, choice (D). Choice (E), the establishment of married clergy in Protestant religions, was a direct result of the Protestant Reformation and answered one of the criticisms of Luther and the other reformers.

Test-Taking Strategy

Remember that all parts of an answer choice must be correct in order for the answer to be correct.

55. **The correct answer is (A).** By 1600, Russia and the Ottoman Empire had expanded eastward and secured their claims to those areas of Central Asia that were home to nomadic invaders. You can eliminate choice (D) immediately because the Khanates of the Mongols were one of the groups that had invaded Europe and the Ottoman Empire. Choice (B) can be eliminated for a similar reason. While Russia is correct, the Mughal Empire is not. The base of the empire was the Mongol invasions into India. Once established, the Mughals drove south farther into India, not back north into Central Asia. The Ming Dynasty in China, choices (C) and (E), is illogical because the Chinese during this period were contracting their contacts with the world, not expanding them.

56. **The correct answer is (D).** The role of the Japanese government to subsidize businesses and the building of infrastructure continued well into the late twentieth century and was often a complaint of foreign competitors who said that this practice benefited Japanese businesses unfairly. Choice (A) is untrue. Workers in neither country were paid more than subsistence wages. Choice (B) is true, both nations had extensive railway systems, but the question asks for a major difference and this statement relates a similarity, so it is not the answer to the question. Choice (C) is incorrect. Japan imported machinery from the West and was less technologically advanced than British industry. Choice (E) is the opposite of the situation. Great Britain was rich in coal resources, whereas Japan had to import its energy sources. This need for energy would be one of the reasons for Japan's aggression in Asia prior to World War II.

ANSWERS AND EXPLANATIONS

57. **The correct answer is (B).** Choice (A), that World War I is the crime of the ages; choice (C), that Russia and Austria are being blamed unfairly; and choice (D), that the nations of Europe are blaming one another are all true about the cartoon, but they do not capture the cartoonist's meaning. Choice (B), that all nations involved in the fighting are to blame for the outbreak of the war, is the only answer choice to deal with the cartoonist's meaning. Choice (E), that war is a terrible crime, is a distracter; it does not relate specifically to the cartoon.

58. **The correct answer is (B).** The author of these words was Josiah Strong, Secretary of the Home Missionary Society. There is no reason why you should be familiar with this person, but his words should signal to you that he advocates imperialism, choice (B). The key words *competition of races* and *Anglo-Saxon* should have clued you immediately to the influence of Social Darwinism and the idea of the fittest race. Choice (C), absolutism, the idea that monarchs have supreme power, is illogical in this context, so it can be easily eliminated. Choice (A), "big stick" policy, from Theodore Roosevelt's well-known slogan "walk softly and carry a big stick" is a subset of the idea of imperialism. So, too, are choice (D), gunboat diplomacy, first used by the British in Egypt in 1882 and later by the United States against the Philippines in 1898, and choice (E), dollar diplomacy, which underlay much of William Howard Taft's foreign policy. All three are specific examples of choice (B), imperialism, making choice (B) the most inclusive and best choice among the answers.

59. **The correct answer is (C).** While the United States did not block the admission of the People's Republic of China to the United Nations, the United States did not support it either, so choice (C) is incorrect. The Eisenhower Doctrine, choice (A), promised economic and military aid to any nation in the Middle East and possible military intervention should any nation in the region be threatened by "international communism." This doctrine was issued after the Suez crisis, choice (E), in which the United States strongly protested the invasion of the Suez peninsula by Great Britain, France, and Israel. The United States introduced a resolution into the UN resolution demanding their withdrawal, and all three nations withdrew in phases. Choice (B), the Marshall Plan, represented huge infusions of money and aid into seventeen European nations to help them rebuild after World War II. Choice (D), deterrence, was one of the approaches to balancing nuclear weaponry with the Soviets. The policy rested on each side's having a huge buildup of weapons, which in theory would discourage the opposite side from a "first strike" because the aggressor knew that its opponent had an equally huge stockpile of weapons that could be turned on it.

Test-Taking Strategy

The key phrase here is twentieth-century revolutions.

60. **The correct answer is (B).** The question is asking you to find the most accurate description of *twentieth-century revolutions*, so you are looking for some large principle, or general statement, about twentieth-century revolutions, not necessarily specific examples. Choice (C), the expansion of Islamic fundamentalism, and choice (D), the nature of the Mexican Revolution as a peasant revolt against the wealthy, are a mix of generalization and specific example. However, choice (B), that twentieth-century revolutions are often based on some ideal, is a more general statement about the nature of twentieth-century revolutions and the best choice to answer the question. Choice (A), that these revolutions generally were undertaken to restore power to the traditional ruling elite, is the opposite of the participants' motives. Choice (E), that the Cuban revolution was atypical in that the people exchanged one autocrat, Fulgencio Batista, for another, Fidel Castro, is not true. The same occurred in Russia where Lenin and then Stalin replaced the tsars and in China where Mao Zedong replaced Chiang Kai-shek, who had replaced a series of emperors.

61. **The correct answer is (C).** Because of the availability of the llama, the Inca practiced a very limited form of pastoralism, which the Aztec, who had no large animals, could not do. Choice (A) is incorrect, because both the Aztec and the Inca developed monumental architecture. Choice (B) is also incorrect because both empires exacted tribute from their dependent states. Although less warlike than the Aztec, the Inca also used force to enlarge their empire, resettling conquered peoples closer to the center of the empire, so choice (D) is incorrect. Choice (E) is partially true, but that still makes it incorrect. The Olmec along the Gulf Coast were the base culture of Mesoamerica, not the Aztec. The Inca did adopt and adapt various elements of earlier Andean cultures.

62. **The correct answer is (E).** All three cities, Kilwa, Mogadishu, and Sofala, were important black African-Arabic cities of the African East Coast. Choice (A) and choice (D) are incorrect because Gao and Timbuktu were important cities of the West African empire of Mali. Don't confuse Gao with Goa, a port in India that the Portuguese seized. Choice (B) and choice (C) are incorrect because Great Zimbabwe was a Bantu city in southeastern Africa. Choice (C) is also incorrect because Benin was an important trading center in the rain forest area of West Africa, as was Nok, making choice (D) also incorrect.

63. **The correct answer is (C).** Unlike the other nations listed, Russia was slow to industrialize and thus lacked an urban working class, which was the base of the revolutions of 1848. Nationalism played a part in the revolutions in Austria, choice (A); Hungary, choice (D); and Prussia, choice (E). Republicans toppled the king in France, choice (B), but the nation turned itself into an empire (not a democracy) that lasted until 1870.

Test-Taking Strategy

Look for clue words in quotations such as enrich a great nation *and* trade *in this quotation.*

64. **The correct answer is (C).** The attribution of this quotation to Adam Smith should have told you immediately that it was about mercantilism. Smith is best known for his theory of the free-market economy in which the "invisible hand" guides self-interest for the benefit of all. An aspect of his view is the operation of mercantilism. Choice (A), the factory system, is the system in which production is brought together in mechanized factories, which replaced cottage industry, piecework, and handwork. Choice (B), industrialization, is the change of an economy from one based on agricultural to one based on industry. The monetary system, choice (D), is the medium of exchange in an economy. Choice (E), capitalism, is an economic system in which all means of production—land, factories, machines, and so on—are privately owned. Profit is the motivating force behind economic transactions.

65. **The correct answer is (A).** All economic classes were raised by the economic benefits of the Industrial Revolution. Choice (B), that the wealthy were the only class to benefit, and choice (E), that the poor became poorer while the middle and upper classes prospered, are the opposite of what occurred, so they can both be eliminated. Choice (C) is illogical. Since the population base was the same, one class could not have grown in size while the other two remained constant. Choice (D) is also incorrect because the middle class, or bourgeoisie, was gaining power and influence as its wealth increased.

66. **The correct answer is (E).** In this *not* question, you are looking for the action or situation that the United States did not face in preserving its security. Choice (E) is about the U.S. economy, not its national security, so that is the correct answer. Choice (A) refers to balancing U.S. interests against those of the Soviet Union during the cold war. Choice (D), balancing defense and domestic priorities, is a statement of the "guns vs. butter" debate that has often marked U.S. foreign policy. For example, the tough choices necessitated by U.S. involvement in the Vietnam War helped to thwart the reelection ambitions of Lyndon Johnson, who saw his Great Society domestic programs fall victim to the costs of the war. Choice (B) and choice (C) are linked. The United States wanted to establish ties with the newly independent nations of Asia and Africa but without seeming to appear highhanded as their former colonial rulers had been and while not provoking the Soviet Union.

67. **The correct answer is (D).** After World War II, the Soviet Union and the United States joined in pushing for the partition of Palestine and the creation of Israel. Choice (A), sanctions against Cuba, is incorrect because the sanctions were levied by the United States for Castro's imposition of a Communist government in Cuba backed with aid from the Soviet Union. The United States had always supported Taiwan's place in the UN and blocked the admission of the People's Republic of China until relations had improved in the 1970s, so choice (B) is incorrect. Choice (C) is illogical because Poland had been one of the Soviet Union's satellite nations in Eastern Europe. Therefore, the Soviet Union would not have supported the new democratic Solidarity government of Lech Walensa in Poland, but the United States would have and did. Choice (E), Salvador Allende, the leftist-leaning Socialist head of Chile's government, was overthrown by a rightist-military coup. The Soviet Union would have had no reason to support this coup, but there is some evidence that the United States did through the CIA.

68. **The correct answer is (D).** If you read the map key and then the map, you will find that most Arab nations are not oil-rich. This is a straightforward visual comprehension question. There is not enough information on the map to be able to determine the truth of any of the other statements. All the other statements are true facts but unrelated to the data on the map. If you had been asked to select the answer choice that most accurately described the impact of their energy resources on Arab nations, then choice (A), the amount of influence Arab nations gained because of their resources, would be appropriate.

69. **The correct answer is (B).** From the beginning when Spain and Brazil established their colonies in the Americas, there was a small ruling elite of the very wealthy atop a widening pyramid of middle class to very poor. Independence did little to change the traditional power and economic structures of these former colonies—even into the twenty-first century. Choice (A), the population explosion, and choice (C), urbanization, are problems but of more modern origin than the issue of the uneven distribution of wealth. Choice (D), lack of natural resources, is incorrect. Latin America is considerably more fortunate than areas of sub-Saharan Africa. Choice (E), hostile environment, is somewhat true in areas such as the Anaconda Desert, the highest Andes, and the rainforest of the Amazon River Basin, but it is not entirely true, so eliminate this answer.

70. **The correct answer is (C).** Developing nations believe they need to exploit their natural resources, including their forests, in order to improve their economies, whereas developed nations believe that these resources, such as the Amazon rainforest, belong to the world because they affect the balance of the natural environment, including the air we breathe. Choice (A), desalinization is a distracter. The process of removing salt from water to make it useable, is a problem developing nations face, but it does not create tensions between developing and developed nations. Choice (B), desertification, is a problem among nations in North Africa rather than an area of conflict between have and have-not nations. Choice (D) is incorrect. Choice (E), urbanization, is a problem facing both developed and developing nations.

SELF-EVALUATION RUBRIC FOR THE ADVANCED PLACEMENT ESSAYS

	8–9	5–7	2–4	0–1
Overall Impression	Demonstrates excellent understanding of world history concepts and outstanding writing; thorough and effective; incisive	Demonstrates good understanding of world history concepts and good writing competence	Reveals simplistic or incomplete thinking and/or immature understanding of world history; concepts; fails to respond adequately to the question; little or no analysis	Very little or no understanding of world history concepts; unacceptably brief; fails to respond to the question; little clarity
Understanding of World History	Insightful; excellent understanding of the question; effective and incisive; in-depth critical analysis; includes many apt, specific outside references; uses all documents; persuasive use of documentary evidence; acknowledges opposing views; consistent use of comparisons between and among societies; effective change and continuity examples	Mostly historically accurate; good understanding of the question; often perceptive; includes specific outside references and critical analysis; uses most documents; has several apt comparisons; some demonstration of change and continuity	Some historical inaccuracies; superficial understanding and treatment of the question; some misreading of documents and lack of historical evidence; mechanical; overgeneralized; few comparisons; little demonstration of change and continuity	Serious historical errors; extensive misreadings and little supporting evidence; completely off the topic
Development	Clear, comprehensive, analytical thesis; excellent use of documents and outside historical knowledge; interesting and innovative use of comparisons; consistent use of theme of change and continuity; thoroughly developed	Adequate thesis; satisfactory use of documents and/or outside historical knowledge; some use of comparisons, theme of change and continuity; competent development; acceptable conclusion	Inadequate, irrelevant, or illogical thesis; little use of documents and/or outside historical knowledge; little use of comparisons; theme of continuity and change; some development; unsatisfactory, inapplicable, or nonexistent conclusion	Lacking both thesis and conclusion; little or no use of historical documents or knowledge; no comparisons or evidence of understanding of change and continuity; no distinguishable development
Organization/Conventions of English	Meticulously and thoroughly organized; coherent and unified; virtually error free	Reasonably organized; mostly coherent and unified; some errors	Somewhat organized; some incoherence and lack of unity; some major errors	Little or no organization; incoherent and void of unity; extremely flawed

Rate yourself in each of the categories below. Enter the numbers on the lines below. Be as honest as possible so you will know what areas need work. Then calculate the average of the four numbers to determine your final score. It is difficult to score yourself objectively, so you may wish to ask a respected friend or teacher to assess your essays for a more accurate reflection of their strengths and weaknesses. On the AP test itself, a reader will rate your essays on a scale of 0 to 9, with 9 being the highest.

Each category is rated 9 (high) to 0 (incompetent).

DBQ

SELF-EVALUATION

Overall Impression _____

Understanding of World History _____

Development _____

Organization/Conventions of English _____

TOTAL _____

Divide by 4 for final score. _____

DBQ

OBJECTIVE EVALUATION

Overall Impression _____

Understanding of World History _____

Development _____

Organization/Conventions of English _____

TOTAL _____

Divide by 4 for final score. _____

CHANGE-OVER-TIME ESSAY

SELF-EVALUATION

Overall Impression _____

Understanding of World History _____

Development _____

Organization/Conventions of English _____

TOTAL _____

Divide by 4 for final score. _____

CHANGE-OVER-TIME ESSAY

OBJECTIVE EVALUATION

Overall Impression _____

Understanding of World History _____

Development _____

Organization/Conventions of English _____

TOTAL _____

Divide by 4 for final score. _____

COMPARATIVE ESSAY

SELF-EVALUATION

Overall Impression _____

Understanding of World History _____

Development _____

Organization/Conventions of English _____

TOTAL _____

Divide by 4 for final score. _____

COMPARATIVE

OBJECTIVE EVALUATION

Overall Impression _____

Understanding of World History _____

Development _____

Organization/Conventions of English _____

TOTAL _____

Divide by 4 for final score. _____

ANSWER SHEET FOR DIAGNOSTIC TEST

Completely darken bubbles with a No. 2 pencil.
If you make a mistake, be sure to erase mark completely. Erase all stray marks.

1 ⊂A⊃ ⊂B⊃ ⊂C⊃ ⊂D⊃ ⊂E⊃	28 ⊂A⊃ ⊂B⊃ ⊂C⊃ ⊂D⊃ ⊂E⊃	55 ⊂A⊃ ⊂B⊃ ⊂C⊃ ⊂D⊃ ⊂E⊃
2 ⊂A⊃ ⊂B⊃ ⊂C⊃ ⊂D⊃ ⊂E⊃	29 ⊂A⊃ ⊂B⊃ ⊂C⊃ ⊂D⊃ ⊂E⊃	56 ⊂A⊃ ⊂B⊃ ⊂C⊃ ⊂D⊃ ⊂E⊃
3 ⊂A⊃ ⊂B⊃ ⊂C⊃ ⊂D⊃ ⊂E⊃	30 ⊂A⊃ ⊂B⊃ ⊂C⊃ ⊂D⊃ ⊂E⊃	57 ⊂A⊃ ⊂B⊃ ⊂C⊃ ⊂D⊃ ⊂E⊃
4 ⊂A⊃ ⊂B⊃ ⊂C⊃ ⊂D⊃ ⊂E⊃	31 ⊂A⊃ ⊂B⊃ ⊂C⊃ ⊂D⊃ ⊂E⊃	58 ⊂A⊃ ⊂B⊃ ⊂C⊃ ⊂D⊃ ⊂E⊃
5 ⊂A⊃ ⊂B⊃ ⊂C⊃ ⊂D⊃ ⊂E⊃	32 ⊂A⊃ ⊂B⊃ ⊂C⊃ ⊂D⊃ ⊂E⊃	59 ⊂A⊃ ⊂B⊃ ⊂C⊃ ⊂D⊃ ⊂E⊃
6 ⊂A⊃ ⊂B⊃ ⊂C⊃ ⊂D⊃ ⊂E⊃	33 ⊂A⊃ ⊂B⊃ ⊂C⊃ ⊂D⊃ ⊂E⊃	60 ⊂A⊃ ⊂B⊃ ⊂C⊃ ⊂D⊃ ⊂E⊃
7 ⊂A⊃ ⊂B⊃ ⊂C⊃ ⊂D⊃ ⊂E⊃	34 ⊂A⊃ ⊂B⊃ ⊂C⊃ ⊂D⊃ ⊂E⊃	61 ⊂A⊃ ⊂B⊃ ⊂C⊃ ⊂D⊃ ⊂E⊃
8 ⊂A⊃ ⊂B⊃ ⊂C⊃ ⊂D⊃ ⊂E⊃	35 ⊂A⊃ ⊂B⊃ ⊂C⊃ ⊂D⊃ ⊂E⊃	62 ⊂A⊃ ⊂B⊃ ⊂C⊃ ⊂D⊃ ⊂E⊃
9 ⊂A⊃ ⊂B⊃ ⊂C⊃ ⊂D⊃ ⊂E⊃	36 ⊂A⊃ ⊂B⊃ ⊂C⊃ ⊂D⊃ ⊂E⊃	63 ⊂A⊃ ⊂B⊃ ⊂C⊃ ⊂D⊃ ⊂E⊃
10 ⊂A⊃ ⊂B⊃ ⊂C⊃ ⊂D⊃ ⊂E⊃	37 ⊂A⊃ ⊂B⊃ ⊂C⊃ ⊂D⊃ ⊂E⊃	64 ⊂A⊃ ⊂B⊃ ⊂C⊃ ⊂D⊃ ⊂E⊃
11 ⊂A⊃ ⊂B⊃ ⊂C⊃ ⊂D⊃ ⊂E⊃	38 ⊂A⊃ ⊂B⊃ ⊂C⊃ ⊂D⊃ ⊂E⊃	65 ⊂A⊃ ⊂B⊃ ⊂C⊃ ⊂D⊃ ⊂E⊃
12 ⊂A⊃ ⊂B⊃ ⊂C⊃ ⊂D⊃ ⊂E⊃	39 ⊂A⊃ ⊂B⊃ ⊂C⊃ ⊂D⊃ ⊂E⊃	66 ⊂A⊃ ⊂B⊃ ⊂C⊃ ⊂D⊃ ⊂E⊃
13 ⊂A⊃ ⊂B⊃ ⊂C⊃ ⊂D⊃ ⊂E⊃	40 ⊂A⊃ ⊂B⊃ ⊂C⊃ ⊂D⊃ ⊂E⊃	67 ⊂A⊃ ⊂B⊃ ⊂C⊃ ⊂D⊃ ⊂E⊃
14 ⊂A⊃ ⊂B⊃ ⊂C⊃ ⊂D⊃ ⊂E⊃	41 ⊂A⊃ ⊂B⊃ ⊂C⊃ ⊂D⊃ ⊂E⊃	68 ⊂A⊃ ⊂B⊃ ⊂C⊃ ⊂D⊃ ⊂E⊃
15 ⊂A⊃ ⊂B⊃ ⊂C⊃ ⊂D⊃ ⊂E⊃	42 ⊂A⊃ ⊂B⊃ ⊂C⊃ ⊂D⊃ ⊂E⊃	69 ⊂A⊃ ⊂B⊃ ⊂C⊃ ⊂D⊃ ⊂E⊃
16 ⊂A⊃ ⊂B⊃ ⊂C⊃ ⊂D⊃ ⊂E⊃	43 ⊂A⊃ ⊂B⊃ ⊂C⊃ ⊂D⊃ ⊂E⊃	70 ⊂A⊃ ⊂B⊃ ⊂C⊃ ⊂D⊃ ⊂E⊃
17 ⊂A⊃ ⊂B⊃ ⊂C⊃ ⊂D⊃ ⊂E⊃	44 ⊂A⊃ ⊂B⊃ ⊂C⊃ ⊂D⊃ ⊂E⊃	71 ⊂A⊃ ⊂B⊃ ⊂C⊃ ⊂D⊃ ⊂E⊃
18 ⊂A⊃ ⊂B⊃ ⊂C⊃ ⊂D⊃ ⊂E⊃	45 ⊂A⊃ ⊂B⊃ ⊂C⊃ ⊂D⊃ ⊂E⊃	72 ⊂A⊃ ⊂B⊃ ⊂C⊃ ⊂D⊃ ⊂E⊃
19 ⊂A⊃ ⊂B⊃ ⊂C⊃ ⊂D⊃ ⊂E⊃	46 ⊂A⊃ ⊂B⊃ ⊂C⊃ ⊂D⊃ ⊂E⊃	73 ⊂A⊃ ⊂B⊃ ⊂C⊃ ⊂D⊃ ⊂E⊃
20 ⊂A⊃ ⊂B⊃ ⊂C⊃ ⊂D⊃ ⊂E⊃	47 ⊂A⊃ ⊂B⊃ ⊂C⊃ ⊂D⊃ ⊂E⊃	74 ⊂A⊃ ⊂B⊃ ⊂C⊃ ⊂D⊃ ⊂E⊃
21 ⊂A⊃ ⊂B⊃ ⊂C⊃ ⊂D⊃ ⊂E⊃	48 ⊂A⊃ ⊂B⊃ ⊂C⊃ ⊂D⊃ ⊂E⊃	75 ⊂A⊃ ⊂B⊃ ⊂C⊃ ⊂D⊃ ⊂E⊃
22 ⊂A⊃ ⊂B⊃ ⊂C⊃ ⊂D⊃ ⊂E⊃	49 ⊂A⊃ ⊂B⊃ ⊂C⊃ ⊂D⊃ ⊂E⊃	76 ⊂A⊃ ⊂B⊃ ⊂C⊃ ⊂D⊃ ⊂E⊃
23 ⊂A⊃ ⊂B⊃ ⊂C⊃ ⊂D⊃ ⊂E⊃	50 ⊂A⊃ ⊂B⊃ ⊂C⊃ ⊂D⊃ ⊂E⊃	77 ⊂A⊃ ⊂B⊃ ⊂C⊃ ⊂D⊃ ⊂E⊃
24 ⊂A⊃ ⊂B⊃ ⊂C⊃ ⊂D⊃ ⊂E⊃	51 ⊂A⊃ ⊂B⊃ ⊂C⊃ ⊂D⊃ ⊂E⊃	78 ⊂A⊃ ⊂B⊃ ⊂C⊃ ⊂D⊃ ⊂E⊃
25 ⊂A⊃ ⊂B⊃ ⊂C⊃ ⊂D⊃ ⊂E⊃	52 ⊂A⊃ ⊂B⊃ ⊂C⊃ ⊂D⊃ ⊂E⊃	79 ⊂A⊃ ⊂B⊃ ⊂C⊃ ⊂D⊃ ⊂E⊃
26 ⊂A⊃ ⊂B⊃ ⊂C⊃ ⊂D⊃ ⊂E⊃	53 ⊂A⊃ ⊂B⊃ ⊂C⊃ ⊂D⊃ ⊂E⊃	80 ⊂A⊃ ⊂B⊃ ⊂C⊃ ⊂D⊃ ⊂E⊃
27 ⊂A⊃ ⊂B⊃ ⊂C⊃ ⊂D⊃ ⊂E⊃	54 ⊂A⊃ ⊂B⊃ ⊂C⊃ ⊂D⊃ ⊂E⊃	

BE SURE TO ERASE ANY ERRORS OR STRAY MARKS COMPLETELY.

ANSWER SHEET FOR PRACTICE TEST

Completely darken bubbles with a No. 2 pencil.
If you make a mistake, be sure to erase mark completely. Erase all stray marks.

1 ⊂A⊃ ⊂B⊃ ⊂C⊃ ⊂D⊃ ⊂E⊃   28 ⊂A⊃ ⊂B⊃ ⊂C⊃ ⊂D⊃ ⊂E⊃   55 ⊂A⊃ ⊂B⊃ ⊂C⊃ ⊂D⊃ ⊂E⊃
2 ⊂A⊃ ⊂B⊃ ⊂C⊃ ⊂D⊃ ⊂E⊃   29 ⊂A⊃ ⊂B⊃ ⊂C⊃ ⊂D⊃ ⊂E⊃   56 ⊂A⊃ ⊂B⊃ ⊂C⊃ ⊂D⊃ ⊂E⊃
3 ⊂A⊃ ⊂B⊃ ⊂C⊃ ⊂D⊃ ⊂E⊃   30 ⊂A⊃ ⊂B⊃ ⊂C⊃ ⊂D⊃ ⊂E⊃   57 ⊂A⊃ ⊂B⊃ ⊂C⊃ ⊂D⊃ ⊂E⊃
4 ⊂A⊃ ⊂B⊃ ⊂C⊃ ⊂D⊃ ⊂E⊃   31 ⊂A⊃ ⊂B⊃ ⊂C⊃ ⊂D⊃ ⊂E⊃   58 ⊂A⊃ ⊂B⊃ ⊂C⊃ ⊂D⊃ ⊂E⊃
5 ⊂A⊃ ⊂B⊃ ⊂C⊃ ⊂D⊃ ⊂E⊃   32 ⊂A⊃ ⊂B⊃ ⊂C⊃ ⊂D⊃ ⊂E⊃   59 ⊂A⊃ ⊂B⊃ ⊂C⊃ ⊂D⊃ ⊂E⊃
6 ⊂A⊃ ⊂B⊃ ⊂C⊃ ⊂D⊃ ⊂E⊃   33 ⊂A⊃ ⊂B⊃ ⊂C⊃ ⊂D⊃ ⊂E⊃   60 ⊂A⊃ ⊂B⊃ ⊂C⊃ ⊂D⊃ ⊂E⊃
7 ⊂A⊃ ⊂B⊃ ⊂C⊃ ⊂D⊃ ⊂E⊃   34 ⊂A⊃ ⊂B⊃ ⊂C⊃ ⊂D⊃ ⊂E⊃   61 ⊂A⊃ ⊂B⊃ ⊂C⊃ ⊂D⊃ ⊂E⊃
8 ⊂A⊃ ⊂B⊃ ⊂C⊃ ⊂D⊃ ⊂E⊃   35 ⊂A⊃ ⊂B⊃ ⊂C⊃ ⊂D⊃ ⊂E⊃   62 ⊂A⊃ ⊂B⊃ ⊂C⊃ ⊂D⊃ ⊂E⊃
9 ⊂A⊃ ⊂B⊃ ⊂C⊃ ⊂D⊃ ⊂E⊃   36 ⊂A⊃ ⊂B⊃ ⊂C⊃ ⊂D⊃ ⊂E⊃   63 ⊂A⊃ ⊂B⊃ ⊂C⊃ ⊂D⊃ ⊂E⊃
10 ⊂A⊃ ⊂B⊃ ⊂C⊃ ⊂D⊃ ⊂E⊃   37 ⊂A⊃ ⊂B⊃ ⊂C⊃ ⊂D⊃ ⊂E⊃   64 ⊂A⊃ ⊂B⊃ ⊂C⊃ ⊂D⊃ ⊂E⊃
11 ⊂A⊃ ⊂B⊃ ⊂C⊃ ⊂D⊃ ⊂E⊃   38 ⊂A⊃ ⊂B⊃ ⊂C⊃ ⊂D⊃ ⊂E⊃   65 ⊂A⊃ ⊂B⊃ ⊂C⊃ ⊂D⊃ ⊂E⊃
12 ⊂A⊃ ⊂B⊃ ⊂C⊃ ⊂D⊃ ⊂E⊃   39 ⊂A⊃ ⊂B⊃ ⊂C⊃ ⊂D⊃ ⊂E⊃   66 ⊂A⊃ ⊂B⊃ ⊂C⊃ ⊂D⊃ ⊂E⊃
13 ⊂A⊃ ⊂B⊃ ⊂C⊃ ⊂D⊃ ⊂E⊃   40 ⊂A⊃ ⊂B⊃ ⊂C⊃ ⊂D⊃ ⊂E⊃   67 ⊂A⊃ ⊂B⊃ ⊂C⊃ ⊂D⊃ ⊂E⊃
14 ⊂A⊃ ⊂B⊃ ⊂C⊃ ⊂D⊃ ⊂E⊃   41 ⊂A⊃ ⊂B⊃ ⊂C⊃ ⊂D⊃ ⊂E⊃   68 ⊂A⊃ ⊂B⊃ ⊂C⊃ ⊂D⊃ ⊂E⊃
15 ⊂A⊃ ⊂B⊃ ⊂C⊃ ⊂D⊃ ⊂E⊃   42 ⊂A⊃ ⊂B⊃ ⊂C⊃ ⊂D⊃ ⊂E⊃   69 ⊂A⊃ ⊂B⊃ ⊂C⊃ ⊂D⊃ ⊂E⊃
16 ⊂A⊃ ⊂B⊃ ⊂C⊃ ⊂D⊃ ⊂E⊃   43 ⊂A⊃ ⊂B⊃ ⊂C⊃ ⊂D⊃ ⊂E⊃   70 ⊂A⊃ ⊂B⊃ ⊂C⊃ ⊂D⊃ ⊂E⊃
17 ⊂A⊃ ⊂B⊃ ⊂C⊃ ⊂D⊃ ⊂E⊃   44 ⊂A⊃ ⊂B⊃ ⊂C⊃ ⊂D⊃ ⊂E⊃   71 ⊂A⊃ ⊂B⊃ ⊂C⊃ ⊂D⊃ ⊂E⊃
18 ⊂A⊃ ⊂B⊃ ⊂C⊃ ⊂D⊃ ⊂E⊃   45 ⊂A⊃ ⊂B⊃ ⊂C⊃ ⊂D⊃ ⊂E⊃   72 ⊂A⊃ ⊂B⊃ ⊂C⊃ ⊂D⊃ ⊂E⊃
19 ⊂A⊃ ⊂B⊃ ⊂C⊃ ⊂D⊃ ⊂E⊃   46 ⊂A⊃ ⊂B⊃ ⊂C⊃ ⊂D⊃ ⊂E⊃   73 ⊂A⊃ ⊂B⊃ ⊂C⊃ ⊂D⊃ ⊂E⊃
20 ⊂A⊃ ⊂B⊃ ⊂C⊃ ⊂D⊃ ⊂E⊃   47 ⊂A⊃ ⊂B⊃ ⊂C⊃ ⊂D⊃ ⊂E⊃   74 ⊂A⊃ ⊂B⊃ ⊂C⊃ ⊂D⊃ ⊂E⊃
21 ⊂A⊃ ⊂B⊃ ⊂C⊃ ⊂D⊃ ⊂E⊃   48 ⊂A⊃ ⊂B⊃ ⊂C⊃ ⊂D⊃ ⊂E⊃   75 ⊂A⊃ ⊂B⊃ ⊂C⊃ ⊂D⊃ ⊂E⊃
22 ⊂A⊃ ⊂B⊃ ⊂C⊃ ⊂D⊃ ⊂E⊃   49 ⊂A⊃ ⊂B⊃ ⊂C⊃ ⊂D⊃ ⊂E⊃   76 ⊂A⊃ ⊂B⊃ ⊂C⊃ ⊂D⊃ ⊂E⊃
23 ⊂A⊃ ⊂B⊃ ⊂C⊃ ⊂D⊃ ⊂E⊃   50 ⊂A⊃ ⊂B⊃ ⊂C⊃ ⊂D⊃ ⊂E⊃   77 ⊂A⊃ ⊂B⊃ ⊂C⊃ ⊂D⊃ ⊂E⊃
24 ⊂A⊃ ⊂B⊃ ⊂C⊃ ⊂D⊃ ⊂E⊃   51 ⊂A⊃ ⊂B⊃ ⊂C⊃ ⊂D⊃ ⊂E⊃   78 ⊂A⊃ ⊂B⊃ ⊂C⊃ ⊂D⊃ ⊂E⊃
25 ⊂A⊃ ⊂B⊃ ⊂C⊃ ⊂D⊃ ⊂E⊃   52 ⊂A⊃ ⊂B⊃ ⊂C⊃ ⊂D⊃ ⊂E⊃   79 ⊂A⊃ ⊂B⊃ ⊂C⊃ ⊂D⊃ ⊂E⊃
26 ⊂A⊃ ⊂B⊃ ⊂C⊃ ⊂D⊃ ⊂E⊃   53 ⊂A⊃ ⊂B⊃ ⊂C⊃ ⊂D⊃ ⊂E⊃   80 ⊂A⊃ ⊂B⊃ ⊂C⊃ ⊂D⊃ ⊂E⊃
27 ⊂A⊃ ⊂B⊃ ⊂C⊃ ⊂D⊃ ⊂E⊃   54 ⊂A⊃ ⊂B⊃ ⊂C⊃ ⊂D⊃ ⊂E⊃

BE.SURE TO ERASE ANY ERRORS OR STRAY MARKS COMPLETELY.

Your everything education destination
the *all-new* Petersons.com

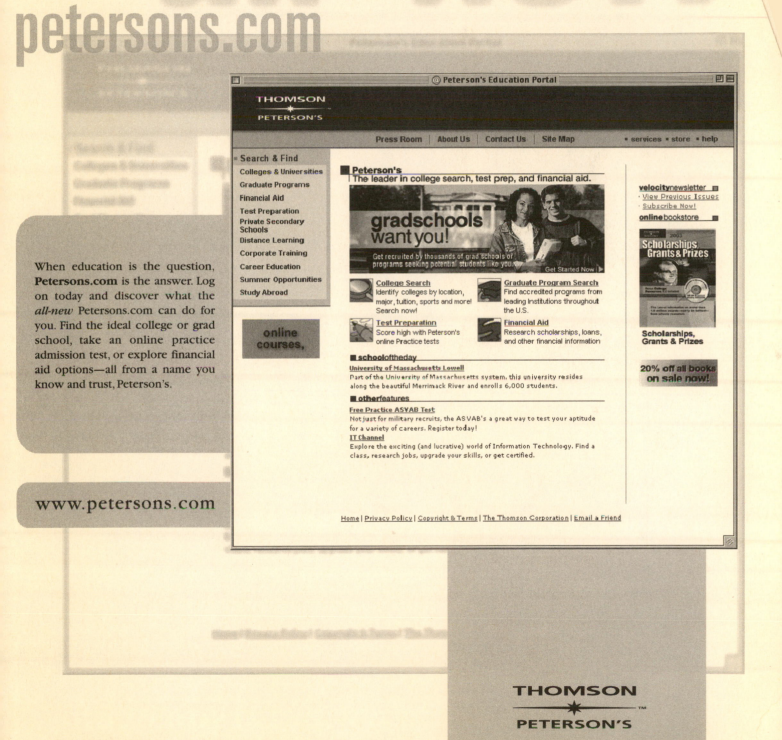

When education is the question, **Petersons.com** is the answer. Log on today and discover what the *all-new* Petersons.com can do for you. Find the ideal college or grad school, take an online practice admission test, or explore financial aid options—all from a name you know and trust, Peterson's.

www.petersons.com